Bauchet, Pierre
Economic planning

ECONOMIC PLANNING: THE FRENCH EXPERIENCE

PIERRE BAUCHET

ECONOMIC PLANNING

THE FRENCH EXPERIENCE

TRANSLATED BY
DAPHNE WOODWARD

WITH AN INTRODUCTION BY
SIR ROBERT HALL

FREDERICK A. PRAEGER, *Publisher*
NEW YORK

Published in the United States of America in 1964
by Frederick A. Praeger, Inc., Publisher
64 University Place, New York 3, N.Y.

First published in France in 1962 under the title of
La Planification Française by Editions du Seuil

Library of Congress Catalog Card Number: 64–16665

Printed in Great Britain

You, Perses . . . put your freight in a large ship; for the greater the lading, the greater will be your piled gain, if only the winds will keep back their harmful gales. I will show you the measure of the loud-roaring sea if ever you turn your misguided heart to trading and wish to escape from debt and joyless hunger . . .

HESIOD

Contents

Foreword

SOME form of economic planning, in the sense of intervention in what individuals would do if left to themselves, is as old as Government itself. But after Adam Smith, it came to be thought that the main function of central or Government planning was to see that market forces had free play and to leave them alone. As a philosophy this did not last long, but there is still a good deal of controversy about what can be achieved by intervention. At one extreme there is full-scale planning of the Soviet type, where the short-term interests of the consumer are regarded as of little importance. Sometimes for similar ideological reasons, but mainly because of the shortage of technical skills and the need for external help, many underdeveloped countries also try for overall planning. At the other extreme are the fully-developed economies of the Western kind, where consumer preference and profit and loss are the driving forces, and where it would only be generally agreed that intervention was necessary to maintain the level of unemployment and smooth out the business cycle.

It is here that the argument is least resolved, but in recent years the case for intervention has become centred on the problem of expansion or growth. This is an argument which cannot be settled on theoretical or general considerations, since so much depends on the way individuals behave in response to various forms of persuasion, inducement or coercion. It is clear, however, that an important factor will be the type of organizations chosen for the application of pressures.

In the post-war period the French have been outstanding both for their growth rate and for the use they have made of planning in a market economy. They have tackled the problem of how to reconcile freedom of choice for the consumer and the business man with centralized direction, and the no less difficult problem of how to reconcile consultation with capital and labour, with Parliamentary democracy. The decision in Britain to establish the

National Economic Development Council (NEDC), with the duty of preparing growth targets and making recommendations about how they are to be reached, is really a decision to adopt the French line.

It is this which makes the appearance in English of M. Pierre Bauchet's a distinguished book on French Economic Planning so timely. He is a trained economist and he has worked for several years in the Commissariat du Plan. He is able to describe in detail the mechanism of planning, its relation to Parliament and the Civil Service, and also its relation to industry through groups representing employers, trade unionists and experts. But he also understands what the organization is trying to do, and thus has made a critical appraisal of the methods available and actually used to get the plan carried out, the difficulties which have been overcome and those yet to be solved. Finally he draws some valuable conclusions, in the light of his own views on the economic and social needs of France, as to where the planning machinery needs to be modified or strengthened.

In Britain and in the United States we are in the early stages of all this. It is not very likely that we shall copy the French in all respects: we have less flexibility in administration, and probably we shall have to pay a great deal more attention to Parliament and to Congress. But we shall at least have no excuse for not knowing how these things have been done in a country where the plan is a reality. Even to say 'we couldn't possibly do that here' takes us a long way to thinking how we could do it.

ROBERT HALL

Introduction

IT WAS while lecturing on Political Economy at the University of Rabat that I first thought of writing my earlier book, *L'Expérience française de planification*, of which the present volume constitutes in effect a revised edition, though nothing of it survives except a few pages from the first and final chapters. It seemed to me that many Moroccan and French students had old-fashioned ideas about the French economic system, the circumstances of which had changed so much since 1940 that the traditional capitalist dogmas had ceased to apply.

I do not feel qualified, however, to put forward a new, all-embracing description of a social structure which is no longer that of the nineteenth century; that would be a perilous undertaking, not only because of its magnitude, but because the present period is one of transition. Changes are occurring faster than ever before, and I must confess that as yet I cannot clearly perceive their dominant and persistent features. Until the pace slackens it will be difficult to get the full picture into focus.

So I have confined myself to describing one element which I hope may prove a useful contribution to modern doctrine. I have studied one aspect of the contemporary scene, the French Plan, and have tried to show that, whatever conservative minds on the Right or left maintain, that Plan exists, and is a sign of the 'wind of change' now blowing through the traditional capitalist structures.

Some people, reading between the lines, will inevitably claim to discover value judgments. They will be mistaken, though a sentence here and there may seem to invite such an interpretation. In describing the merits of French planning, I had no intention of depicting it as the herald of a new social era, glowing with all the virtues of the institutions adumbrated by the nineteenth- and twentieth-century reformers. True, the Plan entails a transformation of the structure of French capitalism which is so radical that people are beginning to wonder whether the system still deserves that name;

but that does not make the Plan a panacea. The revolutionary developments that lie ahead are designed to ensure the emancipation and fulfilment of individual human beings, and this cannot be achieved by means of a plan, however excellent. Besides, the French experiment is still too novel for its effects to be clearly foreseen.

So the following pages do not constitute an apologia. Nor do they offer a comparison with Soviet planning, which would call for more searching analysis and lead, unavoidably, to political and philosophical judgments.

I have stressed the changes that have occurred in the management of private business; but I do not mean to suggest that French planning, with its respect for private ownership of the means of production, is as acceptable to a Socialist as Soviet planning, which is based on public ownership. Many other problems are left unsettled. Do the principles of management of the big Western enterprises still differ considerably from those of the Socialist firms? How should they be amended?

The launching of a fourth Plan (1962–1965) accounts in part, of course, for the appearance of this new book, which is almost twice the size of its predecessor.

But a more important fact is that circumstances have altered. My aim in 1956 was to show in what respects the French system constituted an innovation when compared with Soviet planning. At the present moment Great Britain, Italy, the European Economic Community and even the United States are contemplating the adoption of a similar technique. Hence, it seems to me that to defend the principle of flexibility in planning is now less necessary than to take stock of the experience gained by France in the last fifteen years, draw the conclusions to which it points and indicate its shortcomings.

My wife, who has been closely associated with the preparation of this book, joins me in hoping that it may be of use to those in all countries who are feeling their way towards a new world.

PIERRE BAUCHET

PRELIMINARY CHAPTER

Economic Planning

BEFORE the second world war, any suggestion of economic planning was opposed in France by two schools of thought. The advocates of a free economic system had by that time abandoned the views of Jean-Baptiste Say and no longer denied the recurrence of periods of depression, with their attendant spectres of unemployment and poverty; but they still believed that such situations righted themselves automatically, and they regarded planning with mistrust, as one of many forms of blundering interference which did more to perpetuate the evil than to remedy it. For their theorists, planning was the first step towards the Soviet type of authoritarian socialism.

The Communist leaders, on the other hand, were hostile on principle, for they considered that planning would be futile under a liberal system of government, where the authorities could not intervene forcefully enough. As long ago as 1935, their opposition prevented the Popular Front from drawing up an effective plan; and since the war they have never given full support to planning except from 1945 to 1947, when they themselves were represented in the Government.

As well as this doctrinaire opposition to the idea of an economic plan, there were the obstacles put up by conservatism and individualism in official circles.

A number of trade union leaders and senior civil servants, most of them Socialists, had indeed been convinced for a long time that something must be done to prevent the recurrence of crises and put an end to the vexations of sporadic intervention by co-ordinating all aspects of economic policy. The need for such action had been recognized as early as 1919, in the Clémentel Commission's general report on the organization of national production. A plan was drawn up in collaboration by MM. E. Beaurepaire,

M. Deixonne, F. Dreyfus, R. Lacoste, R. Marjolin, J. Moch, A. Philip and others, and a first attempt to apply it was made during the depression of the 1930's, when the *Comité Consultatif du Perfectionnement de l'Outillage national* (Advisory Committee for the Improvement of National Capital Equipment) was set up by an Act of 28 December 1931 (D.P. 1932, 4, 5) and made loans for financing certain activities.

By 1936, the need for a body with general powers, which could co-ordinate the programmes of the various government departments and settle disputes between them, had become still more urgent, the Socialist Government having found no remedy for the persistent depression. The administrative services could not see beyond the interests of the industries for which they were severally responsible, so they could hardly be expected to devise an overall policy. In 1936 the Ministry of National Economy was created to draw up such a policy and overcome departmentalism. But this too was a failure. The very title of the new Ministry, with the vast number of boards it appointed, many of which duplicated existing agencies, was enough to indicate the misconception in which it had originated; for instead of being placed above the other administrative departments it was on the same level, and in direct competition with them.

The same consideration led in 1941 to the establishment of a *Délégation générale à l'Equipement national*, set up by an Act of 6 April 1941 (D.A. 1941, 233); but the war prevented this body from effectively carrying out its appointed task of drawing up a plan and enforcing its application.

Faced with urgent post-war reconstruction problems, the Government issued an Order (23 November 1944) by which the preparation of a fresh plan for national investment was entrusted to the Ministry for the National Economy, a new administrative service being created within the Ministry for this purpose. Finally, a Decree of 3 January 1946 (B.L.D. 1946, 79), amended by a Decree of 19 May 1953 (B.L.D. 1953, 394) established the *Commissariat général du Plan*, headed by a *Commissaire général*, to draw up the plan and supervise its application.

The 1944 plan of the Ministry for the National Economy had proved unsuccessful, but the new (Monnet) Plan won through because it had a definite initial aim. This was, to convince the Americans that the aid they were giving to France under the Blum-

Byrnes agreements was being put to good use. It was not until later that the range of the Plan was gradually extended.

The creation of the *Commissariat général du Plan* was accepted in 1946 without uproar, because it was only one of a number of measures recognized as unavoidable in that disturbed post-war period. But whereas many other projects launched at the same time are now forgotten, the Plan still survives, followed with interest, if not actively championed, in many trade union and business circles. True, the interest and approval are expressed with some reticence, for those concerned are not eager to be stigmatized as 'Marxists' or 'Socialists' by people whose clouded minds equate planning with the Soviet system. But for all that, there is abundant evidence to show that planning is increasingly important, not to say indispensable, in the establishment of price, production and manpower policies for public and private enterprise.

In the fifteen years during which it has been in operation, the French *Plan de Modernisation et d'Equipement* (Plan for Modernization and Equipment) has brought about a minor revolution, the original credit for which is due to M. Jean Monnet.

M. Monnet, who was born at Cognac in 1888, has spent his whole life tackling new problems in a constructive way, and usually solving them. In the 1914 war he supported the idea of co-ordinating supplies for the allied armies, and helped to organize the committees set up for that purpose. He was among those with whom the idea of the League of Nations originated, and in 1919 he was appointed as its Deputy Secretary-General. During the Second World War his services to the allied cause won him a seat on the British War Supplies Council. After the liberation of his country he led the French purchasing missions to the United States.

Once in Washington, M. Monnet realized that when lend-lease was wound up France would have to think out new ways of making efficient use of the foreign aid which was essential to the reconstruction and modernization of her equipment. To meet this need, a plan for modernization and investment was drawn up under his guidance, including specific proposals for dealing with basic sectors. M. Monnet gave up his post with the Plan in May 1950, when he was appointed President of the European Coal and Steel Community.

Under his leadership the *Commissariat du Plan de Modernisation et d'Equipement*, the smallest of all the French administrative services, had begun to display its truly original features. Its working committees brought together trade unionists, industrialists, farmers, experts and civil servants – men of proved ability who could thus get to know one another personally, unhampered by professional barriers or civil service rank. And together they fixed the targets for the Plan.

The very small permanent staff was recruited in unorthodox ways. Its members came from a wide variety of backgrounds: there was M. Gaillard, the inspector of finance; M. Hirsch, the mining engineer who later became *Commissaire Général*; there was M. Marjolin, the professor of economics, who was to become Secretary-General of O.E.E.C. and later of the European Economic Community; there was M. Uri, the professor of philosophy; and all these worked on equal terms with holders of lesser qualifications, for what counted was a man's abilities, not the letters after his name. Three director's posts were the only evidence of hierarchy, which it was thought should be kept to the minimum to ensure go-ahead methods.

The working timetable was equally unorthodox. At peak periods the planners ignored the claims of evenings and Sundays, and the group study meetings in the Commissioner-General's office lasted far into the night.

In 1950, M. E. Hirsch became Commissioner-General. As a former director of several companies in the Kuhlmann group, the leader of the French Supply Mission at the Allied Headquarters during the war, and a trained engineer with great experience of the business world, he was well fitted for the post; he held it until 1959, when he left to become President of Euratom.

He was succeeded by M. P. Massé, a graduate of the *Ecole Polytechnique*, a civil engineer and a D.Sc. M. Massé had been working in the electrical industry since 1928, had held the post of Director of Investment of *Electricité de France* and subsequently of Deputy General Manager, and was an expert on investment problems.

Led by these men, the *Commissariat* consolidated its position in the French Civil Service and worked out its methods of planning and intervention.

The existence of this French Plan, about which other countries are frankly curious, raises two questions. Why, when planning was rejected until recent years, is it now regarded as a necessity? And how can we describe the manifest differences between the French experiment and that of Soviet Russia?

I. THE REASONS FOR PLANNING

Planning and forecasting now extend beyond national frontiers. The European Coal and Steel Community (E.C.S.C.) not only attempts to co-ordinate the policies of its member countries, particularly with regard to manpower (for instance, by transferring surplus Italian workers), but tries to prepare forecasts and programmes that include them all. The Organization for Economic Co-operation and Development (O.E.C.D.), the European Economic Community (E.E.C.) and the majority of the international organizations, each in its own field, resort to similar methods of forecasting production and trade.

One of the primary aims of planning is to ensure full employment. That idea is enough in itself to show that the French mentality has progressed considerably. Only a few years ago no Frenchman would have been scandalized by the statement that a 'pool' of unemployed was essential to prosperity. Nowadays the big French nationalized enterprises, such as the S.N.C.F. (French nationalized railways), sometimes put up with heavy losses rather than dismiss any of their workers. In using their manpower and other factors of production they all make a careful scrutiny of prospects of expansion. Many factory managers would echo the following statement, quoted from a journal which cannot be accused of Marxism: 'Whether we like it or not, a policy of *laissez-faire* is no longer possible in the production of energy, and in fact no State pursues such a policy at the present time. . . . Government entails making medium-term, long-term and even very long-term forecasts, and expressing the results in practical, well-constructed programmes. . . . Owing to these new developments, with their far-reaching and complex repercussions at national and international level, and to the adoption of increasingly precise methods of econometric analysis and investigation, the planning of an energy policy is a considerable undertaking.'[1]

[1] M. R. Boutteville, Chairman of the *Société alsacienne de Constructions mécaniques*, in *Le Moniteur des Travaux publics et du Bâtiment*, 14 May 1955, p. 11.

Generally speaking, the present readiness of industry and trade to accept the planned system that they rejected until recently is due to their realization – assisted by peaceful competition with the Eastern European countries – that the whole basis of economic activity has been transformed. People have become more willing to organize their lives and more eager to go ahead, and technical innovations are compelling manufacturers to make forecasts. These two changes have been reflected in economic life.

THE NEW ATTITUDE IN FRANCE

It is impossible to analyse in a few words the respective contributions of technical advances and individual behaviour to the development of the superstructure of which economic policy, and planning in particular, forms a part. But planning and forecasting would have been impossible without the radical change of attitude which occurred in the first half of the present century.

Hitherto, the French population, with its Catholic traditions, had shown less interest in technological progress than the Protestant English-speaking countries. This partly accounts for France's backwardness. For a long time Frenchmen ignored the existence of oil in the Sahara and natural gas in the South of France, simply because they felt no 'inclination' for progress – in other words, did not believe in it – and therefore lacked the determination to succeed and to rally all the necessary resources for that purpose.

Mental fixity is a myth invented by bourgeois radicals in the nineteenth century and too readily adopted by the classical economists, Marx, and their successors. All allegedly objective statements about the natural man and descriptions of 'fossilized' classes are equally old-fashioned. Recent experience in France gives food for thought; neither the average manufacturer nor the average factory worker has the same outlook nowadays as in 1936, let alone in 1940. Any attempt to describe them must unfortunately involve a degree of caricature; but it can safely be said that, living as they do in a world with a growing need for unity, the people of today are beginning to recognize that collective organizations are indispensable if the future is to bring that progress to which everyone aspires. In economic matters, this leads them to the idea of planning.

The trend towards organization

People in France are becoming aware that the world, with all its continents and territories, is one and indivisible. During the between-war period they inclined towards isolationism, but easier communications, the mixing of nationalities in the last world war, the very fact that wars can no longer be localized (as was made evident by Suez) and the pressing need for international economic agreements have all helped to open French eyes to the world situation. The problems resulting from the rapid increase of population in North Africa have contributed to the same effect.

If the majority of Frenchmen have admitted the necessity for the Euratom and Common Market Treaties, if they are playing their part in the various attempts at international organization even where they do not share the political views implicit in these, it is because they realize that the world is becoming increasingly unified and that they cannot contract out of it. Pure research, in which, as a people with a long-standing civilization, we like to think ourselves superior, compels us more and more to concentrate on certain fields and to exchange information with other countries. We have come to feel that the attempt to arrive at a synthesis of the laws governing matter and life must henceforth be pursued on a world-wide scale and not merely on a national one.

Not that national sentiment – let alone class consciousness – can yet be dismissed as outdated and useless superstition. In the nineteenth century, the workers' movement, followed by the awakening of the peasants, brought emancipation and progress to millions who had previously been resigned to a life of wretchedness. The same awakening is now taking place among the peoples of the former colonial territories. At the present day, business and political circles in France are being aroused, by peaceful East-West competition and by the constant pressure maintained by the trade unions to ensure wage increases and security of employment, to the urgent need for economic growth and for a policy based on forecasting and planning.

In seeking to defend their interests, men have been led to form groups to fight for their rights. This is a primitive impulse, and leads to associations representing limited interests, instead of to the general organization required for economic progress. The C.G.T.[2] itself is aware of this, for it is composed partly of 'pure' Marxists who would like to weld the workers together in a class war, and partly of reformers who consider that the unions, while continuing to defend their rights, should help to construct new institutions. Many French workers and peasants now feel that systematic opposition alone can no longer solve the problems raised by their country's development.

As already pointed out, the international organizations are upheld in their social and political action by an awareness of world unity. To be more precise, it is the threat to the survival of the human race which results not only from the risk of atomic warfare but even from the preparations made for it, weighed against the benefits to be anticipated from a harmonious development of the different national communities, that has given rise to the United Nations and to the successive disarmament conferences.

In the economic sphere, the still vivid memory of the years of depression in the 1930's, the realization that while France has a wheat surplus, famine is endemic in North Africa – economic anarchy – have helped Frenchmen to appreciate the need for organizations. The leaders of the French economic system are fond of describing themselves in newspaper articles as champions of free enterprise, but it would never occur to them to question the need for Social Security or for the *Commissariat général du Plan*. International bodies like O.E.C.D., E.C.S.C. and E.E.C. also accept the idea – received nowadays even in the most conservative circles – that the virtues of organization excel those of free competition.

The pursuit of progress

Be he industrial magnate or factory worker, the Frenchman is an individualist; but because he feels that the future will bring progress, he now submits to being organized without too much complaint. If space permitted, it would be interesting to quote some recent statements by various company chairmen, to the effect that the cautious management of pre-war days no longer meets the situation, that it has become essential to advance boldly along the

[2] *Confédération Générale du Travail* (largest and furthest to the left of the three French federations of trade unions). (*Translator's note.*)

path of development, with the help of new methods, reorganization and trade agreements.[3]

Though people are not always fully aware of the fact, the general atmosphere of present-day thinking is radically different from what it was before the last war.

In the old days history was regarded as a succession of disconnected, interchangeable events; this made it difficult to formulate a programme of co-ordinated, conscious action, not bounded by the immediate circumstances. People did not know why they were working, let alone whither their work was leading. If the classical economists declared that the world was governed by 'blind' economic and social forces, it was because they themselves were unable to see into the future.

Thanks to the convergent progress of biological, historical and natural sciences, we of today can perceive the close relationship between past and future. Every past development is seen to be the necessary outcome of some earlier development, however far back we carry our investigation. The process is irreversible. Civilizations, men and industries all proceed from a period of infancy to one of maturity. They have their place in history, determined by previous events, while before them lies a future they are shaping and can control. In practical terms this means that the future of the French nation will be the result of its present efforts.

People are beginning to realize that the future is collective, not individual. Its success will depend on their united efforts. 'In the universe, no elementary fibre, as it grows, is entirely independent of the neighbouring fibres.'[4]

This concept of an evolving world, in which the future of any set of factors is conditioned by its present situation, has opened up entirely new fields for action. The 'radiant future' of a nation,

[3] Cf. M. Fr. Albert-Buisson's speech to the General Meeting of shareholders of the Rhône-Poulenc Co. on 7 June 1955 (reported in *Le Monde* of 9 June), in which he said: 'And it is no longer enough nowadays for the head of a firm to manage it cautiously; it is his duty to be bold and, where research is concerned, spendthrift. Unless he is to be outdistanced in national and international competition, he must deliberately accept this new risk, like the entrepreneur as conceived by the classical economists, with their liberal theories. This indicates the scale and complexity of the task that the manager of a business has to carry out, among all manner of different people and circumstances.'

[4] R. P. Teilhard de Chardin, 'L'Esprit nouveau et le cône du temps', in *Psyché*, No. 99–100, p. 50.

like the expansion of a business enterprise, is closely dependent upon present-day policy and behaviour. Blind, hand-to-mouth, individualistic action is making way for a conscious, collective effort to ensure continued progress.

Progress was first evidenced by an increasing number of technical methods which lightened the burden of physical and intellectual labour and reduced even the need for supervision. Activity became more effective and less strenuous, although the new techniques had so far revealed only a fraction of their possibilities.

With more and more surplus energy to dispose of now that machinery had relieved them of manual labour, men could give more time to thought. One consequence of this was the spread of education. The man of today has a new awareness, his reason is in the ascendant. His increasingly rational outlook is in itself a form of progress.

Those who object to anything that is 'collective' will not, of course, agree that a more complex social organization is a sign of progress. Without entering into an argument about the meaning of the word 'collective', which has been distorted by mental images of the Communist countries, we can safely assume that even those who dread the extension of collectivism are in favour of technical improvements and greater rationalization. Would anyone nowadays refuse to make use of motorcars, electric light or refrigerators, and is not everyone eager for greater speed, less effort and more knowledge?

And it is precisely because the modern world has been transformed by technology, that patterns of behaviour have altered.

CHANGED TECHNIQUES

Those responsible for economic activities are thus obliged to envisage collective development.

At this point I should like to emphasize the importance of the changes resulting from technological progress – while pointing out, as Marx did, that technical developments do not entirely shape the lives of individuals or groups, whose behaviour remains largely unaffected by them. However, the acceleration of progress in the twentieth century has strengthened their influence, though in a manner that Marx, writing in the middle of the nineteenth century, could hardly have anticipated; for technology now makes forecasting a necessity, while simultaneously providing the instruments required for it.

Technological developments make forecasting a necessity

The maxim that government is synonymous with foresight is not a new one. But it now expresses a universal and imperative necessity.

Let us take as an example the transformation which has occurred in the production of energy in France. Greater demand has led to a more and more rapid increase in the quantities produced.

Research into sources of supply and methods of production has been intensified – fuel oil research centres and laboratories for the production of atomic, solar and tidal energy are wrestling with the problem of how to satisfy demand. At the same time the old sources of energy are becoming exhausted and new techniques are being invented, so that the capital investment required per unit of energy produced has become increasingly heavy. The volume of investment has grown relentlessly from the small, late nineteenth-century textile mill, by way of the hydro-electric dam of the 1930's, to the atomic plant.

The increasing demand for energy, the exhaustion of certain resources and the very high cost of capital equipment all combine to make forecasting essential. Long before new requirements arise, means of satisfying them must be considered and a research programme initiated, the results of which may take as long as five years to mature. It is by no accident that all the Western countries draw up their forecasts and programmes in the sphere of energy for a period of twenty years or very nearly. The amount of atomic energy that will be available twenty years hence will depend on research which must begin forthwith. Moreover, by forecasting that amount we can decide the rate of investment in the other branches – coal and oil – and *vice versa*. In 1890 a textile manufacturer could set up his plant and order coal for it a year ahead; nowadays the supply of energy at normal prices depends on investments made more than fifteen years ago.

Forecasting is also needed to enable the production of energy to pay its way. Owing to the large scale of capital investment and the negligible cost of maintenance – it takes only a handful of men to look after a dam or an atomic plant – depreciation is now a bigger item than operating costs. Production must be fully absorbed in order to avoid a gap between production and consumption, with 'off-peak' periods. This calls for a nation-wide forecast of consumption, which is tantamount to a prediction of general economic development. And no rational pricing of power can be established without a plan.

The technical transformation and concentration effected in the energy sector have led, among other consequences, to forecasts relating to that sector and to the whole national economy.

What has been said above applies equally to the iron and steel industry, the chemical industry and all other rapidly expanding branches with a growing volume of investment. They all have to grapple with the same difficulties, investing larger and larger sums further and further in advance of the anticipated date of production. The biggest French iron and steel groups can no longer invest without first calculating their prospective sales – in other words, predicting the growth of national production. The new factories being built today will not come into production until 1965. No one will deny that there is an element of risk about decisions based on such increasingly lengthy forecasts, but they are unavoidable for technical reasons.

Automation and its repercussions on employment also oblige us to look ahead. More rapidly now than in the past, technical developments are making workers redundant in some branches and creating a demand for them in others; new skills are needed, while others fall into disuse; women are driven from textile mills and clerks from banks by 'mechanics' and engineers whose task is to service and repair spinning machinery or computers. To prevent serious unemployment in a particular branch of technology, geographical area or industry, vocational training and readaptation centres must be set up to meet the anticipated changes. And as a long-term development, reduced working hours will have to pave the way for the decline in employment which must inevitably result from automation. In short, if the side effects of automation are to be kept down to a minimum, the decisions that guide it must be more and more closely concerted.[5]

One could quote any number of examples of the technical transformation which makes forecasting unavoidable.

[5] See H. de Bivort, 'Automation: some social aspects', *International Labour Review*, December 1955, pp. 467–495.

Forecasts are not confined to single firms or sectors of the economy; they are undertaken on a national and international scale as well. An iron and steel producer no longer takes decisions about future capital investment merely in the light of the circumstances prevailing in his own firm or branch of industry; the reason why French steel firms conform to the levels of output recommended by the Commissions of the Plan is that there is a close connection between the nation's economic progress and its iron and steel output. Prospects for the individual branch, its total purchases and sales, are fairly strictly determined by the prospects confronting industry as a whole. The fact that studies of the relations between different industries are now being widely undertaken is a clear indication that each of them is dependent upon the others.

The interest displayed in such studies by the big American and French firms[6] shows beyond doubt their awareness that expansion is a matter of co-operation.

Private American firms began to make forecasts in the 1930's, but these were usually limited to market studies and did not provide an overall picture of development. It was not until after the last war that models in which these forecasts were presented in relation to national development were worked out by firms such as General Motors, United States Steel and Westinghouse, by private associations such as the National Planning Association, and by certain branches of the administration, including the Bureau of Labor Statistics and the Council of Economic Advisers. Even now there is no comprehensive official map of United States development by which the leaders of public and private business can steer their course. Frenchmen, though slower to be converted to the idea of forecasting, realized immediately that progress could no longer be restricted to a single firm or branch of industry, but must henceforth be shared by the country as a whole.

This applies at the international level too. France's economic growth is bound up with that of her neighbours. The connection is still more evident for a country like the Netherlands, whose economic life is founded on international trade and thus on the activities of other nations. So the forecasts established by the central planning organs in France and the Netherlands include studies of the future of those European countries with which they

[6] Nowadays the big banking houses have their own econometric study units.

principally trade; a country's exports, and therefore its economic growth, depend on the prosperity of its foreign customers.

Even the most self-sufficient countries are affected by this law. It may be pointed out that technological progress brings some degree of independence, by increasing the number of synthetic products which can be manufactured. On the other hand, however, it militates in favour of enterprises which develop a speciality in some vast-scale market, covering several countries. It may reduce a nation's dependence on a particular foreign product, but it also generates organizations that operate in a number of foreign territories. The classic example of this is provided by the international oil companies, such as Shell (Royal Dutch), the motor manufacturers – General Motors or Ford – and the cable firms, joined recently by certain chemical firms (e.g. Unilever) and manufacturers of electrical goods, such as Philips. The international fellowship between firms is closer than that which used to be created by international trade. Nowadays this inter-dependence is so clearly realized that the international organizations – O.E.C.D., E.E.C., E.C.S.C., and so forth – prepare combined forecasts for several countries, as a guide to the policy of each of them.

It is obviously important for any State, however powerful, to have economically 'healthy' neighbours buying its products; a slight 'chill' may so easily develop into 'galloping consumption' and cause a serious crisis that will spread to other countries. A glaring example of this is provided by France's shortsighted treatment of China and of her own overseas territories. Many a crisis would have been avoided if French industry had helped those countries to expand their economy so that the goods they imported could be paid for by their own exports. Instead of forcing the Chinese at the cannon's mouth to open their ports to us we should have made it possible for them to pay for our products.

Because of this interdependence in growth, the forecasts by which decisions are governed in the present-day world must be far-reaching. Thanks to the technological revolution which has occurred in the twentieth century, manufacturers can now form a general picture of the future.

Technological advances facilitate forecasting

The closely-knit structure of the modern world, which is partly the result of technological advances, enables us to make forecasts for consumption and production which would have been impossible in the past.

Only fifty years ago, the idea of predicting the future trend of consumption of a particular product or group of products seemed completely utopian. Scrutiny of the future was rendered illusory by changes in individual taste, fluctuations in agricultural production caused by climate and 'circumstances', and uncertainty regarding family income-levels. Today the factors determining consumption can to some extent be foreseen. Production is less dependent upon climatic variations or mere chance than it used to be, and more closely conditioned by technological discoveries; the appearance on the market of a new fertilizer or a new type of seed affects harvests as much as the climate can do. Incomes still vary, it is true, but in a manner that is more or less understood. And individual taste is to some extent affected by new products: the appearance of bicycles and radio sets in Southern Morocco or television and washing-machines in France, the introduction of the helicopter, and so forth, result in immediate and future sales whose direction and limit, though of course not their exact volume, can be accurately calculated. The way these new products will affect the behaviour of people who like to be 'up-to-date' is indicated by previous examples of social snobbery and by the reaction in countries that acquired them earlier. There is of course an element of uncertainty in that behaviour and sometimes – as with motor-cars, for instance – it fails to conform to prediction; but technical determinism is a good guide to sales trends in certain categories, such as agricultural products and electric household appliances.

Production trends can also be determined beforehand; changes in the principal factors – manpower, scale of investment, markets – can be predicted with great accuracy in many sectors. As a production process grows more complex, it becomes less subject to chance; a good or bad harvest makes less difference to France, where agriculture is a subsidiary activity, than to north Africa. And it is increasingly conditioned by the past and by environment: thus, as we have seen, the production of energy in France in 1970 will depend upon the amount of investment undertaken in the 1960's and upon the volume of French production at the time.

Without exaggerating the extent of social determinism, we have to admit that the increasingly close connection between all technological and economic phenomena, the relationship of present to past and of future to present, facilitates forecasting on a scale that would have been unthinkable not so very long ago.

But forecasting entails the perception and analysis of a complex series of factors – population, income levels, investments, the output of the different branches of industry – all of which influence one another and determine future changes.

Here again, technological advances have opened up new prospects. Scientific progress has made it possible to obtain a view of these complex elements; a skeleton view at present, no doubt, but the details are steadily being filled in.

To give a practical example, computers are now performing services without which forecasting would be impossible. The rapid calculation of such factors as stocks, investments and current expenditure, the present level of which will have a decisive influence on the future, is an essential feature of forecasting; until lately it had to be done by hand, and was thus inevitably somewhat rough and slow, but the new mechanical computers turn out statements in the twinkling of an eye.[7]

Technology makes it possible for firms and governments alike to obtain an overall view of the elements upon which their future will depend.

Lastly, forecasting involves numerous and complicated arithmetical calculations. The changes by which many interrelated sectors of the economy will be affected at the same time are expressed in simultaneous equations. A mathematician of average ability would take months, if not years, to solve these; but an electronic computer can do it in a few hours. Here again, technological progress has equipped our economic leaders with new means of looking into the future.

It seems almost superfluous, in our day, to point out this influence

[7] The comparative accuracy of the forecasts made by American firms when compared with those of European companies is due to the use of modern computers rather than to any new intellectual approach. The nationalized Renault company, which is now equipped with these machines, makes forecasts which sustain comparison with those of General Motors.

of technique in the economic sphere. The ideas of Karl Marx have spread far and wide. But the deductions Marx drew from his principles were – obviously – only applicable to his own period. He prophesied future social developments in the light of the tremendous technical changes he himself had witnessed. But history is now being shaped by discoveries made since Marx's time. And among their other effects, these oblige man to scrutinize the future, while providing him with the means of doing so.

Economic life has been transformed by our present-day awareness of these changes and the consequent alteration in our behaviour.

CHANGES IN ECONOMIC LIFE

Long ago Malthus saw the changes coming. Discussing the relationship between wages and population growth, he declares that the population begins to increase as soon as the minimum living wage is exceeded.[8] He adds, however, that the habits of the people must be taken into account. 'From high wages . . . two very different results may follow; one, that of a rapid increase of population, in which case the high wages are chiefly spent in the maintenance of large and frequent families; and the other, that of a decided improvement in the modes of subsistence, and the conveniences and comforts enjoyed, without a proportionate acceleration in the rate of increase.' He goes on to say that those countries which produce the first result owe this to all the circumstances which contribute to depress the lower classes of the people, which make them unable or unwilling to reason from the past to the future and ready to acquiesce, for the sake of present gratification, in a very low standard of comfort and respectability. . . . Among the circumstances which contribute [to this state of things] the most efficient will be found to be despotism, oppression and ignorance.' Malthus prophesied that once these circumstances had altered, a new type of civilization would be born, one in which man, instead of living in the present, would look backward and forward, and that this would change his behaviour and affect the laws governing population.

These propositions apply to a wider field than that of the laws of population; the whole of our economic life is dominated today

[8] T. R. Malthus, *Principles of Political Economy*, 1820.

by the increasing rationalization which Malthus foresaw would develop when men began to look backward and forward.

The old-style economy had three main characteristics. Its form and ideals were static: it was a circular flow of goods, regarded as flawless so long as goods circulated without a hitch. The accumulation of wealth and of precious metals – chrysophilism – symbolized the ideal and represented a means of attaining it. The system required no concern for the future of the community; economic decisions were taken from day to day, on an individual basis.

The sense of progress and the constantly increasing demand for goods, including energy, are now transforming this attitude. One can no longer talk of an unchanging circular flow in a world where the demand for certain commodities doubles every ten years; there must be expansion, and preferably optimal expansion. To amass precious metals is not in itself a means of obtaining desirable commodities. A blindly individualistic policy is no longer justified in a world where agreements concluded on a continental or even on a wider scale, such as those of E.C.S.C. and Euratom, are paving the way for investment which will not become productive for ten years or more.

In the present economic system the centre of gravity of our activities really lies in the future. Industrialists can no longer act in blind response to the fluctuations of the market. One might almost say that only stockbrokers and greengrocers can still take decisions in the light of the customer's attitude, the state of his purse and the size of his appetite. The producer of steel or electricity is not guided solely by consumer reaction in periodically adjusting his prices or the volume of his output. He takes these decisions on the strength of forecasts he has prepared or helped to prepare, with the approval of the authorities. Dynamic economic growth guided by forecasts is gradually being substituted for static, individualistic rivalry between private persons or groups. This new economic life is exemplified in institutions which vary from one country to another.

The new economic institutions

The development of these has been remarkable, particularly in the traditionally capitalist countries, though not so widespread there as in the Socialist States or the under-developed regions.

In Germany the Government resolutely abstains from any form of intervention, as being incompatible with its proclaimed liberalism. But private firms seem to be taking a growing interest in forecasts and to be co-ordinating their activities, unofficially at least. This tendency will perhaps be accentuated by the present shortage of labour.

The British Government, mindful of the French experiment, set up a National Economic Development Council in July 1961. This is composed of from twenty to twenty-five members, including representatives of the employers, the trade unions, the Treasury and the Board of Trade, with the Chancellor of the Exchequer as its Chairman. Its purpose is to draw up a long-term economic programme in close co-operation with all the interests concerned.

In 1959 the Belgian Government established a *Bureau de Programmation* to draft economic plans for 1965.

In Canada the Federal Government is also contemplating the preparation of programmes, and the Province of Quebec is thinking along the same lines.

In the United States a paper dealing with the potential economic growth of the country in the coming ten years was published in 1954 by a congressional body, the Joint Committee on the Economic Report. Many private groups, trade unions and business firms have made similar studies on their own behalf.[9] Under the U.S. Employment Act of 1946, a new body, the Council of Economic Advisers, was created to keep the President informed about the situation; it suggests what measures are called for to ensure the anticipated expansion of the American economy. This attempt to co-ordinate long-term policy in a country with such a strong liberal tradition in economic matters deserves mention. President Kennedy's Democratic administration has recently taken steps to reactivate the research on development prospects which President Eisenhower had put into cold storage. The President's Economic Report for 1961[10] not only includes an analysis of the situation and a forecast of future activities, particularly from the angle of full employment, but goes on to indicate desirable changes in the use of the nation's resources and proposes taxation calculated to bring

[9] Cl. Gruson, 'La prévision économique aux Etats-Unis', in *Cahiers de l'I.S.E.A.*, Series K., No. 2.

[10] 'Economic Report of the President', Council of Economic Advisers, Washington, January 1962.

these about. Granted, this is not yet a true Plan, merely a set of measures; it has no actual selective effect intended to modify the decisions made by specified industries. Indeed the Report emphasizes (p. 108) that there has been no change in the traditional division of responsibilities between the Government and private individuals.

Turning to the Netherlands, we find that as long ago as 1945 that country felt the need of a research and planning centre to co-ordinate the Government's economic, social and financial policy. This, the Central Planning Bureau, is an advisory body which makes forecasts and suggests what measures should be adopted to ensure a balanced economic development for the country. It makes recommendations to the Government in the form of the annual plans into which its long-term projects are divided. It also gives its views on individual problems arising in a particular branch of industry, and on such questions as the relationship between wages and prices.

In 1955 Italy established a Secretariat to harmonize the activities of the various interministerial committees appointed to study the objectives of a development plan and the problems relating to its application; this is an offshoot of the Interministerial Committee for Reconstruction (C.I.R.), which co-ordinates economic policy. The studies prepared are combined in a 'Plan for the development of employment and income in Italy during the ten-year period 1955–1964'; this surveys the conditions required for expansion in full employment, and suggests what the authorities could do to ensure that development.

On 8 August 1962, under the premiership of Signor Fanfani, the Government appointed a National Commission to draw up economic development programmes. Its thirty-one members include representatives of the employers' and workers' organizations and experts in various fields. This Commission is laying down the main lines of a Plan for economic and social development which will be submitted, in succession, to the Cabinet, the National Labour Council and Parliament.

Japan, too, has an Economic Planning Agency with a Council for the discussion of economic questions[11]. The administration and application of the plans thus produced seem in some ways to be

[11] See *New Long-range Economic Plan of Japan*, Economic Planning Agency, published by the Japan Times Ltd, Tokyo, 1961.

very close to the French system. The Council has some thirty members, appointed by the Prime Minister; they include leading figures in industrial and banking circles, and experts. Expert committees are set up to study the problems of individual branches. When each successive Plan is being prepared, the Government asks the Council to submit a report describing the conditions required for the fulfilment of the economic aims it regards as desirable. Once approved by the Government, this report becomes the Plan. It serves as a general framework within which decisions are annually announced by the State and the industrial activities for which it is directly responsible are pursued. There have already been several of these Plans, the latest of which (1961–1970) calls for the national income to be doubled over the period concerned, at the rate of 6.5 per cent per annum. This requirement is relatively moderate in comparison with its actual growth in the period 1953–1959, which was 8.3 per cent.

Like the plans drawn up in the Eastern countries and those of the under-developed nations, all these new institutions reflect the far-reaching changes which have recently been occurring in economic life. Not all of them are equally extensive. Some are only rudimentary and confine their ambitions to making simple forecasts; others, such as the Dutch Planning Bureau, are merely advisory bodies and do not, like the French organization, undertake the actual planning. A distinction must also be drawn between the different categories of plans.

II. PLANS—THEIR COMMON FEATURES AND DIFFERENT CATEGORIES

Every true plan is the expression of a collective determination to steer the economic system in the direction of what is seen as progress. As distinct from the plans of individual firms, a national Plan constitutes *the action of a community which is subordinating the decisions of natural persons and corporations to the achievement of co-ordinated aims within a fixed period.*

The fact that planning originated in Russia has given the public a false notion of its essential nature, which is characterized neither by authoritarianism nor by the collective ownership of the means of production.

Before a plan can come into existence, co-ordinated fixed-term aims must be laid down; a body of administrative decisions drawn up independently of one another, like those in the 'Report of the President' (of the United States) for 1961, does not constitute a plan. And the merely 'indicative' plan, by which a State attempts only to look into the future without trying to change it, is not worthy of the name.

Lastly, planning must involve a measure of constraint exercised by the authorities upon private individuals and groups; but there is nothing in this to alarm those who have listened to the siren-song of liberalism; for every economic system entails some constraint, and though that established by the plan is different, it is not necessarily stronger. Constraint should, of course, be kept to a minimum by a policy acceptable to all the interests concerned. But since the general interest can never be simply the sum of all individual interests, the chorus of approval will never be absolutely unanimous. Constraint being a necessary aspect of planning, projects such as those drawn up in Germany, or even in the Netherlands, are not to be regarded as plans. Planning presupposes the existence of machinery for its implementation.

Though all plans have certain common features, there is great variety among them.[12] Their purpose is to modify existing structures, but they are closely conditioned by these. They display marked technical, social, legal and political differences. For the sake of simplicity, however, I will distinguish only two categories: imperative plans and flexible plans.

Imperative planning[13] may be defined in M. Bobrowski's words as 'of vast scope and great intensity'.

An imperative plan not only covers every branch of activity, but embraces many aspects of economic life, including volume of output, prices, localization of industries, and employment. It does not analyse all management decisions, but the behaviour of the individual firm is closely controlled by its requirements. In extreme cases the nation may be said to behave like a single firm with a number of factories to manage.

[12] As pointed out by F. Perroux in *Le quatrième Plan français* (P.U.F., series *Que sais-je*, Paris 1962), this variety is even shown in the successive French plans.

[13] This term is borrowed from J. Bénard, 'Problèmes et instruments de synthèse d'un plan indicatif', *Cahiers de l'I.S.E.A.*, Series *D*. No. 10, May 1958.

The imperative plan also has a particular way of preparing its forecasts. It tends to determine final demand, consumption and investment in the light of production targets arranged in an order of priority rather than to take account of the spontaneous behaviour of the agents.

The method of attaining the objectives is also singular. In principle at least, the Plan relies for its implementation on orders; it is controlled by the central planning bureau, by the financial organizations, and above all by the political authority.[14] The entire system is based upon a deterministic belief in the working out of a future clearly defined by its own laws. However, experience having shown that orders must be limited if respect for them is to be maintained, there is nowadays an increasing recourse to market mechanisms and financial incentives; competition is introduced, and profit-making capability invoked.

This type of planning is dependent upon the situation and structures peculiar to Russia. It can cover a huge field, because the collective ownership of the means of production has done away with profit-making in the capitalist sense, by which the policy of individual firms has always been guided. In the absence of other decentralized criteria of selection, of which there is little evidence even at the present day, decision-making is more highly centralized than in the Western economies. Moreover, economic institutions have been influenced by the political organizers, with their dominant principle of 'democratic centralism'.[15]

The social structure, too, helps to account for Soviet planning, particularly for its choice of objectives. For the Soviet planners, individual consumption is a consequence of the priority given to certain production targets, rather than an objective factor. This is because the population, whose income was for a long time very low, could make no wide choice among the goods offered for purchase, and were more or less submissive to the Government's views on the subject.

[14] One of the puzzling features of the system is the question of how contact is maintained between the political authorities and the economic bodies, how the former can keep themselves informed without becoming entirely subservient to the latter. Apparently the fact that the Party membership includes technical experts serves as a bridge, and the politicians are kept sufficiently in the picture to be able to reach and enforce decisions.

[15] See M. Lesage, 'Les Institutions politiques de l'U.R.S.S.', in *Notes et Etudes documentaires* No. 2402, Documentation française, Paris 1958.

The changes now evident in the Soviet system, the greater attention given to the analysis of private consumption, and most of all the attempt to offer financial incentives, bear witness to new developments in the Russian social and political structure.

Flexible planning is exemplified by the French system. The argument about a suitable name for this type of plan shows the difficulty of drawing up a definition of it. The term 'indicative plan' came under fire because it did not cover the practical objectives which are an essential feature of every plan.[16] I personally prefer the traditional term, 'flexible plan'. Such plans, operating within the wider limits of the growth forecast for the whole economic system, deal with a restricted number of targets, usually established per branch rather than per firm, and allowing considerable freedom of action to the entrepreneurs. They lay down fixed objectives for the basic sectors, most of which are nationalized, but only suggest targets for the majority of the manufacturing industries. In an imperative plan the future is rigorously predetermined; in a flexible plan it is merely indicated in its broad lines, the necessary adjustment to unforeseen developments being regarded as a matter for day-to-day action and the operation of automatic mechanisms. These are true plans, however, for their aims are co-ordinated, they have a time-limit, and they employ means of compulsion.

Flexible planning is accurately described in Article 1 of the Act of 23 July 1962 (*Journal Officiel*, 7 August 1962) as 'the framework for investment programmes covering the period 1962–1965, and an instrument for guiding economic expansion and social progress'.

As we shall see when considering French experience, certain special features characterize the preparation of a plan. The authorities cannot regard themselves as having sole responsibility, owing to the existence of a large sector of private production. The discussion of economic questions among the different agents in various committees facilitates the drafting of a plan which private business interests are the more ready to adopt because they have helped to formulate it. The procedure consists in assembling and combining the schemes put forward by individual firms and the trends manifested by the consumers, rather than in setting up targets *a priori*.

[16] See preface by M. P. Massé to the book by F. Perroux already mentioned, and the article by M. Cusenier entitled 'La logique de *Esprit*'.

Generally speaking, the plan is carried out by offering financial incentives, with a minimum of constraints and prohibitions. In at least part of the public sector the financial authority exercised over firms by the Finance Ministry is probably as 'imperious' as the means of application adopted in Soviet planning. But in the rest of the economic field the means of fulfilment – grants, loans, tax relief, public works contracts – are used indirectly and may be more properly described as incentives. Much is achieved by persuasion, by pointing out the advantage to be gained through participation in the system of development outlined in the plan. Many French business leaders are now convinced of that advantage. The wage-earners' organizations would adopt the same attitude if the system of employment were reformed so that they no longer needed to regard opposition as the sole method of advancement, and could have a greater say in the decisions that affected their future.

These features of the flexible plan are well suited to the structure of a country like France. There must be flexibility, owing to the existence of private firms, where decisions are taken in comparative independence, the fact that the powers of the State are limited, and the freedom of choice enjoyed by consumers – or at least by those categories of consumers whose incomes are in excess of their basic requirements.

Plans in under-developed countries, where the social structure calls for original economic methods, differ from both of the types described above. But they do not fall within the scope of this study.

In spite of the differences mentioned, all plans are the same in essence, inasmuch as they reflect a collective determination to steer the economy in the agreed direction of progress. In the economic sphere they denote the transition – made necessary by technological advances and by changes in behaviour – from a Darwinian age when progress depended on survival resulting from natural selection, to a Lamarckian age of survival by calculated inventiveness.[17] This progress is achieved not so much by conflict as by united effort with an eye to the future. The slow, gradual development of French planning shows that we are still at the dawn of the new world.

Moreover, the successive French Plans have taught us by experience that, whatever their merits, they involve political and technical problems which call for unremitting investigation.

[17] See R. P. Teilhard de Chardin, *art. cit.*

From the political angle, without falling into the error of the Marxists and the liberals who declare that any plan must necessarily be imperative, we have to admit that the problem of 'planning versus democracy' has not yet been solved. No way has yet been found of reconciling the co-ordination of decisions regarding prices, production and income with some measure of decentralization, of imposing a necessary degree of constraint while respecting the freedom of firms and individuals, of ensuring continuity of economic management while encouraging the participation of all interested groups. Although a *modus vivendi* has been established in France, this has by no means disposed of the danger that individuals and firms may find their liberty sacrificed to collective constraint,[18] that large firms may invoke that very liberty as a means of bringing State plans under their own influence, and that the technocrats may slowly wrest the economic control of the State out of the hands of the political authority and away from the other groups in the community. The first part of this book will deal with the problems raised by the coexistence of planning and democracy.

From the angle of economic technique, we are faced with the task of drawing up plans which will give the fullest possible satisfaction to the aspirations of the community. It is difficult enough to paint a picture of the future in terms of collective progress and to bring that picture to life, but the planners have to do even more: they have to set before the political authorities, when the time comes to consult them, alternative hypotheses of development from among which they can select the one they prefer, while leaving some degree of freedom to individual behaviour. Their attempt to do this will form the subject of the second part of my book, dealing with 'planning for an optimum'.

Lastly, the existence of a Plan inevitably leads to extensive economic and social changes. Moreover, the Common Market will have repercussions on current plans, and we may wonder whether it will be possible for these to remain purely national. These changes will be considered in the third part of the book.

[18] See F. A. Hayek, *The Constitution of Liberty*, Routledge & Kegan Paul Ltd, London 1960. This writer has the merit of pointing out one of the dangers inherent in planning, – that of freezing methods of thought and action at the time when the forecast is made, so that further development becomes impossible.

Part One

PLANNING AND DEMOCRACY

DIVISION OF FRANCE INTO DISTRICTS FOR PURPOSES OF REGIONAL ACTION (ORDER OF 28 NOVEMBER 1956).

PART ONE

Planning and Democracy

THIS general heading covers two aspects of the subject.

The first relates to the substance of the Plan, which must satisfy the needs of the community, pursue aims of general interest, ensure that they will be fulfilled – in short, be democratic in content.

The second deals with the procedure of decision and action. The Plan must be the expression of a general determination, but it must not make individual choice impossible for persons or for groups; in brief, it must be compatible with a democratic system.

These two problems are in fact inseparably connected, as evidenced by the theories to which they give rise.

A section of economic opinion remains hostile to the idea of planning, in the conviction that no collective economic decision can leave scope for individual freedom of choice: to decide what is in the general interest by starting from individual preferences involves the same difficulties of logic for those who prepare collective decisions and for those who have to interpret them. It is better to leave people quite free, making no attempt to lay down regulations in economic matters – for regulations can never be democratic and they smother the individual initiative which, in the long run, leads to progress. For example, 'the freedom to choose' is by no means incompatible with 'the freedom not to starve to death'; on the contrary, it promotes growth. The Soviet example is adduced to show that the whole concept of planning is radically opposed to that of freedom; that – as evidenced by recent Soviet attempts to decentralize the Gosplan – it requires an enormous, all-powerful central administration, dominating every sphere of economic life. Furthermore, the very notion of a Plan is inconsistent with the activity of a democratically elected parliament, which confines itself to giving *carte blanche* to the executive at stated intervals.

We may regard this attitude as old-fashioned, we may agree that it has now become a matter of course to undertake commitments for the future, thus reducing the opportunities for last-minute decisions, and to draw up Plans because they enable us to control forthcoming developments; but this does not make it any easier to draw up a plan democratically.

The French experiment in planning is to some extent reassuring, of course. It is taking place in a political atmosphere which it cannot so far be said to have rendered anti-democratic. But in its present form it gives rise to a number of queries. While little objection is made to its organization, a good deal of criticism is expressed regarding its range, the methods by which it is put into effect, and the procedure for its political control.

CHAPTER I

Organization of the Plan

THE REASON why the French Plan passed unnoticed for so long is that its 'quantitative' importance in the general field of administration is very slight.

A few figures will make this clear. In 1956 the *Commissariat général du Plan* had one of the smallest budgets in the Republic: its expenditure did not exceed 113 million francs, including equipment and the upkeep of premises; and its staff, consisting of a Secretary-General, a Commissioner-General, a Deputy Commissioner, councillors, secretaries, typists, chauffeurs, maintenance personnel and office messengers, amounted all told to one hundred persons. The staff now numbers 150, chiefly because the Productivity services were amalgamated with it in 1959. This is still far short of the enormous administrative departments employed in the East, and is enough in itself to indicate the profound difference between the two systems of planning.

The French organization is, however, more complex than these figures would suggest, for other government departments and various sections of the community are brought in at different stages while the Plan is being prepared.

I. ADMINISTRATION OF THE PLAN

This is divided into three separate parts: a permanent working administration known as the *Commissariat général du Plan*; a number of Working Parties which, though attached to the Commissariat, are recruited from outside; the *Commissions de Modernisation*, and two supervisory bodies, the *Conseil Supérieur* and the *Comité Interministériel*.

In everyday speech, 'the Plan' means the *Commissariat général*, but in reality the reports are not produced solely by its staff of 150; between three and four thousand other people help to prepare them.

THE COMMISSARIAT GÉNÉRAL

This is headed by a Commissioner-General appointed by decree as the 'permanent delegate of the Prime Minister to the ministerial departments for all aspects of the preparation of the plan'.[1] He is responsible for 'drafting proposals to be submitted for consideration by the Council of the Plan' (which, by a Decree of 19 March 1953, became an Interministerial Committee).

In addition to the Deputy Commissioner and the Secretary-General, the *Commissariat* comprises some forty councillors and heads of mission; it is remarkable for the low average age of its members and for the wide range of activities they represent.[2]

They are divided into sections, one for each of the principal segments of the economy: agriculture, chemicals, building, energy, the manufacturing industries, overseas, iron and steel, transport and communications. There are divisions to deal with economy, finance, manpower, regional development and productivity, and various other services such as a bureau of personnel and a reference unit.

THE 'MODERNIZATION COMMISSIONS'

These are set up whenever a new Plan is to be prepared. The Prime Minister appoints them by a decree giving effect to the proposals of the Commissioner-General, and they are composed of civil servants, representatives of the employers and of the industrial and agricultural unions, and experts.[3]

These Commissions, which constitute the really original feature

[1] See Art. 3 of the Decree of 3 January 1946, amended by a Decree of 16 January 1946 (Appendix 1).

[2] In 1956 they were as follows: five agricultural engineers, six industrial engineers, one Inspector-General of the National Economy, one Inspector of Finance, one geographer, one H.E.C. (*Hautes Etudes Commerciales*), one records expert, one University professor, three specialists on the French overseas territories, two legal experts, one civil administrator and three economists. Since then, the tendency has been towards more specialized recruitment, with an appreciable increase in the number of engineers and of former students of the National School of Administration attached to the Finance Ministry.

[3] Whereas the members of the British National Economic Development Council are appointed by the organizations they represent.

of the French system, make proposals for their respective branches and submit them to the Commissioner-General, whose task then is to co-ordinate the projects. Since the Commissions include representatives of the administration, business leaders, experts and wage-earners, they are able to thresh out the different opinions on the development of each individual branch with very useful results, particularly as their organization is directly responsible to the Executive. This close collaboration between the Government and the different branches of industry, with its representation of all social categories, marks the inception of a revolutionary development whose potential effect on our traditional institutions has not yet been generally realized.

The active participation of all those concerned, and of the different Ministries, which too often tend to work in watertight compartments, is noteworthy in itself. Moreover, an attempt is made – though not always successfully – to avoid sterile controversy by ensuring that the Commissions will be representative of the human element rather than of groups of interests, and to obtain the widest possible agreement about development prospects, rather than to secure majority votes. There is no hard-and-fast rule as to the proportion in which the different groups are represented. All this takes us a long way from the established attitude of parliamentary democracy, and emphasizes the desire for collective rather than majority decisions.

Each Commission has its own field. The 'vertical' Commissions, one for each sector,[4] numbered seventeen for the third Plan; for the fourth Plan there are twenty-three of them.[5] The 'horizontal' Commissions (finance and manpower) deal with problems common to a number of branches. In addition there are Commissions for Productivity and Research, and a Committee on Regional Plans about which we shall have more to say when discussing regional development.

[4] A sector consists of a group of enterprises having their main activity in common.

[5] They deal with Agriculture, Craftsmanship, Building and Public Works, Fuel, Chemistry, Trade, Fats, *Départements d' Outremer*, Energy, Cultural Investment, Health and Social Investment, Investment in Schools, Urban Development, Housing, Agriculture and Food Industries, Manufacturing Industries, Mines and Non-ferrous Metals, Sea Fisheries, Postal and Telecommunications, Broadcasting and Television, Iron and Steel, Tourism, Transport.

When the third Plan was being prepared, the 612 members of the nineteen Modernization Commissions comprised:

Civil Servants	113
Technical Experts	134
Heads of businesses	206
Trade union representatives (including twenty-five farmers)	82
Representatives of the leading State institutions (the *Conseil d'Etat*, the *Cour des Comptes*, the Universities)	23
Representatives of finance and banking	13
Miscellaneous (business representatives, hotel-keepers, craftsmen, members of the medical profession, representatives of family organizations)	41

They were not, however, the only people concerned with the Plan, for each Commission had several working parties to study finance, foreign trade, demographic problems, the development of subsidiary branches, and other special questions. In all, about 3,000 people helped to draw up the third Plan, either as members of the Commissions or of the working parties.

For the fourth Plan, the figure is even larger. The total membership of the Commissions is 991, as against the previous 612, and those contributing in other capacities bring the number of participants to 3,137, including:

Farmers	107
Heads of businesses (including craftsmen)	715
Civil Servants	781
Trade union representatives (industry and agriculture)	281
Representatives of employers' associations	562
Miscellaneous (experts)	691

Studies of existing conditions in each branch, and proposals for its expansion, are drawn up by the appropriate group in the light of a general policy approved by the Government and of a general forecast of economic trends prepared by the Finance Ministry's *Service des Etudes économiques et financières* (Bureau of Economic and Financial Studies – S.E.E.F.) in consultation with the

Commissariat général. Thus, from the outset there is some degree of co-ordination between the reports of the various Commissions, which are further adjusted in course of preparation, to avoid incompatibility between the policy of individual branches, and are finally combined and summarized in the Commissioner's general report.

THE CONSEIL SUPÉRIEUR AND THE COMITÉ INTERMINISTÉRIEL

Under the Decree of 19 March 1953 (B.L.D. 1953, 394), the *Conseil Supérieur* and the *Comité Interministériel* were entrusted with supervisory duties.

The original intention was that the *Conseil* should act as a kind of super-Commission, in which the leading representatives of the employers and workers would discuss and approve the trend of the Plan as a whole, as the Commissions did for the individual branches. Its twenty members, representing the various national activities involved, were not convened to debate the third Plan, however – partly because the main interests were in any case given opportunities for expression in each Commission, and partly because of the danger that general discussion might call in question the decisions already taken by the working parties.

As for the Interministerial Committee set up to follow the preparation and application of the Plan, it was supposed to hold a meeting at which the activities of the different Ministries would be co-ordinated, and then forward the general report on the Plan to the Cabinet. But this task is now carried out by the Ministry of Finance, Economic Affairs and the Plan, which functions rather like the British Treasury, and both the *Comité Interministériel* and the *Conseil Supérieur* were shelved for a time. Nevertheless, the *Conseil* was reconstituted by a Decree of 12 July 1961, the *Comité* having been revived by a similar Decree on the previous day (see Appendix I).

The *Conseil* was consulted rather precipitately (at the beginning of October 1961), even before the Commissions for the fourth Plan had finished their work. It is to some extent redundant, for a Decree issued on 4 October 1958 had established procedure for consultation with the *Conseil Economique et Social*, which includes representatives of the same interests as the *Conseil Supérieur*.

This complicated administrative structure already gives some idea of the *Commissariat*'s special position in the French administrative machinery.

THE REGIONAL BODIES

The increasing lopsidedness of regional development in France, the bloated expansion of Paris and the fact that some areas of the country were dying of inanition, combined to oblige the authorities to turn their attention to regional problems. A wider distribution of effort, the determined encouragement of local initiative, and the desire to keep a check on how funds were being spent, have stimulated attempts to co-ordinate the measures adopted and fit them into the Plan.

Geographical considerations gradually intruded themselves. The first Plan barely touched on the problem of regional equilibrium, but its successor laid down three well-defined courses of action. A Committee on the Plan was set up in the Moselle Department, its title being changed in November 1951 to that of *Comité d'aménagement du Plan d'Equipement de la Moselle* (Development Committee for the Moselle Investment Plan). A special Commission was appointed for the development of the Bas-Rhône-Languedoc area. And lastly, a Decree published in January 1955 established a Commission on the use of natural gas resources and the promotion of industrial development in South-West France.

A Decree of 30 June 1955 laid down a system of 'regional action' programmes to combine all these activities in a national framework. The preamble to this Decree says that the aim of the programmes will be to contribute to the 'Plan for Modernization and Investment' under which they are to be drawn up, and to ensure the co-ordination of public and private resources in the regions concerned. Stress is also laid on one of the Plan's essential features, the participation of representatives of private enterprise in working out the programmes.

Regional Development Plans were provided for by an outline-law on building activities, adopted on 7 August 1957, and a Decree of 31 December 1958 announced that these would be amalgamated with the regional action programmes, to form 'regional plans for economic and social development' under which long-term forecasts would be established and targets selected. Efforts could then converge towards these as part of the national Plan.

It took seven years to prepare these regional plans,[6] largely owing to the absence of any regional economic administration and indeed of a suitable geographical framework. Decree No. 60-516, of 2 June 1960 (*Journal Officiel*, 3 June, p. 5007), which made certain readjustments in the administrative districts, was needed before some thirty local authorities decided to adapt the geographical boundaries of their services to those of the twenty-one districts into which the Order of 28 November 1956 had divided the country for purposes of regional action (see map p. 29).

But even so there were no regional organizations. Moreover, apprehension regarding possible regional demands was so great at the initial stage that the preparation of the regional plans was entrusted to secretaries who had very little contact with the local authorities. Their reports were drafted in the office of the *Commissariat général*, under the supervision of what was at first known as a *groupe de synthèse* (co-ordinating group); its composition has since been slightly altered and its name changed to *Comité des Plans régionaux*. It included the Deputy-Commissioner for the Plan, together with representatives of the different Ministries, of the Prefects of the *Départements* concerned, and of the local authorities. *The Comité national d'Orientation économique* (National Committee for Economic Guidance) was consulted before a decree was published to announce that the Ministers had reached agreement and approved the plans.

The creation of genuinely regional bodies was a very slow process. A Decree of 7 January 1959 set up in each 'regional action district' an Interdepartmental Conference composed of the regional Prefects, the Inspector-General of the National Economy and certain regional officials. One of the Prefects, known as the 'co-ordinating Prefect', acts as Chairman, and each district thus has its permanent organization to study and co-ordinate public utility programmes and the implementation of the regional plans.

Side by side with these, there are the Regional Expansion Committees, the status and composition of which were established by Decree No. 61–72 of 20 January 1961 (*Journal Officiel*, 21 January 1961, p. 867); they bring together representatives of the various

[6] The first reports were drawn up in 1956, the last did not appear until 1962.

occupational and social categories in their respective regions, and have only advisory powers.

Both these bodies will have an important role to play when the time comes to work out the operational stages of the regional plans. This phase, of which I shall have more to say later on, is to begin in 1962.

A number of private, semi-public and public institutions take part in this regional activity. These need only be mentioned briefly. They include the *Sociétés de Développement régional* (Regional Development Associations – S.D.R.) for which provision was made in one of the Decrees of 30 June 1955, and which are formed by certain banks and industrial firms to encourage the regional population to put their savings into local investments. As well as these, there are the Investment Associations, joint (government-private) economic bodies co-ordinated by the *Société centrale pour l'Equipement du Territoire* (Central Association for the Development of the Territory), the function of which is to carry out large-scale public utility schemes such as housing projects and motor highways, etc.[7]

II. THE POSITION OF THE COMMISSARIAT IN RELATION TO OTHER GOVERNMENT BODIES

This may be assessed by considering the prerogatives of the Commissioner-General and the links between the *Commissariat* and the outer world.

PREROGATIVES OF THE COMMISSIONER-GENERAL

The Commissioner-General is responsible by law for the co-ordination of French economic policy. Article 3 of the Decree of 3 January 1946, amended by a Decree of 16 January 1947, describes him as 'the permanent delegate of the Prime Minister to the

[7] There are now six bodies responsible for public utilities on the national scale – the *Compagnie nationale du Bas-Rhône-Languedoc*, the *Société pour la mise en valeur agricole de la Corse*, the *Compagnie d' aménagement des Landes de Gascogne*, the *Société du Canal de Provence*, the *Compagnie d'aménagement des Coteaux de Gascogne* (authorized by a Decree of 14 April 1960 to launch the first part of its programme), and the *Société des friches et taillis pauvres de l'Est*. In addition, a *Société centrale d'aménagement foncier rural* was formed in 1960 to facilitate the migration of agricultural workers by providing housing and other amenities for them.

ministerial departments for all aspects of the preparation of the Plan', while Article 4 states that help is to be furnished to him by the Civil Service and the appropriate Ministers.

He undertakes surveys, or has them carried out by various other ministerial departments, and all programmes with a bearing on the country's economic activities are put before him. In point of fact, however, he has never supplanted the interministerial committees in the task of unifying economic policy as a whole.

Nevertheless, his scope has gradually extended. At first he was responsible only for the development of basic industrial production, but he soon took over agriculture, the Overseas Territories, building, and finally the manufacturing industries. The Plan, which was based on a real, nation-wide conception of equilibrium, came in course of time to deal with monetary problems – such as the financing of investments – the distribution of certain forms of revenue, regional development and social questions. It now covers the whole field of economic growth, its prospects and the conditions required for it. In 1959 the *Commissariat à la Productivité*, which had taken over the activities of the earlier Productivity Agency, was reabsorbed by the *Commissariat du Plan*, the official title of which then became *Commissariat du Plan et de la Productivité*.

As time went by, the personal relations between the Plan and the different Ministries grew closer. The opinions of the planners receive greater attention, particularly from the Ministry of Finance, and the usefulness of the working Commissions as 'round-table' meetings is universally acknowledged. No one would dream nowadays of suggesting that the *Commissariat* be abolished outright.

At the same time, however, other government bodies have come into existence, independent of the *Commissariat*, but with the powers usually attributed to a planning organization. These include the *Service de l'Aménagement du Territoire* (Territorial Development Board), which should originally have been attached to the Plan, but was allocated, previous to some recent indecisive changes, to the Ministry of Reconstruction and Housing.

Nor has the Plan brought about the gradual amalgamation of the economic departments of the various Ministries which pursue parallel aims, such as the Directorate of Foreign Economic Relations at the Ministry for the National Economy and the Directorate of Foreign Finance at the Finance Ministry. Lastly, the failure of the Plan to act as an over-riding authority for the arbitration of disputes led to the formation of interministerial commissions just at the time when political stability was strengthening the authority of the Ministers' personal staff: all these struggled to occupy the vacant position of co-ordinating authority, and filled it in an extremely unsatisfactory manner.

LINKS BETWEEN THE COMMISSARIAT AND OTHER ADMINISTRATIVE BODIES

In its role of adviser, the *Commissariat* does not trespass upon the province of any other authority. Its links with other administrative bodies fall under two headings. In the first place, as the permanent delegate of the Prime Minister, the Commissioner-General takes part, or is represented, in the work of a number of organizations and is consulted before certain decisions are adopted. In the second place, the *Commissariat* is directly responsible to the Prime Minister, although from 1954 to 1962 it was attached to the Ministry of Finance and National Economy.[8] It serves as a round table, a meeting place for all the Ministries.

1. *The Commissioner's participation in other bodies*

As the delegate of the Government, in permanent contact with the various Ministries, the Commissioner-General attends interministerial meetings; at the legislative level he is consulted by the Commissions appointed by the Chamber of Deputies and the Senate; he is a member of the *Conseil national du Crédit* and of the board of directors of the *Fonds d'Aide et de Coopération* (Fund for Aid and Co-operation – F.A.C.)

He belongs to, or is represented on, a variety of commissions and committees, including the Steering Committee of the *Centre de Recherche, d'Etudes et de Documentation sur la Consommation* (Centre for Consumer Research, Study and Information – C.R.E. D.O.C.) and the *Comité de Coordination des Etudes statistiques* (Co-ordinating Committee on Statistics), to say nothing of the numerous international expert committees of the Organization for Economic Co-operation and Development (O.E.C.D.) and the European Coal and Steel Community (E.C.S.C.).

[8] Since April 1962 it has again been responsible to the Prime Minister.

At times collaboration with certain Ministries becomes particularly close, as when the experts of the Finance Ministry and those of the *Commissariat* meet to compare views on economic and financial questions. During the actual preparation of the Plans, the *Commissariat* works in the closest possible association with several administrative bodies, such as the Department of Economic and Financial Studies (S.E.E.F.) at the Ministry of Finance, the National Institute of Statistics and Economic Studies (I.N.S.E.E.), the National Institute for Demographic Studies (I.N.E.D.) and the Centre for Consumer Research, Study and Information (C.R.E.D.O.C.). Together they forecast trends in population and output of consumer goods, and draw up expectational models. But – though this is contrary to both the spirit and the letter of the law (the Decree of 3 January 1946) – the ministerial Departments are not obliged to follow the suggestions of the *Commissariat*.

2. *The* Commissariat *as a round table for the Ministries*

The *Commissariat* has become increasingly popular as a centre for round-table discussions. The meetings of its Commissions have brought home to those attending them the value of a neutral ground where private interests, civil servants, and even the different departments of one Ministry, can come together and air their differences, uninhibited by considerations of personal status. New commissions and committees are always glad to meet on the *Commissariat*'s premises, with a member of its staff participating or attending as an observer, when they have to deal with some urgent problem such as decentralization, regional development, the resettlement of repatriates or the water supply – to mention only the most recent topics. This increases the influence of the *Commissariat* and safeguards it from any possible danger of being thrust into the background.

III. THE PREPARATORY STAGES

Since the various Civil Service departments are not in sole control of economic development, preliminary studies are needed to ascertain what spontaneous tendencies are revealed by the behaviour of its various agents and to decide what general aims shall be laid down for them. We will consider this phase of forecasting before describing the work done in the Commissions and the final synthesis.

THE PRELIMINARY FORECASTS

These are begun a year ahead of the Plan itself and are worked out jointly by the *Commissariat du Plan* and the S.E.E.F. For the fourth Plan, this phase of operations lasted from the spring of 1959 to July 1960. Forecasting for the fifth Plan started early in 1962. These forecasts, which will be described in detail later on, explore the field of the Plan by investigating, for the period of time it is to cover, the prospects of development of the economy, which is divided for this purpose into some thirty sectors. They are made first for a long term (ten or fifteen years) and then for the period of the Plan (four or five years), present several hypotheses, each corresponding to a different annual rate of growth (3 per cent, 4½ per cent and 6 per cent were considered in the preliminary forecasts for the fourth Plan) and indicate which is the most feasible. The authorities consulted can thus select, in the light of full information, whichever annual rate they consider will lead to maximum expansion while maintaining equilibrium in fundamentals – full employment, equality of investment and savings, stable public finance and maintenance of the balance of payments.[9]

Since the fourth Plan, the forecasts have been submitted at this stage to the Investment and Planning Section of the Economic and Social Council, which gives its opinion on the rate of growth and on any special features of the Plan – such as, in 1960, the structure of needs and the necessity of giving priority to collective consumption.

On the strength of this information the Government draws up its 'instructions to the Commissioner-General on the preparation of the Plan', indicating the rate of growth (5 per cent for the fourth Plan) to be taken as a working hypothesis,[10] and laying down the principal objectives of the Plan – to aid the new States in the French Community, to provide more housing and more capital investment in education, health services and town planning, and to guide each sector of activity along agreed lines.

[9] See lecture given in London by M. Massé on 22 April 1961 (a roneo document), p. 18.

[10] The Government also recommended consideration of a rate of 5½ per cent, and this was the one finally chosen.

THE WORK OF THE COMMISSIONS

The membership of the Commissions is announced in the *Journal Officiel*. For the fourth Plan, they set to work in July 1960 and finished in July 1961. They look into and elaborate the general preliminary forecasts, which are given to them together with the Government's instructions. The 'vertical' Commissions then proceed to investigate conditions of growth in their respective branches, including possible markets, the most economic production techniques and the necessary factors.[11] The 'horizontal' Commissions classify the information thus obtained to make sure that fundamental equilibrium (of manpower, balance of payments, savings and investment) will be preserved.

During the preparation of the earlier Plans the Commissions completed their work in one stage, but for the fourth Plan it was divided into two consecutive stages. They carried out their first studies and combined these in a provisional synthesis (December 1960). In the light of the adjustments then effected to harmonize their respective projects, they afterwards made a fresh series of separate studies, based on a growth objective of $5\frac{1}{2}$ per cent per annum. This is a cumbersome process to complete in the brief space of a year, and is likely to be reconsidered.

THE NATIONAL SYNTHESIS

Finally, the reports of the different Commissions are amalgamated by the S.E.E.F. and the *Commissariat du Plan*. The *Commission de l'Equilibre et du Financement* takes over the combined report, which is prepared in consultation with the vertical Commissions and the Ministries concerned, particularly the Ministry of Finance, and submits it to the Government. The Government settles any controversial points of policy and passes the result to the *Conseil Supérieur du Plan*, after which it goes before a plenary meeting of the Economic and Social Council. Finally, the Plan is submitted to the two houses of Parliament – though this has not been done on every occasion. Only the second and fourth Plans were put before Parliament, and even then with some delay, the fourth Plan not being submitted until the spring of 1962.

[11] See Appendix V for the questionnaire sent to the Commissions.

THE REGIONAL PROGRAMMES

The preparation of the third Plan included that of the first regional programmes, intended to give planning a geographical dimension. But seven years went by before, in 1962, these programmes – now known as 'Regional Plans for economic, social and territorial development' – were extended to cover the whole country.

Their purpose is to help each region to take stock of its circumstances, problems and potentialities, to define the aims and trends its economy should pursue, to co-ordinate the action of the different regional authorities, and to provide guidance for local effort.

The preliminaries are simple. The Committee on Regional Plans, of which the Commissioner-General of the Plan is Chairman, supervises the preparation of the report, which is drawn up by a civil servant. The individual plans are first submitted to the recognized Regional Expansion Committees, then referred to the *Conseil national d'Orientation économique* (National Council for Economic Guidance) and, after that body has given its opinion, embodied in a Decree.

In their initial stage – since when they have been appreciably improved – these plans had one great defect: they did not lay down a definite policy with clearly specified stages of application and methods of finance. In the fourth Plan, however, a new procedure was adopted. For the period 1962–1965, each regional plan is divided into operational sections (*tranches opératoires*), the completion of which will be mandatory. These will be worked out principally by a nation-wide 'Interdepartmental Conference' with the assistance of the Regional Expansion Committees, and then submitted to the Committee on Regional Plans. Thus, while still indicative in character, the regional plans will act as a geographical extension of the National Plan, and be financed from the same sources, funds to cover the cost of the year's share being included in the annual budgets of the appropriate Ministries.

The fifth Plan will take in all the regions while still at the preparatory stage, so that its geographical extension will not be a separate, subsequent development.

This new procedure represents a considerable innovation, which will have to be judged in the light of experience. The Plan will no longer merely pay lip-service to the aim of geographical balance, for certain measures will be localized. Instead of simply being consulted, the regional authorities are to be closely associated with the preparation of some at least of the suggested programmes.

After considering these successive phases in the preparation of the Plan, we may now inquire whether its present organization is satisfactory.

IV. POWER TO ARBITRATE, AND DEMOCRATIC PARTICIPATION

I shall deal later with the problem of political control of the Plan; for the moment it is enough to say that its organization should include the following two features: the *Commissariat* must have powers of arbitration, so that it may be able to settle the conflicting claims of rival groups and even of opposing interests in administrative circles; and the active forces within the nation must be closely associated with the preparation of the Plan, through the representation of the different social categories or local groups.

POWERS OF ARBITRATION

The *Commissariat* is not merely an advisory and consultative body, like the Dutch Planning Bureau or the Council of Economic Advisers to the President of the United States. It is not divided from the Executive. The Commissioner-General, personally or through his representatives, participates in the work of bodies whose decisions are enforceable. He thus exerts an appreciable influence over economic and business life, for the decision to grant government loans to firms through the F.D.E.S. to finance capital investment rests partly with him.

But the Commissioner-General is not a kind of super-Minister, co-ordinating economic and financial policy. He seems to prefer not to make full use of the powers conferred on him by law. Every Commissioner has maintained this attitude of cautious moderation – no doubt because they all remember the failure of the Economic Ministry set up in 1936. The highly mistrustful attitude of the different Ministries, each jealous of its prerogatives, and the privileges enjoyed by certain national Companies, have done more to prevent the *Commissariat* from taking a strong line, and been a greater threat to its survival, than have the political forces which are hostile to the whole idea of planning. For fear of losing the support of the Civil Service, the Commissioners have elected to pursue a conciliatory policy rather than to assert their authority by insisting upon co-ordination. There is reason to believe that had they behaved otherwise, the Plan would have foundered. This is borne out by the experience of other countries, such as the Netherlands.

So the *Commissariat du Plan* is something more than an advisory board and something less than a real centre for the co-ordination of economic policy. Is it desirable for it to go further in the second of these directions? Without advocating the Soviet degree of centralization, or denying the progress achieved by the use of the *Commissariat* as a platform for discussion, one may acknowledge that the evidence is in favour of a change.

As things are, every Ministry retains its prerogatives. Each of them invariably tries to push ahead with its own projects and to set up new bodies for the purpose, regardless of duplication with other branches of the Civil Service. The Fifth Republic, like the Fourth, seems unable to reduce their number. This means that responsibility for foreign trade, technical assistance, territorial development and the supervision of public corporations and decentralized community schemes is divided between a host of authorities, making it impossible to devise an overall policy for major problems such as co-ordination of transport, loans, etc.

Team-work has no doubt improved in some cases, owing to the slowly but surely increasing influence of the Ministry of Finance. But that influence, however undeniable, is not yet – as some remarks made in *The Economist*[12] might suggest – strong enough to render the Plan expendable. It has in fact been coloured by the Plan. Moreover, it is limited by differences of opinion between the departments of the Ministry and apprehensions aroused by the autocratic behaviour of its financial magnates.

This difficulty cannot be overcome by setting up more and more Ministries and interministerial committees, by Cabinet interference

[12] See 'Planning like the French', *The Economist*, 28 October 1961, p. 314.

or by appointing a host of commissions of private experts.[13] On the contrary, an efficient arbitral body can only be created by making the planning procedure less cumbersome and thoroughly overhauling the structure of the executive.

1. Buoyancy and elasticity are characteristics of youth and efficiency. Institutions, like individuals, are apt to grow ponderous as they grow older. Up to now, the French Plan has escaped that danger. But as its range increases it becomes more meticulous in detail, and the threat is already apparent. In preparing the fourth Plan the working Commissions were obliged to draw up two syntheses in less than a year, which is too much to ask of them, at least in the conditions under which the secretaries now have to work. Furthermore, at the present stage of ideas and of economic organization it is impossible to trace the results of the alternative policies to their final conclusion, to determine the ultimate effect of a given policy on the pattern of private consumption, to choose between increased consumption and reduced working hours, etc. If the planners are to weigh the merits of the possibilities confronting them, the Plan must not be too detailed, it must keep to the essentials of economic life.

2. To ensure that the Plan shall play its proper leading role, government action must be concentrated, and based on an improved system of technical study.

The fate of the short-lived Ministry for the National Economy demonstrated the futility of creating a separate body for concentrating government action. What is needed is co-ordination at the highest ministerial level, perhaps under the leadership of a super-Minister for Economic Affairs, perhaps through a small panel of Ministers headed not by the Finance Minister but by a Minister of Planning and Productivity.

Such a Minister would have under his immediate authority the present planning services, those responsible for regional development, and some of those at present attached to the Budget and Treasury Departments of the Finance Ministry; this would ensure the co-ordination of economic and financial policy.

[13] There has recently been a tendency to commission private research organizations to undertake surveys, when the Government finds it embarrassing to make a decision.

There should also be a small panel of Ministers – the heads of certain of the present Ministries, reorganized into larger units (Ministry of Technology, Ministry of Communications, Ministry of Social Welfare, Ministry of Finance) – which would deal with all important matters having economic repercussions, including orders placed by the armed forces, on which in the past the economic authorities have not been consulted. 'This grouping of the principal Ministries would be accompanied by some readjustment of the administrative structure – rendered necessary by the increased importance of the Plan as a factor in economic and social life – and by the establishment of machinery for consultation and supervision in which the different social and professional categories would be represented, as a parallel to the political supervision of the Executive which is traditionally exercised by the Parliamentary Commissions.'[14]

Lastly, if the Plan is to play this leading role, facilities for study must be adequate, and research should not as a rule be entrusted to private bodies, and in particular not to the managements of firms – as it too often is at present, so that the planner has no say in the scope of the problems he is required to consider, or even in the solution adopted for them. To avoid this erosion of control, the heads of the appropriate Civil Service departments might appoint small study groups, one for each of the chief national products. These groups, working in consultation with the S.E.E.F., would follow the development of their respective branches, noting how progress conformed to the forecasts made in the Plan and what changes were needed. They would act as 'feelers' for the Plan, and would have extensive facilities for investigation; but they would not be satellite bodies, liable in the long run to usurp the power of independent decision and thus disrupt the unity which is the Plan's chief merit.

To ensure that this concentration of authority would not ultimately degenerate into authoritarianism, opportunity must also be provided for the participation of the active forces in economic life, and particularly of the different social groups in the community.

[14] See *La planification démocratique* (p. 29), issued by the Club Jean Moulin, Paris 1962.

PARTICIPATION OF SOCIAL GROUPS

The preparation of the Plans affects interests which it is desirable to associate with any decisions reached, if only to facilitate their enforcement.[15] This consideration was reflected in the composition of the Commissions appointed when the very first Plans were drawn up, and is now evidenced by the participation of the *Conseil Economique et Social* and of the *Conseil Supérieur du Plan*.

1. *Conseil Economique et Social*

This, first consulted when the fourth Plan was being prepared, seems exceptionally well qualified to represent the various economic and social interests involved. But its present composition should be amended, to make it fully representative even of interests which are not effectively organized, such as low-income groups and immigrants.

The *Conseil Economique et Social* should play a twofold part, advising the Government on economic and social problems and advising Parliament whenever that body is brought into close association with the planning process. On such occasions the specialized sections of the *Conseil* would collaborate with the Parliamentary Commissions.

This would of course entail more extensive preliminary consultation of the *Conseil*; at present only its investment and planning section is called upon, and its discussions are not made public. The whole *Conseil* should be associated with the planning, and should discuss not merely rates of expansion but all the basic choices of policy to be made in such matters as family welfare, overseas territories, military expenditure and so forth. The *Conseil Economique et Social* should also be responsible for supervising the fulfilment of the Plan.

2. *Conseil Supérieur du Plan*

As we have already seen, this body had never found a niche for itself, but merely duplicated the work of the *Conseil Economique et*

[15] In addition to the organized social groups, which can bring pressure to bear, there are others – old people, youth, immigrants and so forth – which are inadequately represented and whose voice ought to be heard. That is why I speak of 'social groups' rather than 'pressure groups'.

Social. Nowadays it considers the draft Plan prepared by the Commissioner-General for submission to the Government and gives its opinion thereon, and it supervises the application of the Plan year by year.

Being a comparatively small body, it might play a genuine, active part in the actual planning. The Plan, being flexible, depends for its fulfilment on the participation and approval of the interests involved. Flexibility is demonstrated by a number of contracts between the public authorities and private enterprise. Could such quasi-contracts be extended to groups such as wage-earners, entrepreneurs and Civil Service departments; covering both the requirements of economic growth and the distribution of its benefits? That would entail, at the very least, a far-reaching transformation of present attitudes.

3. *The Modernization Commissions*

These, both in composition and in the part they play, are probably the most original and the least criticized feature of the Plan.

Their role is essentially an advisory one; they forecast the development of production and the market prospects for their respective branches, and provide information about structural changes and the conditions governing investment and finance. The fact that they do not make decisions leaves the individual members free to form and announce their opinions, more especially as no vote is taken at the end of their deliberations. This resembles the procedure followed at the meetings held by the workers' syndicates of Soviet firms. The advantage is that such discussions are not bogged down from the start in declarations of principle; since the debate will have no immediate consequences in the form of a vote or other decision, the parties are more inclined to pursue it until at least a partial agreement is reached – to seek for points of agreement rather than of difference. Since economic progress depends on agreement there is good reason for encouraging the various groups to arrive at it, rather than exacerbating their differences as a majority decision is apt to do.

To go no further than consultation involves the danger that the central authority will feel at liberty to decide matters as it chooses. But the duty of preventing this must be left to a political institution, not to technical bodies like the Modernization Commissions.

The Commission might be strengthened by entrusting the most important among them – whose membership would in that case be reduced – with a continuous role in the supervision of the fulfilment and revision of the Plan.

Above all, they should be given a greater part in preparing the Plans. Hitherto, at least so far as the manufacturing industries are concerned, each Commission has simply taken up the forecasts included in the Government's instructions for its particular branch of the economy, and discussed their soundness. Incidentally, some reports give most of their space to means of action which are more in the nature of claims, demanding financial facilities, tax relief or the amendment of regulations, while 'constructive' proposals are scarcely touched upon.

To enlarge the role of the Commissions does not mean extending the scope of the Plan, which must remain buoyant so that it can systematically review every possible course of development. It is understandable that successive governments should hesitate to intervene further in economic matters, particularly at the level of the firms. But the Commissions, if they were less interested in claims on points of detail, could devote their attention to the principal decisions affecting development, such as the choice to be made between important but incompatible projects put forward by different firms in a particular branch (the motor industry for example), or between expansion in two different sectors.

An enlargement of the role of the Commissions would mean that the statistical information – mostly from managerial sources – at present available to the experts and the union representatives would have to be appreciably improved, and that the authorities must resolutely adopt the practice of arbitration between the expansionist ambitions of rival firms. The dearth of information except from the management angle could be remedied, and praiseworthy efforts to that end have already been made by the I.N.S.E.E. This lack is largely responsible for the sense of isolation still felt by the workers' representatives in the Commissions. As M. Eugène Descamps said on 26 February 1961,[16] 'when the Plan is being drawn up in the Commissions and Working Parties . . . the union

[16] See *Le Monde*, 27 February 1961, under the heading 'La vie économique et financière'. M. Descamps included these remarks in a lecture he gave in the series on Democratic Planning organized by the Socialist Study Centre.

militants are handicapped . . . not so well armed as the managers.' Their own sources of information are insufficient.

To alter the composition of the Commissions in the manner advocated in some quarters would not meet these needs. It has been suggested that representation should be strictly tripartite (one-third trade unionists, one-third management, one-third experts). That would be a reversion to vote-counting, and would render these technical and advisory bodies completely sterile. It would mean abandoning the basic principle that the members of the Commissions are appointed on their personal merits, not as representatives of rival interests; and although the wage-earners and employers often select their own representatives, that principle does make it possible to slip some really impartial members into the Commissions.

Although a rigidly tripartite system seems inadvisable, it would be a good thing to include more workers, who are often too few to gain a hearing, and to appoint their representatives as Chairmen of some of the Commissions, which has not been done up to now. This would strengthen the trade union influence, which is at present too small despite the inclusion, since the fourth Plan, of the C.G.T. and of *Force Ouvrière*. Ensuring their representation in each of the Commissions and working parties, in addition to the work they have to do elsewhere, lays a heavy burden on the unions, particularly as they are divided into three organizations. The C.F.T.C. has made the biggest effort, providing 160 militants out of the 250 union representatives who participated in the fourth Plan.[17]

Some people think group participation should be broadened by reviving the equi-representative consultative bodies which were set up after the Liberation to advise the heads of the technical Ministries. It is felt that these would help to protect Ministers from the pressure of private interests. That aim is laudable in itself, but group influence is weakened rather than reinforced by creating too many advisory bodies, to which regional representation would have to be added. The effect is not only to stimulate rivalry among the bodies themselves, but to disperse the comparatively small resources in men and money which the workers and peasants, for

[17] The C.G.T. (*Confédération Générale du Travail*), *Force Ouvrière* and C.F.T.C. (*Confédération des Travailleurs Chrétiens*) are the Communist, Socialist and Christian trade union organizations among which the French workers are divided. (*Translator's note.*)

instance, can bring into the field. Better results would be achieved, in my opinion, by reshuffling the existing advisory bodies.

In considering the question of group participation, we should not underestimate the obstacle constituted by the determination of individual organizations to avoid committing themselves, to keep their fighting force intact.[18] This applies not only to the workers' side, where each of the three trade union federations is reluctant to give undertakings which may be turned to its disadvantage by its rivals; the employers' organizations, too, reserve the right to demand changes in regulations, or financial advantages for their members. Group commitments would become even more unreliable if the Plan were to proceed from the study of the technical conditions of expansion to incomes policy, for that is the crucial point of the struggle. As the Dutch experience showed, it is rash, at least at the present stage, to hope for any lasting agreement on this subject to which both sides would be loyal.

Thus, group representation is bound to result in unreliable, short-lived definitions of 'the general interest', which must be carefully watched over and constantly amended.

PARTICIPATION AT THE BASE; REGIONAL BODIES

There is, however, an unquestionable need for planning to be shared by other groups than those at the summit. Lack of a sense of involvement among the actual firms is the cause of indifference and misunderstanding which are holding up the progress of the Plan. Interviews on the French radio and television have shown that the man in the street knows nothing about the Plan, and that his ignorance is shared even by the staff of some public corporations.

A sense of involvement is impossible without at least some

[18] In the lecture quoted above, M. Descamps emphasized the prime importance of a free hand for the unions at all levels of economic life, from the base (legal recognition for factory branches of the trade unions, wider powers for wage-earners in the joint managerial committees) to the summit of the *Commissariat du Plan*, not forgetting the need to provide each region with equi-representative economic bodies.

While alert to seize any opportunity – such as those which occurred in 1936 and 1945 – for making great advances in social matters, the C.F.T.C. means to be represented in the existing institutions in order to fight every step of the way. Even in a socialist economy, the trade union movement will not rest content with a merely contributory role.

contact between the different levels of a firm; and here the joint-management committees and other organs of liaison fall far short of their purpose. Opposition by the groups at the base is preventing collaboration at the summit, in the Commissions of the Plan, or is at least hampering it.

Even if co-management were a reality, it must be remembered that the French Plan is seldom carried down into the individual firms; there is general agreement to stop short of that; the personnel could not take direct responsibility for applying the Plan in each enterprise.

But joint study of the aims of the Plan, undertaken at the base – at least in each branch, if not in every firm – would make a useful contribution to general co-management by providing a basis of discussion. For the time being it seems unwise to count on participation at the level of the firms, owing to trade union rivalry, the narrow-mindedness of a proportion of employers, lack of means and the absence of precedent in such matters. This gives all the more importance to the regional bodies, which stand half-way between the State and the individual firms.

It became evident at a very early stage that the Plan must have a regional structure in order to reduce friction between decisions taken at the centre and independent interests, and to establish that flow between the base and the summit which is the essence of a democratic institution. Does the creation of new regional organizations mean that the Plan has been effectively decentralized? A few brief comments on the developments of the last few years will provide an answer to that question and suggest whether it is desirable to go further.

At the institutional level, the part played by the local bodies has gradually increased since 30 June 1955, when the regional development programmes first saw the light of day. Those programmes are now known as 'regional plans for economic, social and territorial development', and they supplement the national Plan by applying the Government's decisions within the compass of the local economy. They are drawn up by the *Commissariat Général du Plan*, this being essential to ensure that they will fit into the national Plan; but the local authorities, the Interdepartmental Conference and the recognized Expansion Committees are consulted, and are responsible for working out how the operational sections of the Plan should be put into effect.

At the same time the number of organizing committees, development associations and investment associations is increasing. Some of the development associations act as banks, accepting subscriptions, floating loans, and advancing funds within a particular region. The investment associations, which are financed jointly by public and private money, act as contractors for public works of local interest, such as housing and area development.

This plethora of organizations should not deceive us, however. The creation of institutions with a localized activity does not lead automatically to decentralization, though without it there is little they can do.

More often than not, the regional development associations are simply a screen for the big organizations in Paris. Local authorities have less and less control over the decisions of private financiers. The last attempts at regional financing are being crushed by the centralization of the banking system – accelerated by the introduction of automation in accounting – and by the destruction of the machinery of local finance, to which the recent Stock Exchange reforms dealt a new blow.

Administrative decentralization, too, is only a pious hope. The French Civil Service, operating through the narrow channels of the ministerial departments, is still highly centralized. The regional directors have no power to undertake studies or to co-ordinate the surveys carried out by public and private bodies, which in any case are sometimes so unrelated as to be of little use. At the executive level the division of authority between an *Inspecteur général de l'Administration* seconded for the purpose and an *Inspecteur de l'Economie nationale* does little to camouflage the plain fact that all important decisions are made in Paris by the individual Ministries and carried out by the authorities in the geographical Departments. As a result, the regional programmes are split up among a variety of national and regional bodies. The 'nationalization' of local public expenditure on road maintenance, education and health is continuing, often at the demand of the local authorities themselves, who are anxious to be relieved of the expense. The consultation of local groups is slowly becoming an empty formality.

It is true that a few recent announcements, such as a circular sent out on 10 July 1961 with reference to the law laying down a programme of sports equipment, which was printed in the *Journal Officiel* of 17 January 1962, have embodied measures of administrative decentralization. But these have been extremely tentative and related only to matters of minor importance, such as felling the trees along a highway, advancing ready cash to local government authorities, and so on. I should add that a Decree of 11 April 1962 introduced – as an experiment, in four Departments – a new method of organizing the departmental public services under the control of the Prefect.

This timidity is accompanied by a signal poverty of economic and political ideas for decentralizing decision-making. Little has been done to relate economic decisions to local circumstances, despite the study of regional employment trends and the attempt to localize the activity of certain branches of industry, which were initiated by the fourth Plan. It still seems impossible to decide upon the most suitable location for most branches, or to choose between sending workers to the industries and moving the industries to where labour is available. I am not confusing location theory with the theory of decentralized choice, but only pointing out that the ineffective pursuit of the former is a barrier to the formulation of the latter. If we are unable to estimate the cost of setting up a particular activity in a particular place, how can we decide to entrust it to one local authority rather than another, and what criteria of management are we to propose to the chosen authority?

The theory of decentralized choice is marking time in any case, its progress halted by insistence on a quantitative concept of the economy which is too ambitious in theory and insufficiently adaptable in practice. In attempting to work out systems in which the independent decisions of individuals could be combined in a harmonious economic pattern, its exponents have repeatedly been brought to a standstill by the difficulty of expressing the personal preferences of consumers in quantitative terms and arriving at the sum of them.

Many of its advocates, while awaiting the anticipated progress, have taken refuge in an attitude of 'all or nothing'. As no one knows how these independent centres could steer the machinery of production, the economy is handled as though such centres did not exist. Centralization then seems to be the only rational method.

But in any realistic approach the independent centres must play their part. It is utterly irrational to ignore the preferences of producers and consumers, for the purpose of the economy is to consider and satisfy them. The only logical solution is that advocated by Pareto, by which politics is called upon to elucidate what economics cannot discover for itself. The creation of local bodies which could give expression to *preferences* that elude economic calculation but can be ascertained through local representatives would offer a way of escape from the deadlock created by excessive reliance on economic statistics. But many of those responsible for our economy are persuaded by their mistrust of any argument that cannot be reduced to figures, and their determination to ignore political attitudes (which in France have admittedly been too often indistinguishable from local demagogy) to withhold all power from the local bodies and to deny the possibility of fruitful consultation with them.

Two courses of action might put more energy into the present half-hearted attempts at decentralization and increase the value of consultation with the groups represented in the recognized Expansion Committees.

The regional bodies should be given more responsibility. The preparation of the regional plans might be entrusted, at least in part, to representatives of the regions concerned, who would report to certain interdepartmental bodies. The activities of the Prefects would be co-ordinated by a permanent civil servant, with authority over the appropriate departments of the relevant Ministries. The central authorities would cease to exercise supervision and control over local decisions in matters of minor significance. Most important of all, the local finances should be thoroughly overhauled and the decentralized authorities left to handle the funds earmarked for various duties which would now be entrusted to them. If those duties were clearly defined, the present disorderly trend towards the nationalization of all expenditure would be brought to a stop.

After sixteen years, the French planning organization has won for itself a place which has no precedent and which is in many respects satisfactory; it is more than an advisory organ, though less than an executive body. But the balance between the exercise of powers of arbitration and the consultation of the groups involved is not yet firmly established.

The *Commissariat du Plan* is continually subjected to the centrifugal force of the Civil Service departments and the pressure of conflicting interests, which threaten to reduce it to the status of a mere adviser to the Executive.

CHAPTER II

The Substance of the Plan

WHILE few people know anything about the administrative structure of the Plan, one meets frequent references to decisions 'taken within the framework of the Plan', and it seems to embrace large areas of the nation's activity.

To form a clearer idea of its substance, we need only read the general reports prepared for the four successive Plans. These analyse the economic situation and its requirements, and then lay down objectives. While the analysis of the economy and its prospects of growth is fairly comprehensive, the definite targets are few – too few, according to some critics.

I. ECONOMIC ANALYSIS AND ALTERNATIVE LINES OF DEVELOPMENT

Economic expansion is an integrated process, and any attempt to dissociate from it aspects regarded as subordinate must necessarily be arbitrary. For instance, expansion in consumption, in export trade and in capital investment all depend upon an increase in domestic production, while investment for purely social purposes does as much as the fulfilment of economic programmes to keep the wheels of the capital goods industries turning. Hence, analysis is applied to the widest possible field and strives to cover the development of all sectors of economic life.

ANALYSIS

It is true that in the first Plan this dealt only with the industries forming the six basic sectors (coalmines, electricity, iron and steel, cement, agricultural machines and transport). But in the aftermath of the war it was a matter of urgency to make good the destruction and backwardness in some branches which were holding up the resumption of the country's activities; food was scarce, reserves exhausted, raw materials in short supply, public utilities inadequate, and transport – harbour facilities, railways, merchant shipping – insufficient. Bottlenecks were preventing the re-establishment of the circle of exchange, which was needed to revive production as a whole. The first Plan was therefore confined to a few priority branches, the development of which could be predicted without a survey of the whole economic field.

On the other hand the general economic situation during the period of the second Plan (1952–1957) demanded a more far-reaching analysis. By that time the economy was no longer one of scarcity; productive capacity had been restored; but there were piecemeal surpluses that were difficult to absorb, the income of some sections of the population was too low, and prices were too high to face international competition, now growing more dangerous owing to the liberalization of trade. On this occasion, therefore, analysis was carried into spheres which the first Plan had only mentioned in passing, the credit for this extension being partly due to the S.E.E.F., which had made great progress under the leadership of M. Gruson.

It covered every aspect of agriculture; to the questions of agricultural machinery and fertilizers, which had been included among the basic sectors of the first Plan, were added those of agricultural training and research, the spread of new methods, and the redistribution of land.

In the industrial field, the Plan set itself to clarify the situation of the manufacturing industries, which had hitherto been considered solely in terms of the needs of the basic sectors, and tackled the problem of grouping certain firms and reconverting others.

The second Plan also covered part of the social field. In 1946, the improvement in the standard of living of the population had been approached chiefly from the angle of food supplies. Building had been considered only in terms of the modernization of material, whereas in 1952 certain aspects – housing, school equipment, health services – were stressed because of their social importance.

Regional problems also began to receive attention. Some less favoured areas, such as Savoy and Lorraine, being densely populated, suffered from chronic under-employment, and it was decided that suitable industrial and commercial activities should be set up there as a stimulus to development. Regional policy was an essential factor in the equilibrium of the second Plan.

Most important of all, improvements in national accounting enabled the second Plan to forecast development not merely sector by sector, as before, but for the country as a whole; there was to be a 25 per cent increase in the national product, which would demand an increase of 20 per cent in agricultural output, 25 per cent in industry, and 60 per cent in building. The Plan then outlined the conditions required to ensure expansion with full employment, a stable currency and balanced foreign trade. Employment figures were given for each sector, side by side with those for investment.

In short, the second Plan, after analysing each sector not merely from the economic but also from the psychological and social standpoint, went on to present a picture of overall economic growth.

The third Plan (1958–1961) carried analysis still further, in several directions.

Improved statistics, continued progress in national accounting, the greater number and growing expertise of the members of the different Commissions, administrative officials and trade union representatives, made it possible to assemble a body of information which was absorbed into the nomenclatures of the national accounting system and covered about 112 branches. With the exception of a few types of production, in particular that of the military arsenals, the entire range of economic activity was included in the Plan's analyses and forecasts.

Some hitherto neglected subjects now came to the fore. A section on social investment was singled out from the rest; plans for each region began to be drawn up by specially devised methods, and certain factors required for general equilibrium were defined.

The most original feature of the third Plan was the care with which the forecasts of national development were drawn up and co-ordinated. The Commissions were invited to study the prospects of overall growth indicated under broad headings (industry, agriculture, trade). They split these up and criticized them in relation to their own sectors. A general synthesis was then prepared, giving an extremely detailed analysis of growth, which covered production, consumption, investment, government expenditure, foreign trade, the monetary flow of expenditure and savings or financing from reserves. True consistency tests were used for the first time.

In the fourth Plan (1961–1965) analysis, though not appreciably extended, was perfected. This applies particularly to the study of inter-industrial relations and final demand (which in point of fact does shed new light on such matters as town-planning, cultural equipment, and the water supply), and it has thus become possible to make a more accurate assessment of the prospects and conditions of development in each branch. Hypothetical development at various price-levels is considered, and so is the relationship between investment and output. The desirability of maintaining regional equilibrium has led to the forecasting of possible disruptions of balance in employment in each region covered by the Plan, in the light of the hypotheses of development it sets forth.

UNCERTAINTIES

As analysis and forecasting become more searching, however, new factors of uncertainty make their appearance. Some of these, it is true, are the result of shortcomings in the present-day methods and system of analysis, and they are tending to diminish. But we are more conscious of them nowadays. For instance, there are still gaps in our knowledge of the different economic sectors, the types of firm that compose them, their geographical distribution, the techniques they employ, and what increase in productivity they could achieve. Forecasting is hampered by the lack of a firm policy in many fields.

Other uncertainties are an inevitable feature of any planning system and can never be eliminated. They relate first and foremost to the behaviour of consumers, which is fickle and hard to predict. Analysis of the factors that govern their purchasing habits is still at the elementary stage. In the manufacturing industries, especially the motor industry, it is never certain that production will conform to the Plan. In the second and third Plans, for instance, it exceeded the forecasts.

Furthermore, any system based on forecasting is affected by unexpected changes in the economic situation. When the third and fourth Plans were drawn up, it was anticipated that France's foreign relations would undergo changes, that the franc area would be affected by political trends, and that the establishment of the

Common Market would affect our dealings with other countries. Though these changes have not radically altered the terms of trade, they have led the business world to adopt certain new attitudes, with repercussions on the general equilibrium. In other respects, too, France has felt the backwash of the fluctuations in the international economic situation, while the availability of manpower and the investment outlook have been influenced by methods adopted to stabilize the currency and balance trade, and by uncertainty as to how long the burden of military expenditure must be sustained.

DEFICIENCIES

In the first place, these occur in the picture of certain economic sectors about which little is known. The activities of the Defence Services have not been closely studied (though some progress may be noted), and this is regrettable, considering the size of the orders they place and the changes of pattern that occur in them. The banking sector is alone in having been entirely passed over so far as structural analysis is concerned; the *Commission de l'Equilibre et du Financement* confines itself to the study of conditions of financing and monetary circulation. Since the banks play a leading part in financing investment, which is the cornerstone of planning, this omission is gravely felt.

In the second place, there are deficiencies relating to aspects of economic life which have not been thoroughly studied, though the fourth Plan does touch upon them. Scant attention is paid to income distribution, regarded not from the functional angle, but from that of social and occupational categories. This is undoubtedly a delicate subject, but its neglect means that little is known about the differences between categories of wage-earners and between incomes in the various regions, or about the groups in the community which have no one to speak for them. In other respects as well, the regional studies are very incomplete.

Lastly, the study of alternative possibilities of development does not seem to have been carried far enough as yet. Only the situations resulting from a variety of rates of growth have been outlined. It would be desirable to know more about the consequences of a reduction in working hours, the restriction of certain types of consumption, a change in orders for the armed forces, increased aid to the under-developed countries, pensions for aged workers, and a different distribution of public funds among the geographical areas. The political authorities with whom the decisions rest could then take them more confidently than they do at present. I shall return to the question of alternatives when discussing the optimum.

The above-mentioned uncertainties and deficiencies would have been a very serious matter if the detailed forecasts given in the French Plan were tantamount to fixed targets. But these are not established for the whole economic field.

II. THE TARGETS

Side by side with the general prospects of development, certain specific objectives are written into the Plan, as 'basic operations' or 'essential tasks'.

Of course, every branch of economic life contributes to the prosperity of the whole, and therefore none must be neglected. But when we consider the activities of the different sectors, we find that some receive no mandatory instructions, while others are narrowly supervised. The report on the fourth Plan emphasizes (Bill No. 1573, approving the Economic and Social Development Plan, p. 50) that 'a distinction must be drawn between basic products and services and the almost infinite variety of manufactured goods. In the case of the former, the programmes must be carried out, under pain of endangering the growth objective. In the case of the latter, a certain flexibility is possible, even desirable, and products may be substituted for one another in the light of price trends and consumer preferences.' The production of television sets is a different matter from that of steel.

Targets are established not only for the productive sectors but for public expenditure, especially on social investment, *and in general, for all aspects of economic life which the Government deems to be essential and can regulate by means of the effective instruments at its disposal.*[1] There are even some targets not immediately reducible to quantitative terms, such as the restoration of regional equilibrium.

[1] The distinction between 'targets' and 'instruments' is a matter of governmental intention. Investment may be described as a target or as an instrument, according to the line of reasoning adopted.

It is difficult to pick out what may be strictly described as 'targets' from the Plans, as the term is sometimes used rather loosely in the Commissariat's reports. For example, in the agricultural report drawn up for the fourth Plan, the 'targets' are the production levels which are regarded as desirable but are unlikely to be observed, owing to spontaneous over-production. Generally speaking, the Commissioner-General's report presents certain aims as being much to be desired, saying that 'the State must . . .' or 'should . . .', but without suggesting any very precise means of action in regard to them. These include the co-ordination of transport and the reconversion of shipyards. At the other extreme there are subordinate activities, normally left to private initiative, on which in certain circumstances the Government may have to bring pressure to bear: there is a kind of shadowy no-man's-land between objectives and mere predictions.

But the outstanding characteristic of French planning is, indeed, the small number of targets it sets up. Are there enough of them?

THE 'BASIC SECTORS' OF THE FIRST PLAN

The first Plan did not present a detailed statistical analysis of the entire economy, but confined its study to the 'basic sectors'. This produced a number of 'basic programmes' in which targets were established for the productive capacity of coalmines, electricity, iron and steel, cement works, agricultural machinery and transport, and proposals were made regarding the investment thought necessary for modernizing them. No distinction was drawn between actual objectives and mere suggestions for the future of the various sectors of the economy, though the latter were vaguer and less essential.

According to Article 1 of the Decree of 3 January 1946, the purpose of the Plan is 'to increase production in metropolitan France and the overseas territories and their trade with the rest of the world . . . to increase the productivity of labour to the level of those countries where it is highest, to ensure full employment, to raise the standard of living of the population, and to improve conditions of housing and community life.'

THE 'BASIC OPERATIONS' OF THE SECOND PLAN

The programmes of the 'basic sectors' of the first Plan were succeeded by the 'basic operations' of the second Plan (Law of 27 March 1956, *Journal Officiel* of 1 April 1956). In other words the true – i.e. imperative – objectives were now carried beyond the economic and statistical sphere. They comprised programmes of reform with lists of indispensable measures for each branch, tied to the fulfilment of the production targets, together with proposals for long-term psychological action, laying particular emphasis on support for scientific research, the popularization of modern techniques and methods, and efforts to foster a new, competitive spirit.

The reason for thus stressing 'basic operations' in the second Plan was that, as I said before, the economic situation had by now developed to a point where it was no longer sufficient to get rid of the bottlenecks in the basic sectors, which had rightly been the chief concern of the first Plan. Scarcities had to a great extent been made good, and the next requirement was to balance markets, reduce prices to a level at which they would be internationally competitive, and raise the inadequate incomes of some sections of the population. If productivity was to be increased and costs reduced, measures of reform would have to go hand in hand with the investment programmes. And something must be done to achieve greater adaptability, for rigidity of structure was a source of inflation and threatened to interfere with the resumption of expansion in 1952–1953.

The second Plan, unlike the first, expressed its targets in terms of production, not merely of capacity; for now that scarcity was a thing of the past, capacity would not necessarily be used to the full. The study was being refined.

The ultimate aim was to increase the national product by 25 per cent between 1952 and 1957.

THE 'IMPERATIVE TASKS' OF THE THIRD PLAN

When the time came to prepare the third Plan, the situation again called for general objectives differing from the 'basic operations' of the second Plan; these were known as 'imperative tasks'. This occasion produced a general plan for development in a form which proved to be final and permanent and was retained for the fourth Plan.The rapid expansion continued, though there were some instances of disequilibrium. In 1957 and 1958 the balance of foreign trade was so unfavourable that the suspension of payments was even contemplated – as though foreign countries could be expected to bear part of the cost of the improvement in French living standards. Within the country, the rise in the nation's unproductive expenditure – particularly for military purposes – and in private consumption (6 per cent per annum), combined with inflation, threatened to reduce investment in the basic sectors, and consequently their future output. The anxiety thus caused was aggravated by the need to secure regional equilibrium and to help the newly independent countries.

In the light of this situation, the specific objectives of the third Plan, as set forth in Article I of the Decree of 6 January 1946, were as follows:

1. To increase domestic production by 27 per cent between 1956 and 1961, with an increase of 30 per cent in industrial output and 20 per cent in agricultural output, the product being obtained by an increase of 28 per cent in investments and resulting in a 24 per cent rise in consumption.

2. To restore the balance of payments by cutting down imports, expanding the manufacture of goods suitable for export, and modernizing the production system, which must be rendered competitive in the Common Market, by specialization, the regrouping of firms, and other measures.

3. To provide the capital equipment essential to expanding future production, avoiding bottlenecks and increasing public utilities.

4. To undertake investment for social purposes, such as housing or education, where there were backlogs to be made up and the needs of a growing population to consider.

5. To promote vocational training and encourage research.

6. To intensify the effort to make the best possible use of national resources by setting strict limits to the growth of Paris and its suburbs.

7. To provide increased technical assistance to the underdeveloped countries, and in particular to the overseas countries of the franc area.

These specific targets were set forth in detail for each sector, in statistical terms wherever possible, and otherwise by laying down programmes, according to the method first adopted in the second Plan.

THE OBJECTIVES OF THE FOURTH PLAN

The attention newly devoted to these social aspects is indicated by the title of the fourth Plan – 'Plan for Economic and Social Development', by Article I of the Act of Parliament approving it (*Journal Officiel*, 7 August 1962) and by the inclusion of a special chapter on the subject.

The foremost place is given to assistance to the poorer regions of the country, to the under-privileged sections of the community (old people, wage-earners, craftsmen and small farmers) and to the less developed countries. In this connection there is a reference to the work of the *Conseil Economique et Social*. 'The opinions we have assembled seem to point to the desirability of greater reliance upon collective goods. For there is reason to think that the consumer society foreshadowed by some aspects of American life – which finds its shrewdest critics among the Americans themselves – turns ultimately to seek futile satisfactions, the effect of which is merely to aggravate dissatisfaction.'[2]

Stress is also laid on the need for large-scale investment to compensate for the shortage of labour, maintain the balance of payments and modernize the army.

These considerations are reflected in the following target figures:

1. *Gross national output to be increased* by 24 per cent between 1962 and 1965 (an annual increase of 5½ per cent), and production per branch to be stepped up as shown in Table VII (page 172).

This entails for:

– *Agriculture*, an expansion of markets at a time of constant and increasing competition from cut-price world surpluses, and an intensification of the measures laid down in the third Plan.

– *Energy*, a reduction of traditional sources of supply – especially coal, the national output of which is to be reduced from 58 to 55 million tons between 1960 and 1965 – and an increase in fuel oil and gas output.

– *Metals*, an increase of approximately one-third in the

[2] Bill approving the Economic and Social Development Plan (No. 1573), p. 18.

production capacity of iron and steel (24·5 million tons in 1965), and a larger production of aluminium.

– *Chemical and manufacturing industries*, developments governed by the increase in home demand and by the new situation resulting from the Common Market.

– *Transport*, the nationalized railways (S.N.C.F.) to be converted to diesel fuel and modernized; completion of 50 per cent of the programme of by-pass motor highways and 25 per cent of arterial motorways, covering, in all, 1,835 kilometres; continued equipment of three large seaports (Dunkirk, Le Havre, Marseilles); development of the Seine and the Canal du Nord, widening of the Dunkirk-Valenciennes Canal, expedited study of the Rhine-Rhône Canal project,[3] and initial study of a medium-range supersonic airliner.

– *Telecommunications*, lines in operation to be increased by 40 per cent.

– *Trade, public services, tourism*, an appreciable increase in activities, necessitating structural changes and considerable expenditure.

2. *The balance of payments stability to be consolidated.* By 1966, even if there is no acceleration of the Rome Treaty, tariff protection against the Common Market countries will have fallen to 20 per cent of its 1957 level, while moving in the same direction in respect of third countries. Some loosening of economic ties within the franc area will also do its part towards endangering the foreign trade balance on which we rely in order to help the under-developed countries, meet payments on our foreign debt, and even build up a surplus.

3. *Investment to be increased* in order to permit of expansion together with a further growth in the provision of collective goods. The share of national income invested is expected to increase from 20 per cent in 1961 to 22 per cent in 1965, as shown in Table I, resulting in a proportionately smaller rise in consumption.

It is to be hoped that a national incomes policy may be pursued at the same time, but this is not actually specified in the Plan.

Though the number of dwellings built is not to increase greatly (350,000 in 1965, i.e. 10 per cent more than in 1961) unless the rate of repatriation from overseas accelerates, they will be of better

[3] This study was introduced into the Plan on an amendment voted by the Senate.

Table I

DISTRIBUTION OF RESOURCES AVAILABLE IN 1965[1]

	Increase (in milliards of francs)	*Percentage increase* (1965–1961)	*Percentage of total increase*
'Economic' investments	10	28	16
'Social' investments:			
housing	3	25	5
collective goods	3·5	50	5
Civil Service consumption......	3	22	5
Private consumption	43	23	67
Miscellaneous	1·5	not given	2
TOTAL....	64	24	100

[1] See Bill approving the Economic and Social Development Plan (*op. cit.*), p. 37.

quality and more spacious. Among the other 'social' investments, prominence is given to town-planning, teaching, cultural equipment, health and welfare equipment, and scientific and technical research.

4. *Regional economic expansion to be promoted* by giving a lead to the backward regions and co-operating with those which are already expanding.

Are these objectives sufficiently numerous and definite?

INCREASING THE NUMBER OF OBJECTIVES

Desirable as it may be to increase the number of objectives, this can only be done in so far as means of compelling compliance with them are available; otherwise the Commissioner-General's report would degenerate into a string of pious hopes. But government intervention is limited by pressure from the private sector and by international competition, felt more keenly since the Common Market came into operation: and it is quite as important to realize this as to prepare forecasts.

Without going into the details of all the projects it would be desirable to carry out – they include a radical overhaul of the banking system, the co-ordination of transport, and the reconversion of the naval shipyards – we will confine ourselves to considering two large categories which a number of people think should be included in the Plan – targets for individual firms, and targets of income distribution.

Hitherto the Plan has set up no targets for individual firms except where a firm, practically speaking, embraces a whole industry, as in the case of energy. Planning at present deals with entire branches of the economy. Some people recommend that it should be carried down to the firms, but in principle this is undesirable. It would make the task of the central organization so complex that the efficiency of the Plan would suffer; the planners would not be able to see the wood for the trees; they could not be expected to adjust their planning to the constantly changing life of the individual firm, and the effect on the firms themselves would be paralysing. In certain eventualities, such as the lack or dearth of a particular product or the under-development of a particular region, the authorities might undoubtedly play a bolder part than they do at present in setting up firms, enlarging them or, on the contrary, closing them down as a means of reducing surplus productive capacity. But it would be unrealistic to attempt to draw the individual firms into a system of planning which is already unwieldy – except in the case of highly concentrated branches with strategic importance.

In the immediate post-war period the Plans paid more attention to economic requirements than to social needs. This was reasonable enough, in view of the urgent problems of reconstruction and development that had to be faced, the fear that – as experience between the wars had shown – recovery might be impeded by the adoption of ill-considered social policies, and the belief that the Plan would in any case be of 'social' benefit by increasing production to the maximum, adjusting output to the needs of the consumers, and preventing slumps and unemployment.

However, by the time the second Plan was started the planners had already realized that the human element – the motive-power and the essential purpose of the desired expansion – did not necessarily develop harmoniously in any and every form of that expansion. So the second Plan gave priority to certain branches because of their importance to the community. Among these were housing, health services and schools.

To set up targets for income distribution would carry the planners far beyond the present 'social plan', which deals with collective and individual investment (housing, hospitals, roads, schools, etc.) and makes recommendations concerning the incomes of small wage-earners, farmers and old people and the provision of welfare services. No comprehensive picture showing the desirable distribution of income among the different social and occupational categories has so far been presented, and there is no 'national wages policy'. Many obstacles stand in the way of both.

In point of fact, our knowledge of the income distributed among the members of a particular group in the community is even more defective than our information concerning the different categories of income. Thus, we not only lack a firm foundation for a policy of income-distribution, but we have no standards by which to guide it; for how are the merits of each category of claimants to be assessed?

Extremely simple hypotheses as to distribution of income among the various groups are, of course, worked out as a means of discovering rapidly whether the real balance between resources and employment is not radically incompatible with the circulation of money in those groups, their savings and their expenditure. But these hypotheses have never built up a completely realistic picture, for the attempt to do so has always run into apparently insuperable difficulties.

The moment we turn from working hypotheses to specific decisions, political problems come to the fore again. From what angle is income-distribution to be approached? In the social atmosphere which prevails in France there can be no question of increasing output in a greater proportion than wages on the plea that investment – and consequently profits – must be stepped up so as to produce more goods. For it may be argued, in crude terms of profits and wages, that in the private sector at any rate, the former might be used in part to increase the private consumption of the holders of the capital, rather than to add to investment. It is difficult to ask one section of the community to make sacrifices from which it will not necessarily benefit later on, but which may work out to the sole advantage of another section.

On the other hand, are the wage-earners to be promised the equivalent of the increase in production, or more? The respective groups concerned could find arguments to prove the unfairness of either policy, for both of them are too rigid.

The most important question is whether the governments of our Western countries have the means of compelling all parties to comply with such a Plan. Profit-control is ineffective, and only a scale of taxation calculated to a hair's-breadth could restrict the entrepreneur's margin of profit without reducing investment. In their anxiety to avoid inflation, the authorities try to control wages, the only form of income that is open to inspection. But even here, local labour shortages and the dearth of key workers lead to unplanned rises which they are powerless to prevent. Their helplessness in the matter of income-distribution was never more clearly demonstrated than in 1956, 1957 and 1958, when incomes were soaring and the only way to restrain them was by tacit complicity in a slow rise of prices which wrought havoc among the lowest income groups – the small wage-earners and small investors.

One may even go further and wonder whether, if the increases in wages and other types of income which are regarded as compatible with expansion were publicly announced, some groups in the community might not feel encouraged to demand, or award themselves, even larger increases than those actually envisaged; for some people, whose standard of living is steadily rising thanks to increased regional prosperity or to greater efficiency on their own part, will regard the forecasts as a minimum. The Government might feel compelled to make a systematic underestimate of potential rises in income, as indeed happened in one Western European country where social forecasting had been very detailed.[4]

Moreover, as matters now stand in France, the principal groups in the community are hostile in practice, if not in theory, to any fully-fledged 'Social Plan'.

The employers are not in favour of a policy which might restrict their freedom of action; they are well aware that the lowest wages, left to themselves, tend to lag behind the rate of expansion, and they take advantage of the resultant margins of profit; besides, they are afraid that mistakes might be made at the expense of their firms.

Strange as it may seem, the trade unions are even less eager for the strict regulation of wages. Some of them fear that government intervention would not be impartial. They urge 'the necessity of defending the legitimate demands of the workers, even including the right to fix wages by agreement, against the danger of a unilateral, restrictive system of wage increases, which is at present taking shape under cover of the Plan.'[5] Besides, the trade unions are afraid that so long as the means of production and profit-making are in private ownership and remuneration is left to the

[4] Everyone knows about the so-called 'constructive unions' which are responsible for enforcing a wage-policy drawn up by the Government.

[5] P. Lebrun, addressing the 1961 C.G.T. Congress.

discretion of those who control them, wages alone would in practice be regulated.

So although a guided distribution of incomes is extremely desirable, both in the interest of social justice and in that of economic equilibrium, it would be impossible without a fundamental change in the mentality of the parties concerned and in the institutions involved. If the question of distribution were raised again in the Plan as matters stand, it would be liable to cut short the Commissions' tentative discussion about means of growth, or to place it in the wrong light.

Even at the present stage, however, a social plan should go further than mere suggestions; it should determine rates of increase for the S.M.I.G. (*salaire minimum inter-professionel garanti*) and for pensions, lay down methods of redistribution of profits through taxation – deal, in fact, with all aspects of the matter in which the State already intervenes – and make a periodical review of wage-scales.

To sum up, the analysis made in the Plan should be extended to certain subjects, such as military and financial activities, about which too much discretion has been observed until now. Planning may be carried down to the level of the individual firms, but this should not be done too readily. Lastly, there is no immediate prospect of planning being applied to incomes, though information may be assembled and a few obviously urgent measures introduced.

More ambitious objectives would also require greater means of enforcement.

CHAPTER III

Means of Enforcement

WHILE the need for planning is now almost unquestioned in France – for it is a remarkable fact that the Plan has not been disavowed by any government, even by those which advocate economic liberalism – there is considerable controversy as to how the different measures can best be enforced. Some think the Plan should comprise a set of general instructions, with only limited powers of constraint, while others would like the means of enforcement to be greatly amplified.

In its present form the Plan satisfies the first group better than the second. It comes before Parliament as a set of instructions, intentions and guiding principles; none of these has the force of law; they merely announce and pave the way for a limited number of subsequent measures. This is not a satisfactory state of things.

Looking back at the period immediately following the liberation of France, one may be led to false conclusions. In those days the authorities were obliged to be autocratic in the distribution of raw materials (steel and non-ferrous products) and foreign currency, because scarcities made stringent economy unavoidable. As early as 1944–1945, when there was no such thing as a Plan, the Directorate of Economic Programmes worked out a system of unconditional orders, with priority in the allocation of ferrous metals. From 1946 to 1948 there was a triple set of controls.

Programmes for the manufacture of 'trade catalogue' equipment, tools and dies, were drawn up for commercial vehicles, machine-tools, alternators and transformers. Their makers were entitled to a quota of scarce raw materials, such as steel; and the finished products were allocated to industries requiring capital goods. This system worked well, and there was no need for the enforcement of a law passed on 11 May 1946 (D. 1946. 223), which made provision for compulsory programmes.

This law provided that orders could if necessary be placed with particular firms, within the compass of the programmes drawn up by the Ministry of National Economy, so as to compel them to manufacture certain specified goods; refusal would entail penalties which might go as far as the requisitioning of the plant. Though never actually applied, this is one of the most radical planning measures ever enacted.

In many cases the investment itself was subject to preliminary control. By an Order of 27 October 1945 (Article 16), anyone proposing to erect a building above a certain size must obtain permission to apply for a building licence. Applications went before an interministerial committee of which the Minister of National Economy was chairman. Until 1948 this formality served to ensure that a project did not exceed the practical possibilities, and the licence gave the right to a quota of cement and steel. Now that materials are no longer in short supply, it serves as an economic 'visa' vouching for the usefulness of the work, and carries weight with the various credit organizations.

The third measure of control was the study of the individual investment programmes, which had to be submitted with estimates of the quotas of materials and tools required.

The decision as to which investment projects should be authorized in the private sector was made for the basic industries by the *Commissariat général du Plan*, and for other sectors by the appropriate Directorates, the last word being left to the Directorate of Industrial Co-ordination at the Ministry of Industrial Production.

These authoritarian interventions were justified during the period of scarcity. By 1949 this was practically at an end, and official means of enforcement took their final shape.

I. THE PRESENT POWERS

The only authoritarian measures still maintained are the building permit, the authorization to set up in the Paris district, and the permit to open a petrol refinery. The second of these (established by a Decree of 5 January 1956) is among the steps taken to check the convergence of industry upon Paris and its suburbs. It applies to any expansion, or addition of new activities amounting to more than 10 per cent, by any firm within a certain radius of Paris which has premises exceeding 500 sq. metres and a payroll of more than fifty employees.

Peremptory orders are avoided so far as possible, out of consideration for the freedom and independence of the firms.

Great allowance is made for psychological factors. Experience has shown that those associated with the preparation of the Plan do their best to see that it is carried out; in many cases it is in their own interest to observe the growth-targets prescribed for each segment, since the resultant equilibrium is favourable to markets and resources.

But as individual interests are not always identical with the general advantage, some degree of constraint remains indispensable. This is exercised by financial methods in preference to the compulsory measures adopted before 1959. Thus, the twin features of the French Plan are the small number of its means of enforcement and the importance of the financial measures at its disposal. After considering the public financing of investment we shall pass to the financial incentives, and then review various other measures.

DIRECT FINANCING BY THE BUDGET AND THE TREASURY

Taking 'public' to mean government funds and those of the specialized finance institutions, direct financing takes three main forms: budgetary appropriations, tax exemptions, and loans from the F.D.E.S. (Economic and Social Development Fund).

1. *Budgetary appropriations*

The Budget contributes in several ways to the fulfilment of the Plan. It makes direct provision for a considerable proportion of investments;[1] in 1961 the amount was four thousand million francs, so that with the loans made by the Development Fund, this accounted for a total of over nine thousand million francs, or one-fifth of the total volume of investment in metropolitan France. Appendix IV and Table II show the appropriations for each sector of the national economy, and the pressure exercised by action within the Budget. The activities of the different sectors are also guided to a great extent by the orders they place with other branches, such

[1] More especially in the building industry.

as the engineering and electrical industries. The Budget had indeed become a main guiding force of the economy, owing to the amount of investment expenditure – larger than before 1940 – for which it is responsible.[2]

Table II

INVESTMENT FINANCING IN METROPOLITAN FRANCE

	1956	1961
	(*Frs. thousand million*)	
Public funds	8·6	13·3
Internal resources of specialized bodies and insurance companies	2·6	4·7
Money market: Loans from specialized bodies	0·6	1·6
Money market: Other loans and issues of securities	2·8	7
Medium-term borrowing	3·6	6·2
Balance of other expenditure and resources	15·6	21·8
TOTAL	33·8	54·6
(Gross fixed asset formation in metropolitan France)		
Percentage of fixed asset formation in metropolitan France:		
Public funds	25·3 %	24·4 %
Specialized bodies, insurance companies and money market	18·3 %	24·3 %
Medium-term borrowing	10·5 %	11·4 %
Balance of other expenditure and resources	45·9 %	39·9 %
TOTAL	100 %	100 %

Source: VIIth Report of the *Conseil de Direction du Fonds de Développement économique et social*, p. 9.

The most justifiable criticism levelled against public loans is that of unreliability; entrepreneurs are given no guarantee as to what commitments they can make for expenditure during subsequent financial periods. The programme-laws, supplemented in some cases by outline-laws, are supposed to guarantee them a prescribed sum to cover the duration of the Plan. This system has found one of its most recent applications at regional level: programme-laws on public investment now specify the sums to be spent on the under-developed regions.

[2] Apart from investment, the Budget governs the operation of the public services, which are labour-intensive and deal with a considerable volume of goods and funds. For instance, a reduction in the numbers called up for military service makes additional manpower available in a period of labour shortage such as the present.

The general situation of the country is also influenced by the balancing of the Budget and the means by which this is achieved – whether by borrowing, by taxation, or by cuts in expenditure.

2. *Tax allowances*

It is not only prices and consumption that are influenced by direct and indirect taxation and affected by changes in the rates or incidence of a tax. Each successive Plan has recommended the use of taxation as a means of encouraging savings, housing construction or the mechanization of agriculture, or of promoting regional development.

Sometimes these means of influence have been thought unsuitable for use as they now stand, and attempts have been made to amend them. Long lists of reforms are given in the various Plans.

Among these, measures affecting direct taxation are the most numerous. Of particular importance is the institution of the value-added tax, which was introduced by M. Lauré as a substitute for the tax on production. Under the earlier system, investments were taxed twice over – once when bought, and again at the sale of the finished product, which included part of their cost. At present, only value added is taxed, the cost of new capital goods being deducted from the sales figure. This gives selective encouragement to investment; exemption has been confined to investments made in conformity with the Plan. Technical difficulties still impede the full application of this principle in certain sectors, such as energy production and shipbuilding, though it was extended to the latter in 1959 and the fourth Plan recommended a further widening of its field.

The conditions at present applying to issues of new capital by companies are such as to penalize this form of investment financing, and led the *Commissions de modernisation* of the third Plan to recommend readjustment of the profits tax, which companies are required to pay both on distributed and on undistributed profits.[3]

The effect of other reforms is to modify the structure of firms and of markets. Numerous measures, including tax relief, have been introduced to expedite mergers, specialization, and the grouping of firms. A Decree of 30 June 1955 made provision for setting up groups of industrialists who would take combined and systematic action to promote rationalization and reconversion.

[3] See *Rapport de la Commission de Modernisation de la Sidérurgie pour le troisième Plan*, p. 140.

Prompted by the wish to increase 'fiscal neutrality', the fourth Plan advised more generous tax allowances for parent companies and subsidiaries, employers' credit associations and finance companies.

3. *The transactions of the F.D.E.S.*

In recent years, government loans have increased to an extent sufficiently evidenced by the few figures given in Table II.

Remembering that loans totalling over four thousand million francs are included under the heading of 'Public funds', it will be realized that half the investments carried out are financed by public loans.

Immediately after the Liberation, the Government began their attempts to use the credit system as a means of influencing economic development. Credit was at that time considerably disorganized, though derived from public sources. There was no co-ordination of the allocations made to the different sectors of the economy; Budget appropriations for petrol research jostled with reconstruction loans and with special accounts opened by the Treasury in favour of the hotel industry.

It was soon realized that all aspects of financial policy needed to be overhauled and steered along the lines laid down in the Plan. The nationalization of the Banks and the creation of the *Conseil national du Crédit* (National Council on Credit) quickly proved to be insufficient. The *Conseil national*, set up on 2 December 1945, is a kind of small parliament with thirty-eight members, seventeen of whom are trade union representatives. It is consulted on general credit policy, draws up finance plans (laying down priorities for the floating of loans, which require the approval of the Ministry of Finance) and gives its opinion on all proposals for the distribution of funds. In practice, however, the infrequency of its meetings, its narrow field of recruitment and its lack of an independent administration have combined with the wishes of the legislature to prevent it from becoming, in financial matters, the equivalent of the *Commissariat du Plan*. Little by little its role has been reduced to laying down the broad lines of credit policy.

Thus, the attempt to steer economic development has led to increased reliance upon government lending, which now extends to a great number of branches. Bank loans are at present left to the

Banque de France, while the Treasury, in agreement with the Plan, concerns itself with financing investment.

This is done by issuing Treasury Bonds and drawing upon deposits. The principle underlying all legislation on this subject is that any capital investment projects financed or carried out by the State must fit into the Plan (Law of 28 October 1946, Art. 4). This means that the credits required for the Plan have to be shown separately in the Budget and that one body must be responsible for drawing up detailed programmes. These conditions are satisfied in part by the *Fonds de développement économique et social* (Economic and Social Development Fund: F.D.E.S.).

This Fund has a dual aspect. It is financed by a special Treasury account, set up by a Decree of 30 June 1955 (D. 1955. 341) supplemented by a Decree of 18 October 1955 (B.L.D. 1955. 1010). It follows up the loans and advances which the Finance Minister is authorized to make as a contribution to financing the projects set out in the *Plan de Modernisation et d'Equipement* and in the regional expansion programmes, such as those relating to building, rural equipment, increase of productivity, industrial and agricultural conversion, and industrial decentralization.[4]

Thus, the Fund's transactions embrace most of the public lending previously allocated by several different funds, including the *Fonds national de Modernisation et d'Equipement*, the *Fonds national d'Aménagement du Territoire*, the *Fonds national de Productivité* and the *Fonds de Construction, d'Equipement rural et d'Expansion économique*. It has recently taken over responsibility for all real-estate operations launched by local authorities for which public loans are required.

Some forms of aid or public lending are still outside the sphere of the Fund, such as those granted by the *Fonds national pour les adductions d'eau* (National Fund for Water Supply), set up by a Decree of 1 October 1954 (D. 1954, 414) to promote the extension of the water supply, and by Section A of the *Fonds national d'Aménagement du Territoire*, which exists to encourage the establishment of new factories in certain parts of the country.

Out of a total of approximately 12·55 milliard francs of public funds allocated for financing investment in 1960, the *Fonds de*

[4] See Appendix II for the Decrees of 30 June and 18 October 1955, setting up the *Fonds de Développement Économique et Social*.

Table III

USE OF F.D.E.S. FUNDS IN 1960[1]
(millions of New Francs)

Sector	*Loans by the F.D.E.S. and H.L.M. (low-rent housing construction)*		*Loans by agents on F.E.D.S.*	
Agriculture	18		176	
Farmers		—		167
Regional development		18		—
Agricultural industries		—		9
Energy	2,226		—	—
Nationalized coalmines		150		—
Nationalized electricity		1,620		—
Compagnie nationale du Rhône		130		—
Nationalized gas industry		156		—
Gaz de Lacq (S.N.P.A. – G.S.O.) (natural gas deposits)		—		—
Atomic energy		170		—
Fuels		—		—
Bureau de recherches minières		—		—
Transport	417		—	
S.N.C.F. (State Railways)		200		—
R.A.T.P. (Paris public transport)		—		—
Local railway lines		—		—
Road transport		—		—
Sea transport		—		—
Air transport		150		—
Independent ports		8		—
Paris airport		50		—
Inland water transport and canals		9		—
Post Office and Telecommunications		—		—
Industry, Trade and Services	—		299	
Minerals and non-ferrous metals		—		—
Iron mines, iron and steel		—		16
Engineering and electrical industries		—		—
Building and building materials		—		—
Chemicals		—		45
Textiles		—		—
Other industries		—		—
Trade		—		—
Tourism		—		47
Services, miscellaneous and unclassified		—		191
Cultural and Social Equipment				
Hospitals		—		—
Broadcasting and Television		—		—
TOTAL FOR ENTERPRISES	2,661			475
Households (including leasehold housing)		2,026		—
State		—		—
Local authorities		60		40
TOTAL		4,747		515

[1] See Report of the *Conseil de Direction du Fonds de Développement Economique et Social, 1961–1962*, pp. 38–39.

développement distributed 5·25 milliard among the different sectors of the economy (see Table III).

The Fund not only functions as a special Treasury account; its Governing Body studies the equipment programmes – thus replacing the *Commission des investissements* (Investment Commission) which is to be dissolved – and gives financial expression to the course mapped out by the Plan.

It consists of a Governing Body (*Conseil de direction*) and a number of expert committees. The Governing Body, which has the Finance Minister as its Chairman, is composed of the Ministers and Under-Secretaries of State directly concerned with economic matters, the Governor of the *Banque de France*, the Directors of the *Crédit national* and the *Crédit foncier* (land bank), the Commissioner-General for the Plan, the Commissioner-General for Productivity, the Directors of the *Caisse des Dépôts et Consignations* (Deposit and Consignation Office), the *Caisse nationale de Crédit agricole* (Loan bank for farmers), the *Prix et Enquêtes économiques* (Prices and economic surveys), the Treasury and the Budget. Applications are investigated by the appropriate technical Ministry and then passed to this Governing Body, which entrusts the preliminary study of them to the expert committee on the particular subject. There are twelve of these committees; their members are appointed by agreement between the *Commissariat du Plan* and the Ministries concerned. Committee 1 deals with State intervention to promote investment by industrial and commercial firms in the private sector; Committee 2 deals with investment by local authorities, etc.[5] The unanimous opinion of these committees on any particular point has the weight of a decision by the Governing Body.

The Governing Body in the broad sense has complex powers:

It considers the capital investment programmes presented by the civil service departments and the nationalized industries, and all other programmes financed with direct or indirect help from the State. It gives its opinion on the order of priority of the projects passed, their timetable, and the best method of financing them. These general powers extend over several years for the purpose of drafting the programme-laws, and over twelve months for the programmes which have to be prepared by 30 September of each

[5] See Appendix III, Structure and organization of the Governing Body of the Economic and Social Development Fund.

year and carried out during the following year. In the course of the year, the Governing Body discusses any suggestions for amending these programmes, and is periodically informed of their progress.

It gives assistance to the Finance Minister in operating the Economic and Social Development Fund, and is consulted as to the amount and distribution of the Fund's annual expenditure and the conditions on which it grants loans. The agreements concluded with the agencies through which the loans are issued are submitted for its consideration.

It also has special functions connected with reconversion and with regional policy.

Before the Budget is adopted, the Fund's committees are consulted, jointly with the *Commissariat du Plan*, on the investment proposals it contains and the means of financing them, and these are then passed by the Governing Body. The latter brings out a report covering all investment expenditure financed from public money.[6] After the Budget is adopted. the Governing Body completes the details of different projects and supervises their implementation.

A special account for 'Loans by the Economic and Social Development Fund' was opened by the Finance Act of 26 December 1959 (*Journal Officiel*, 26 and 27 December 1959) and the full particulars of its organization were laid down in Decree No. 60–703, of 15 July 1960 (see Appendix II). I need not describe its method of operation in detail, but its main purpose is to rationalize the form in which the Fund's various accounts are presented. The traditional public accounting system, and in particular the special allotment accounts, did not lend themselves to the new functions of a banker-State.[7]

The *nationalized industries* are in a rather special position. Theoretically, the Government can dictate their policy in the matter of prices and capital investment, for which the authorization of the appropriate Ministers is required – to say nothing of subsequent measures of supervision, such as the auditing of their accounts by the *Commission de vérification des comptes des Entre-*

[6] The *Rapport du Fonds de développement économique et social*, published by the Imprimerie Nationale, is a valuable working document.

[7] The *Caisse des Dépôts et Consignations* also advances loans on deposits by private individuals or groups.

prises publiques (Auditing Committee for the accounts of nationalized industries).

In practice, they are more independent than might be supposed from a study of the legislation dealing with them.

Nevertheless, their financial requirements and the large amount of public money spent on them do enable the State to guide their investment policy to some extent; indeed, the Governing Body of the Economic and Social Development Fund draws up an annual investment programme for each of them, giving full details of different methods of financing. The public sector is less independent than private industry, especially those of the nationalized enterprises which need public funds. But firms that can balance their own budgets – the R.N.U.R. (*Régie Nationale des Usines Renault*), for example – have much the same freedom as their private competitors, except for a few constraints inherent in their public status, such as the ban on the issue of shares.[8]

Table IV

FINANCING INVESTMENT BY THE NATIONALIZED INDUSTRIES, 1961[1]

	Millions of NF.
Own resources	1,990·1
F.D.E.S. (grant)	2,300
Caisse des Dépôts (utilization)	220·8
Public loans	1,640·8
Foreign loans	25·5
Increase in medium-term bills outstanding	28·4
Carried forward	– 24·3
Investment total	6,181·3

[1] Source: Seventh report of the Governing Body of the F.D.E.S. (*op. cit.*), (p. 22).

One reason for the considerable sums allocated to the nationalized industries – in addition to the Government's wish to keep down prices – was that they have no capital, in the sense in which that concept applies to private limited companies. Their very costly investment programmes thus had to be financed entirely by loans; and – again unlike the capital of a limited company – not only did the loans carry interest, but they had to be repaid in annual instalments. For this reason, the second Plan proposed that the *Charbonnages de France* – the nationalized coalmines – be given a

[8] See my book, *Propriété publique et planification* (Cujas, Paris 1962).

non-repayable 'capital endowment', to enable them to compete in the E.C.S.C. on equal terms with foreign coalmines in private ownership. Similar endowments were later given to other nationalized industries, including Electricity, Gas, and the Paris Public Transport system.

FINANCIAL INCENTIVES

There are several ways in which the Government can intervene to ensure fulfilment of the programmes laid down in the Plan, including those in the private sector.

First comes the control of credit. It is true that by tacitly agreeing to refrain from influencing the banks, even the nationalized ones, in the choice they must make among applicants for loans and the aims to be promoted thereby, Governments have deprived themselves of a powerful weapon. But long-term, rediscountable loans exceeding 2.5 million francs made by the *Crédit national* are granted only after a succession of permits and discussions, including consultation with the *Commissariat du Plan*, and are allocated by preference to projects that further the aims of the Plan. In the case of medium-term rediscountable loans, the requirement of conformity with the Plan is much less strictly enforced, though the *Commissariat* is consulted if the sum to be borrowed exceeds one million francs. Short-term loans are not subject to this kind of supervision. Not that either medium-term or short-term borrowing goes entirely unquestioned; but though the *Banque de France* closely scrutinizes all transactions from the banking point of view, it has not so far shown any concern to promote the aims of the Plan.

Another means of intervention is the control of bond issues on the Stock Exchange. When these exceed a specified amount, permission must first be obtained from the Treasury, which lays down an order of priority and a timetable for the issues.

The State has a considerable variety of other means of persuasion. It guarantees public loans, or makes grants towards the payment of interest on them, to institutions and undertakings whose activities fall within the framework of the Plan (Laws of 31 December 1953 and 7 February 1954), or to assist conversion, concentration, specialization or decentralization.

It also gives special investment bonuses to firms setting up in the depressed areas of Western France or in one of the five 'critical zones' of which I shall have more to say in connection with regional planning (Decree 60–370, of 15 April 1960).

Mention should also be made of the tax relief used to steer new firms to certain parts of the country and of the 'letters of approval' which authorize the *Caisse nationale des Marchés de l'Etat* (State Marketing Fund) to contribute to the cost of stocks and help to launch new manufactures.

Lastly, the interim Plan for 1960–61 provided for the conclusion of *quasi-contracts* with the manufacturers of capital goods, by which a firm undertakes, in return for some financial support from the authorities, to carry out a clearly defined programme of investment, research and production, of special interest to the national economy. This method seems likely to spread.

OTHER WAYS OF STEERING THE ECONOMY

The Government investigates the legal obstacles to expansion, and proposes amendments.

Some of these deal with financial machinery and the structure of firms. Others relate to market organization, such as the creation of the *Fonds de Garantie mutuelle et d'Orientation de la Production* (Mutual Guarantee Fund for the Guidance of Production), for the benefit of farmers. Others, again, refer to business property or the system of land tenure.

It would be possible to give many examples of reforms introduced in these and other spheres, including the retraining of labour, decentralization, and price-fixing for the principal commodities and basic services.

Price-fixing in general plays an important part. An Order of 30 June 1945, which is still in force, declares that 'the prices of all goods and services shall remain unchanged . . . at the levels established by decisions adopted since 1 September 1939'. Subsequent decisions have ratified the price-increases which have taken place since 1 September 1939, or have modified the price system. As a result there are now three different situations.

(1) The prices of primary products, such as wheat, steel, coal and aluminium, are still controlled.

(2) Those of many manufactured goods – engines, household appliances, agricultural equipment, etc. – while free within certain limits, are nevertheless subject to government control or supervision.

(3) Textiles and footwear are completely free.

In addition to these permanent forms of supervision there are others, in theory of a temporary character; the Government is empowered to issue decrees 'freezing' all prices, even those which were formerly non-controlled. In point of fact, price-freezing has been constantly maintained since 1952, though waived in some cases to permit adjustments.

These wide powers of regulation should not be overestimated, however. Price-control is easier in the basic sectors than in the manufacturing industries or in trade. In the former category, specific commodities, such as steel or coal, are produced by a comparatively small number of firms, making it easy to verify the application of prices which are fixed in relation to a base period. Whereas in the latter category a very slight difference in quality, which is always possible, can place the product in a different class: the price of aluminium can be controlled, but not the price of saucepans.

Outside the basic industries, price-control is feasible only in concentrated manufacturing activities, such as the motor industry, or in contracts for the supply of equipment to the nationalized industries – for example, turbines.

The system of penalties is such as to reduce the Government's powers still further. Until 1955 the Minister for Economic Affairs could impose fines and order confiscation, and the Prefects could close down an offending outlet. But these powers, held to be incompatible with republican concepts of legality, were abolished by an Act of 28 November 1955, or rather transferred, for the most part, to the judicial authorities. Since judges are always reluctant to put a small factory owner or a shopkeeper out of business, infringements of the law go largely unpunished. A measure enacted on 16 November 1957 attempts to correct this laxity by empowering magistrates to close an offender's premises as soon as his offence comes to light, before the case is tried. But the chief impediment to effective discipline is shortage of staff in the bodies responsible for inspection and for economic surveys.

Hence, though price-control is theoretically widespread, it is confined in practice to the primary branches, the development of which is thus hampered to the advantage of less important segments in which prices are comparatively free. Nevertheless, as a feature of general economic policy it has a definite part to play.

Repercussions are produced not only by the average level prices of basic commodities and utilities, but also by the rates established for different categories of users. The introduction by *Electricité de France* of its so-called *tarif vert* ('green tariff'),[9] and the changes in fares made by the S.N.C.F., represent steps towards a price system which will reflect real production costs.

A very effective influence is exerted through government purchasing and the orders placed by the nationalized industries. The greater the proportion of its output sold by a particular industry to the public sector, the more readily it will submit to guidance. It has thus been possible, through indirect pressure, to rationalize the structure of the heavy engineering and electrical industries.

In practice, the exercise of these powers of action involves all the firms, public and private, in a maze of incentives and prohibitions and creates a dialogue with the authorities. A firm may wish to expand; but if its premises are in the Paris area it will be forbidden to do so on the spot; it must apply to several Ministries, and to the Plan, for suggestions as to where it should move and for the material and financial advantages and the tax allowances to which it then becomes entitled. Another firm may want to begin manufacturing a new type of capital goods; it will try to secure quasi-contracts for the purpose.

The Plan's hold on the firms depends not so much on whether they are public or private undertakings, as on the nature of their output and their financial position. If they belong to what are called the basic sectors (transport, energy, metal production) or if they are very large (chemical manufacturers), price-controls and the fact that, since their function is to provide fundamental products or services, they must often carry a heavy burden of capital investment, will lead them to apply to the authorities for tax concessions, loans on favourable terms from the F.D.E.S., and permission to raise their prices. Their contact with the State is closer than that of the manufacturing industries because their products are a determining factor of growth, and means of coercion are more numerous.

But are they sufficient?

[9] The new scale of charges for high-voltage current introduced by *Electricité de France* in 1957.

II. INADEQUACY OF THE MEANS OF ENFORCING FULFILMENT OF THE PLAN

The satisfactory fulfilment of the first Plans is not enough to dispel all apprehensions. There were some shortcomings, which showed that the powers of enforcement were not strong enough. Private capital tends to be withdrawn from branches which are declining, or which offer small profits, and invested in others, the development of which may not be of the first importance. Government funds have sometimes been enough to ensure growth in the former – the iron and steel industry is a case in point; but some sectors, including the manufacturing industries, reveal deficiencies which have never been made good. On the other hand, official intervention has been powerless to prevent the unnecessary squandering of capital in shipbuilding, motor-car manufacturing and petrol retailing.

According to the fourth Plan, investment is to expand with appreciably greater speed in the near future. Not only is the annual rate of increase of the gross domestic product to be raised from 4·5 per cent to 5·5 per cent in the coming four years, but in 1965 the ratio of investment in that product will be 22 per cent, as against 20 per cent in 1960. Are the present forms of intervention adequate to guide, and especially to increase to such a degree, investment in each sector?

In selecting its targets, the Plan takes account of the development trends indicated by the preliminary forecasts; so it is legitimate to suppose that given more effective means of fulfilment, the planners would become more ambitious.

The effectiveness of such means depends partly on their number, and partly on their continuity and co-ordination.

THE NUMBER OF MEANS OF ENFORCEMENT

If by the means of enforcement we are to understand the legal arsenal available to the authorities, the impression is that this is adequate. Not all its weapons are employed with equal frequency, some indeed have fallen into disuse; but it would be pointless to pass new legislation while neglecting what already exists. There is great readiness to make use of incentives to stimulate expansion, though these might be better co-ordinated and more discrimination should be shown in granting credit facilities, including short-term loans. But the authorities are reluctant to impose penalties for non-fulfilment of the Plan, and even more unwilling to take over the tasks abandoned by private initiative. Their assistance is taken for granted, but the burden it imposes is resented. At the very least, a firm that fails to reach the target assigned to it should forfeit the financial advantages granted by the State as its part of the bargain. Taxation might even be employed, or credit manipulated, to penalize firms that make excessive profits or put them to undesirable use. But the imposition of penalties, let alone the dismissal of offending managers, cannot be made common practice unless the Plan's objectives are to be described more fully and the firms given strict injunctions. The attempt to lay down such injunctions has proved extremely difficult, and their number must be restricted if the Plan is to retain its flexibility.

The Government might spur certain branches to greater effort by threatening to take over any tasks they refuse to carry out. But since 1946 it has shrunk from using this weapon,[10] except on a very small scale in the petrol industry. Government take-overs cannot solve all problems,[11] but there is no other way of making good the deficiencies of private initiative.

If the Plan is to be effective, it must be carried out consistently. What is done by the *Commissariat du Plan* in this respect?

THE ROLE OF THE COMMISSARIAT DU PLAN, OR CONSISTENT FULFILMENT

Thanks to its wide connections and the advice it provides, the *Commissariat du Plan* plays an important part, even more important than the documents reveal. All the same, the fulfilment of the Plan still leaves much to be desired from the standpoint of continuity and co-ordination.

Continuity

No Plan which comes under fire every year at Budget time can serve its purpose. A Plan is supposed to facilitate the unremitting

[10] The introduction to the fourth Plan (see Bill cited on p. 40) suggests that the State might be asked to take shares in newly formed companies.

[11] See P. Bauchet, *Propriété publique et planification.*

effort required by the circumstances of present-day economic life, to ensure that firms shall be able to pursue their activities and to prevent an excessive strain on the exchequer.[12] But the multi-annual Plan – whether French or Russian – does nothing of the kind; it offers no more than a moral undertaking that a certain policy will be carried out.

Continuity is, of course, a matter of political determination rather than of legislation comprising financial pledges, which can be evaded. But such pledges have their value.

Article 2 of the Act of 27 March 1956, approving the second Plan for Modernization and Investment, provides, for certain sectors of the Plan, 'programme-laws' that include financial appropriations for the period concerned, together with measures of reform. The loans are to be spread over several years. These 'programme-laws' have many advantages. They make it possible to undertake work that will cover a number of years (e.g. successive highway extensions); entrepreneurs can confidently lay down long-term investment policies and make favourable terms with their suppliers for orders divided into annual instalments. This reduces costs and keeps down the price to the public.

In principle, these multi-annual schemes – the authorities will not allow them to be discussed afresh when the annual Budgets are presented – are worked out by the Plan. But the preparation of the second Plan, in which they were recommended, was finished by the time they were begun, and the task of drawing them up devolved upon the committees of the Governing Body of the Economic and Social Development Fund. For the third Plan, these committees were instructed to refer the projects for approval to the Plan's Modernization Commissions – a convenient procedure, for the committees, being comparatively small, can draft proposals more easily than can the Commissions, which are bigger; while as the committees include in their ranks a number of members of the Commissions there is little danger of opposition from that quarter. The projects are then submitted to the *Conseil supérieur* of the Plan and to the Minister of Finance. Special powers have sometimes been granted – to the Mendès-France Government, for example – to enable the programme-laws to be cast in the form of decrees.

But not all sectors of activity have programme-laws, though they

[12] In Russia, the principal plans are the annual ones, not the Five-Year Plans.

have been drawn up to deal with electrical engineering, the electrification of the nationalized railways, the infrastructure of air transport, Postal and Telecommunication services, shipbuilding and health and social equipment. They have not always been adopted as soon as the relevant Plan was launched; there has sometimes been a lapse of several months or even years, during which the old ways have continued. Moreover, they do not always cover the whole period of the Plan,[13] but may be limited to two years.

Above all, there is no standard form of programme-law; those dealing with the electrical industry,[14] for instance, differ considerably from those relating to merchant shipping:

– The former are no more than an expression of intention; the approval of the authorities must be obtained each year for the forthcoming commitments and expenditure, and this may lead to reconsideration of the whole programme as laid down in the Plan.

– Whereas the latter provide an absolute guarantee of continuity, for they involve approval of the programme. Their annual adoption is simply a (statutory) confirmation of 'services voted'.

If some of the programme-laws have thus been drained of their substance, it is partly because the Finance Minister has found no other way of resisting the political pressure which attempts to enforce them in all directions, although in some branches they are not essential and merely impede the Government's necessary freedom to intervene. There should be a definite ruling as to the branches where programme-laws are needed and those where more elastic formulae are applicable. Present policy is confused, and lends itself to the most divergent interpretations.

In any case, even where they are essential, programme-laws must necessarily differ according to whether they entail loans from the F.D.E.S., as in the case of *Electricité de France*, or Budget subsidies (granted without security). The loans are only intended to supplement the working capital fund if it is not large enough to

[13] They do not always cover the entire period of the Plan, for the simple reason that it is difficult to estimate investment needs in detail so far ahead. For example, the last programme-law on Electrical Equipment (October 1961) laid down the programmes for 1962 and 1963, in continuation of the programme-law of 31 July 1959 which had approved the programmes for 1960 and 1961.

[14] In point of fact these comprise two programmes. One, approved by the law, was a guaranteed programme, while the other, which might later be submitted to Parliament, was aleatory.

finance needful investment; the extent of the deficit not being foreseeable, the programme-law, in its present form, can only suggest an approximate total figure, and requires renewed approval each year. Whereas a programme-law covering Budget subsidies intended to finance an investment programme carries with it the approval of the programme, i.e. of fixed credits which cannot be questioned at the beginning of each financial year. Hence, the programme-law on shipbuilding subsidies ensures real continuity. But though continuity is the very essence of the Plan, it is not provided for the investments of public corporations which borrow public money through the F.D.E.S.

Programme-laws should enable public utility undertakings to abide strictly by the terms of the Plan. It is not enough to lay down programmes in terms of value or credit. If the sums lent can be devoted to purposes other than those for which they were originally granted, the programme is not binding. This means that if public corporations are to spread their investment programmes over several years and keep them in conformity with the Plan, the programme-laws must be amended. They should be submitted at the same time as the Plan, and be of a different nature from those adopted hitherto. They should lay down – in the branches where this is feasible – work programmes of a compulsory nature; though these should be subject to revision in the final years of the Plan (but not before), because it is impossible to draw up projects in minute detail for a five-year period. Approval of the programme should no longer relate to the financial appropriations, but to the actual work proposed, irrespective of whether it is to be financed by F.D.E.S. loans or by Budget subsidies. Thus, even in the former case, the Plan could not be altered by a budgetary measure. All decisions made by Parliament, by the Civil Service and by the firms themselves must be brought into alignment, and the necessary elasticity preserved.

It is true that the economic situation may make it imperative to slow down the programmes if the demand for capital goods proves to be straining capacity, or to speed them up in the event of a depression. But the estimates of F.D.E.S. loans given in the programme-laws need only be approximate, as they are today, and the Budget subsidies would be no obstacle to variations in the pace of investment over the whole period. The entries for payments would be adjusted in due course by the Finance Ministry, price fluctuations being taken as the reason for accelerating the programmes or slowing them down.

Under the existing system, some of the programme-laws do not carry approval of the programme and of the expenditure it involves, so that the Plan is liable to be called in question in each successive year[15] whereas the reforms outlined above would leave only expenditure open to adjustment. However, it would still remain to co-ordinate all measures for the fulfilment of the Plan.

Co-ordination

In agriculture, for instance, the Plans have stressed the fact that an increase in meat production – desirable both from the standpoint of domestic consumption and for export purposes – would be possible only if a whole series of related decisions were applied. Agricultural prices must be adjusted, to reduce the price of cereals, where the margin of profit is excessive, and bring about a definite increase in the selling price of meat; stockbreeding subsidies must be granted to relieve breeders of the burden of preliminary expenditure and ensure them against risks; and there must be support for the export market, which would also benefit livestock production. Similarly, in industry, financial policy should be supplemented by measures of price-control – including more especially a rational scale of charges to be imposed upon the nationalized undertakings providing transport and energy – and by a customs policy, all directed towards promoting the development of well-defined branches and areas.

Little progress has been made, however, in co-ordinating the means of enforcement available to the various Civil Service departments. The problem is usually camouflaged by listing the 'means of fulfilment of the Plan', without explaining who possesses them and whether there is any connection between them. The layman imagines that they are either controlled or extensively

[15] Not that the entire fabric of the Plan is subjected to reconsideration; but substantial alterations, not always logically accountable, are made for various reasons. Sometimes, as a result of political pressure, Budget appropriations are diverted on such a scale that it becomes impossible to finance the investments of public utility undertakings (pressure from agricultural interests has more than once endangered the financing of the large basic sectors). At other times, certain Civil Service Departments may think fit to reject the course laid down in the Plan.

co-ordinated by the Commissioner-General. But as we have seen, he has no such authority over other Ministries, and his means of enforcing the application of the Plan are tortuous and restricted.

The *Commissariat du Plan* is in close touch with certain executive bodies, including the Finance Ministry. The Commissioner-General works with the *Conseil national du Crédit*. He co-operates with the Social and Economic Development Fund in using public money as an instrument of control – an important one, as we have seen; he has a seat on the Governing Body of the Fund; the chairmen of many of the expert committees are his representatives, being likewise the chairmen of the corresponding Modernization Commissions (this applies to Committee 4, Energy, Committee 5, Overseas Countries, Committee 6, Agriculture, Committee 8, Transport, etc.). The secretariats of many of the committees have their offices at the *Commissariat*. The committee leaders are appointed by agreement between the Commissioner-General and the Minister concerned.

The Commissioner-General makes proposals for financing investment, drawing these up each year in the light of meetings held by the Fund's committees and its Governing Body, on which he is represented, and in agreement with their views. These proposals are discussed with the Finance Ministry and with the parties to whom they apply, after which the Minister's decision is notified to the Governing Body of the Fund. Once the Budget has been approved, the Plan and the Fund make joint arrangements for supervising the work to be done, and are responsible for revising the programmes if need be.

As we already know, the programme-laws are drafted by the Fund's committees, in agreement with the Modernization Commissions of the *Commissariat du Plan*.

Consultative machinery has been set up to associate the Commissariat with decisions regarding the loans for long-term investment that are granted by the specialized finance organizations, and the rediscountable medium-term loans. The Plan plays a much more active advisory role than a mere reading of the relevant documents would suggest, especially with regard to long-term credit, where it co-operates with the F.D.E.S. The *Commissariat* also undertakes direct supervision of the investment programmes of the administrative services and the nationalized enterprises.

The *Commissariat du Plan* and the Treasury collaborate in the control of funds distributed in instalments out of a bulk appropriation. It was thought expedient to stipulate in the Act of 10 August 1948 (Article 4) that the release of each successive instalment should be conditional upon the satisfactory progress of the work in hand. The Finance Ministry not being equipped to undertake the requisite economic and technical analysis, the *Commissariat du Plan* was made responsible for the investigations and might be asked to issue a visa authorizing each investment credit. No visas were actually issued, but the idea made its mark, and in practice the Treasury takes account of the *Commissariat*'s views on the progress of investment.

But the Fund – and consequently the Plan – does not supervise all loans made by the specialized bodies (the *Caisse des Dépôts et Consignations*, the *Crédit agricole*, the *Crédit national* and the *Crédit foncier*).

The Budget forecasts take into account the development prospects for the different branches and the conditions required to ensure equilibrium, which are described in the Plan; and in a more general way, the Finance Ministry spontaneously consults the *Commissariat du Plan* on various matters.

The fact that such consultation is spontaneous gives it particular significance. There are several reasons to prompt it. For one thing, the investment analysis, for which the Ministry is not equipped, has always been undertaken by the Plan. And still more important, the Finance Ministry realizes the value of fitting its decisions into the general picture of economic development.

This should not be taken to mean that the Finance Ministry falls in readily with the *Commissariat*'s suggestions. While it now appreciates the importance of co-ordination, it does not consider itself to be committed by all the opinions expressed. On the other hand, no Plan can be put into operation without the agreement of the Finance Ministry; so that as the Ministry is powerful and the Minister is in present circumstances a stable factor, the *Commissariat du Plan* seeks advice as frequently as it offers it.

The influence of the *Commissariat* over the other means of fulfilment of the Plan is less direct.

Being represented on the Steering Committee of the *Fonds d'Aide et de Coopération* (Fund for Aid and Co-operation, F.A.C.), it keeps abreast of decisions concerning investment in the newly independent countries. It also takes a hand in deciding the decentralization policy, through membership of the '5th January' Committee which considers applications from firms in the Paris area for permission to expand, and owing to the important part it plays in the preparation of the regional plans. Furthermore, being closely associated with the *Commission des Comptes de la Nation* (Commission on National Accounts) and the *Comité de Coordination des Etudes Statistiques* (Co-ordinating Committee on Statistics), it is helping to foster information services, which are very backward in France.

Conversely, a number of Ministries and Departments which take part in the work of the Modernization Commissions – among them the Directorate of Economic Relations with foreign countries at the Ministry of National Economy – are thus made familiar with the general outlook of the Plan.

But the influence of the *Commissariat* over all these bodies depends on the goodwill of the Ministries and other authorities that determine economic policy. It cannot control all decisions on the subject.

The voluntary co-ordination promoted by the *Commissariat* in the national interest has narrow limits, partly because every branch of the administration wants to go its own way and partly because of the unco-operative attitude of some financial and other bodies who refuse to follow the lines laid down in the Plans.

The comparative stability of ministerial appointments under the Fifth Republic, and the increased powers of the executive, have made little difference in this respect. The Ministers and their personal staff – whose influence is increased by the impression that they are there to stay – are no more inclined than formerly to accept any measures of co-ordination which are not forced upon them under the present Civil Service system.

Only by radical changes can these difficulties be overcome.

III. HOW TO ACHIEVE MORE COMPLETE FULFILMENT

Contrary to the view sometimes expressed, the greater effectiveness of the Plan is not a matter of altering its entire character and making it compulsory.[16] Apart from necessary political developments, better trade union organization and closer co-operation among the pro-planning elements in Parliament, an overhaul of certain public institutions, administrative departments and firms would be enough to put fresh vigour into the application of the Plan.

REFORM OF THE PUBLIC SECTOR

The first step towards the fulfilment of the Plan would be to overhaul the State machinery, for the better co-ordination of its activities and in order to ensure that, in the first place, the State shall obey the precepts of its own Plan. This involves the entire structure of the State, with the Civil Service and the nationalized firms.

1. The trouble with the *State organization* is that the conditions governing economic decisions are chaotic, and that the Ministry of Finance has too much power.

As keeper of the public purse, the Ministry of Finance tends to claim the functions of arbiter and the right to decide what expenditure is justified – thus usurping the prerogative of the head of the Government. There is no question as to the competence of its senior officials and their increasing awareness of economic problems; but this attitude leads the Ministry to take on too many tasks and overburden its upper levels in a way that sometimes brings their work to a standstill. Moreover, it irritates the other branches of the Civil Service, which dislike being kept in leading-strings. The staff of the Finance Ministry have no direct contact with the general public, and are often less well informed about practical problems than the technical Ministries and the local authorities, whose views they are apt to override. And the division of major decisions between the Prime Minister and the Finance Minister adds to the difficulty of co-ordinated planning and balanced application of the Plan.

16 It is amusing to note that members of the parliamentary Centre often call for stricter and more compulsory planning, whereas the Left, being well acquainted with the abuses and dangers attendant upon a mandatory system, would prefer planning 'to remain indirect, confined to incentives and suggestions, particularly where wages are concerned' (P. Lebrun, addressing the C.G.T. Congress, *op. cit.*).

Even if a 'Minister for the Plan' were appointed and given authority over certain departments, or put at the head of an inter-ministerial committee representing the Ministries with direct economic interests, he would be powerless unless the administrative machinery had previously been overhauled.

The technical Ministries should have small study-groups to work in consultation with the *Commissariat du Plan* and follow the trend of production of the primary commodities. These would prepare technical studies, assemble information needed in the preparation of the Plan, and supervise its fulfilment, at any rate in the matter of investments deemed to be essential. Thus, without sacrificing flexibility to an obsession with detail, the Plan could obtain information independently of the employers' organizations, which are at present its only source.

Financial responsibility might be shared out in a different manner, and in some cases entrusted to the Prime Minister himself or to the Minister for the Plan, thus ensuring united action and avoiding dispersion of authority among different Ministries and arguments about decisions: a Credit Department could be responsible for questions concerning the finance firms, a Revenue and Taxation Department would not only raise funds by taxation but would also distribute the gains resulting from economic growth; a Foreign Exchange Department would deal with the balance of payments; and a Budget Department would help to improve liaison between the Budget and the Plan. As suggested by the Economic Council (Opinion of 18 November 1961, published in the *Journal Officiel* of 12 December 1961), the adoption of the Finance Bill should be preceded each year by the study of documents comparing the Plan's forecasts up to the year concerned with the results achieved, and the investments still to be made out of public money with the appropriations requested in the Budget.

2. *The Civil Service* in France maintains an exceptionally high standard of efficiency, but a few observations on this topic will not be out of place.

The Civil Servants responsible for the fulfilment of the Plans are in permanent contact with the productive sectors, public and private. But, more especially in a period of rapid economic progress, their income does not keep pace with that of the industrial managers they are supposed to supervise. When the gap is too wide the standard of supervision declines, unless an economic crisis is expected to reverse the situation. Actual peculation is extremely rare in France, but the hope of a post in the semi-public or private sector sometimes leads to negligence or complicity prejudicial to the fulfilment of the Plan. It is essential to revise the salary scale and to take a firm line with pressure groups. Apart from this, the French Civil Service, with its rigid caste system and its division into watertight compartments, prevents contact between the different Ministries, so that even the senior personnel, completely wrapped up in their day-to-day business, lose track of events in the outside world; they have no time to consider long-term prospects or to form a broad view of the situation. It would be a good thing to transfer certain functions and responsibilities to the local authorities, releasing them from irksome controls, and to arrange 'circuits' of Civil Servants through the Finance Ministry and the technical Ministries, thus bringing a breath of fresh air into the departments concerned.

3. *The public services* have a decisive contribution to make to the fulfilment of the Plan, but they do not always play their part. The authorities should be more alive to their potential influence and should encourage them to adapt their development policies and schedule of charges to the aims of the Plan. It would be a good thing if a special Agency were made responsible for the extent of their contribution,[17] increasing it where private initiative falls short, and reducing it wherever it is redundant. The same authority should deal with the development of subsidiaries of the nationalized firms, where confusion often reigns. Proper co-ordination of the stocks and supplies which account for much of the activity of certain private branches would be another effective and hitherto neglected means of intervention.

A final essential is the *co-ordination of investment of public funds* made by the State, the local authorities and the national corporations; for the contact established through the Commissions of the Plan has not succeeded in breaking down the isolationism of the agents involved, or of the Ministries to which they are responsible.

[17] It would be particularly desirable to form public companies in the weaker branches of the engineering industry. And urban development would be facilitated if more land came under municipal control and real-estate companies were set up to administer it (See P. Bauchet, *Propriété publique et planification*, pp. 305, 306, 307).

CONTROL OF CREDIT AND SELF-FINANCING

To bring *private firms* into the scope of the Plan is an even more delicate task, for despite the considerable inducements now offered, the individual businesses are still definitely independent. They can refuse to follow the Plan's suggestions, or they can exceed them. The increased pace of investment advocated by the fourth Plan raises difficult problems of finance. As the Commission for Equilibrium and the Financing of Investment (*Commission de l'Equilibre et du Financement*) pointed out in its report,[18] the pressure exercised on prices by competition from foreign goods makes firms inclined to husband their own resources and rely increasingly upon credit. But they hesitate to borrow more than the banks are willing to advance them. Consequently, if the aims of investment are to be maintained, there must be careful steering of the available savings, and extensive self-financing makes this difficult. While some degree of self-financing is inevitable, at least under a system of private ownership, it has obvious social and economic disadvantages. 'It raises prices at the expense of the consumers, which means chiefly the wage-earners. It aggravates inequality by giving the shareholder, in the form of extra wealth, what could otherwise be passed to the consumer in the form of price-reductions, and by concentrating that extra wealth in a few hands. It may also disturb economic balance and even cause recessions, by breaking the traditional circuit between savings and investment. Lastly, and above all . . . self-financing, by leaving firms free to take their own decisions, makes them more independent of the Plan.'[19]

The demand for the control of self-financing has become a slogan. If the meaning is that it should be closely regulated, or even that the sums thus used should be absorbed by taxation and redistributed under a different system of investment, then we might as well bring the independence of the individual firms to an end and transform them into national undertakings, as is done in Soviet planning. It is sometimes suggested that the margin available

[18] See *Résumé du rapport du Groupe de l'Equilibre*, issued by the *Commissariat Général du Plan* as a roneotyped document in June 1961 (Annex III).

[19] Albin Chalandon, 'A la recherche d'une politique économique', *Le Monde*, 30 May 1962.

for self-financing in the different branches might be regulated by some method more precise than discriminatory taxation. If the margin were too small, the public authorities, after making sure that this was not due to inefficient management, would take steps – by raising prices or by some other method – to enable investment to be financed. If the margin were too large, it would have to be reduced. But it is to be feared that a too stringent regulation of margins would lead to close economic control of prices and of wages. While the former is necessary for all basic commodities, it cannot be extended to the whole economy if planning is to remain elastic. As for wage-regulation, it is rejected even by the trade unions, who are more anxious than anyone for self-financing to be standardized. It has the approval of the political parties on the Right, who wish to check the rise in the cost of living. But they reject any type of planning that restricts the firm's freedom to dispose of its own funds.

Hence, the control of self-financing cannot be carried far without causing an upheaval in our economic system. If it proves inadequate, public ownership will have to be extended and planning made mandatory. But without going so far as that, self-financing could be brought within bounds by using and strengthening the existing machinery for financial planning, which poses the problems of steering investment and of distributing the extra wealth it produces. The first of these could be solved by adopting a more consistent policy of financial intervention.

A *Direction du Crédit* (credit-steering board) might take over and extend the responsibilities of the Treasury, the F.D.E.S. and the *Conseil national du Crédit*, receiving reports from the *Banque de France* on the state of its commitments and reducing the investment targets laid down in the Plan to financial terms. It could establish criteria for the acceptance of loan applications, and supervise the observance of its policy by the nationalized banks, in particular.

The banks' regulations would be amended in such a way that instead of being guided exclusively by the traditional commercial considerations when granting loans, they would make their selection with a view to promoting schemes laid down as priorities in the Plan and brought to their knowledge by the *Direction du Crédit*. But if credit is to be selective, the bankers must be provided with a clear and detailed statement of its guiding principles. Many people, but not all, consider that an investment bank should be established to carry out the State's banking functions, determining its strategy in this sphere and the extent of its participation, and financing projects such as loans and bond issues in cases where private initiative lags behind.[20] But if the nationalized and semi-nationalized banks are prepared, after reorganization, to carry out all these tasks under the guidance of a supervisory body, there would be no need to create yet another institution in an already overcrowded field.[21]

The whole credit apparatus thus placed at the service of the Plan's investment programmes would be closely co-ordinated with budget policy, giving a unity of action which has so far been confined to a few special cases. The granting of subsidies, fiscal policy, including methods of amortization, monetary policy and loans – even, in some cases, short-term credit – would be decided by a single authority. Large-scale investment projects, too, should be submitted to the judgment of this central authority, which would make a detailed review of methods of financing them, as the F.D.E.S. does nowadays for undertakings assisted by public money.

Thus made to feel a hand on the rein, any large firm, even one with 90 per cent of self-financing and particularly aloof in its attitude towards the suggestions of the Plan, would try to fall into line. Fiscal sanctions and shortage of funds would compel it to do so.

Other means could be adopted to reinforce the guidance thus given to firms in their savings policy. To say no more about building licences and the wider adoption of quasi-contracts, market control is a method that might be explored. The Government market (purchase of current goods and investment) accounts for 10 per cent of total national resources. In the case of some products, including heavy electrical equipment and certain electronic goods,

[20] See F. Bloch-Laine, 'Pour une réforme de l'administration économique', *Revue économique*, November 1962, and *La Planification démocratique*, Club Jean Moulin, p. 38.

[21] The present system is anything but unified. The national companies have made no effort to pull together. There is, indeed, a certain amount of contact between the specialized institutions (the *Caisse des Dépôts*, the *Crédit national*, the *Crédit foncier*, the *Crédit agricole* and the *Caisse de Coopération économique*), but their credit policy is unco-ordinated and in some cases conflicting. Moreover, the status of some of them is ambiguous; this applies for instance to the *Crédit national*, a semi-public limited company responsible for granting long-term loans on privileged conditions.

the public sector has a monopoly of purchasing; the system of placing orders is antiquated and fails to recognize their importance as a means of applying the Plan. Yet public orders act as a stimulus to other buyers, enable production capacity to be used to the full during a seasonal or permanent lull, and are a means of bringing pressure to bear on suppliers. The creation of the *Commission Centrale des Marchés* (Central Marketing Commission) at the end of 1959 was merely a first step in this direction.

The battle against inflation and self-financing

Self-financing also, in its own way, impedes the fulfilment of the Plan. It enriches owners and middlemen or bankers who speculate on the stock-market. An increase in the rate of growth of the economy and of industrial firms invariably leads to an ill-regulated rise in certain types of income. In that sense, self-financing is an obstacle to growth. The workers, whose wages are held to a fixed ceiling in order to make self-financing feasible, become aware of the prosperity resulting from their efforts, and make impracticable demands for parity. The Plan should at least envisage means of reducing speculative rises by imposing a capital gains tax on Stock Exchange transactions and reorganizing the flow of money through the banks.[22] The measures proposed for this purpose in the fourth Plan were surprisingly meagre, considering that an annual rate of economic growth of $5\frac{1}{2}$ per cent must inevitably result in inflation.[23]

The speculative aspect of the wealth accruing through self-financing, for which capitalists have hitherto borne the entire blame, has obscured the problem of its distribution. All the schemes put forward, such as the award of wage-bonuses and the constitution of pensions funds in each branch of industry, or at national level, are confronted by two difficulties: how are they to be introduced without causing inflation, and how can equitable treatment

[22] The *Commission de l'Equilibre* has made no serious analysis of the banking system.

[23] The fourth Plan suggests no means of enforcement commensurate with the ambitious aims set forth, for example, in Part I of the Bill. This weakness is underlined by insistence on the need for a neutral fiscal policy and the absence of any important measures of taxation apart from exemptions granted to dealings between parent companies and their subsidiaries, the wisdom of which will be questioned by anyone acquainted with the abuses to which they give rise.

be given to workers in all the different branches, when self-financing is not on the same scale throughout?

OTHER MEANS OF INTERVENTION

In other fields, particularly that of consumption, guidance can be ensured by control over the announcement of prices for certain manufactured goods, and even more by indirect taxation. Stricter use of the present powers of intervention would result in greater efficiency. Production in the priority sectors could also be encouraged by stimulating technical research, particularly in capital goods.

If the threat of setting up public companies were added to these measures, investment could undoubtedly be guided along the desired lines. Instead of calling for the close control of self-financing, even to the confiscation of the resources involved, or for the other impracticable policies frequently advocated nowadays, sometimes merely to catch votes,[24] it would be more effective to make better use of the existing means of intervention. In particular, the banking system should be reorganized (although there have been changes in its legal status, it has not in fact been seriously reformed). Only if experience showed these measures to be inadequate should there be any question of extending public ownership and introducing mandatory intervention, with its attendant political risks.

[24] Discussion of the fourth Plan by the Economic and Social Council, reported in *Le Monde*, 19–20 November 1961.

CHAPTER IV

Political Control of the Plan

THIS has two aspects. The first, which I will only indicate briefly, relates to the control of the administrative machinery set up to implement the Plan. The French Civil Service has no particular penchant for 'technocratic dictatorship'. But colourless parliaments and an unstable executive, indifferent to economic matters, have made it easy to shake off the constraints of the past, and some people, not sorry to see that the politicians who used to oppose their plans are now reduced to impotence and without popular support, would gladly perpetuate a situation where they can uninterruptedly, and in their opinion efficiently, direct the life of the nation, which they are apt to regard as a firm run by 'technicians'.

This situation has its perils. There is no established hierarchy among the Civil Service departments. With a weak or non-existent legislature they are relieved of external pressure and the rifts between them widen accordingly. Clans or castes exist in their ranks, and the rivalry among these is not always for prestige; the private interests which formerly made use of members of parliament now try to influence some of these clans, even those which are supposed to be supervising them. In the absence of any 'counterbalancing power', such influence goes unchecked. In a more general way, the persistence of this state of things might give rise to a fully-fledged oligarchy, which must always be anti-democratic, although to obtain a key post the right qualifications are as important as discreet log-rolling.

The second aspect, with which I shall deal more fully, is the control of the Plan itself.

The Decree of 5 January 1946 did not specify what form the political control of the Plan was to take. The new institution, co-existing with the traditional parliamentary system, might have turned in a completely different direction from the one it is now following. The laws that set it up, including the Decree of 16 January 1947 in which the French Cabinet finally adopted it, placed the Commissariat in the governmental sphere. In course of time, the executive might have tightened its hold.[1]

But that is not enough. The Plan must be supported by representatives of all the principal views of economic policy; this is the very basis of democracy.

In actual fact, the gradual withdrawal of parliamentary participation, for reasons I shall try to make clear, is now endangering the political control of the Plan. On the other hand, certain social groups are intensifying their intervention. How far should they be allowed to go?

I. THE LINES FOLLOWED BY PARLIAMENTARY CONTROL

As pointed out by M. Jean Rivero,[2] parliamentary control is exercised indirectly, through the funds required for implementing the Plan. The financing of investment, partly with public money, is necessarily decided by votes in both Houses.

THE FIRST PLAN

The system of parliamentary control began to take shape during the period covered by the first Plan.

It was a loose system. The Bill of 30 March 1947, which determined the size of that year's appropriations for reconstruction and capital equipment, allocated the first credits required for the

[1] This assumed the executive to be aware of the conditions required for development and of the alternative methods of achieving them. It is difficult for men who have not received special training to acquire such knowledge, but without it they cannot fulfil their task. The same problem arises in every country, including Soviet Russia, where the inclusion of Party representatives in Gosplan apparently serves to keep the political leaders informed. Nor must the executive consist exclusively of technicians or administrators, who might tend to act as representatives of the various administrative oligarchies and the interests sheltering behind these.

[2] Jean Rivero, 'Le problème juridique du Plan', *Droit social*, No. XXXVI, March 1951.

fulfilment of the Plan, but made no distinction between these and the rest of the Budget. The programmes were approved in the framework of the powers conferred upon the Minister responsible, and the credits to pay for them were voted year by year.

The Act of 7 January 1948 – supplemented by that of 21 March 1948 – marked a step in the direction of stricter control. A separate body, the *Fonds national de Modernisation et d'Equipement*, was set up to finance the activities laid down in the Plan, for which the legislature earmarked definite sums.

This state of things was unsatisfactory both for the two Houses of Parliament and for the executive. The former, by voting sums already allocated, were approving policies they had been given no opportunity to discuss beforehand, while the principle of voting credits on an annual and therefore precarious basis was unacceptable to the authors of the Plan, continuity being its essential requirement.

In 1948 and 1949 Parliament reiterated its desire to approve the Plan itself, with all dispatch; but its approval was not asked.

The Plan having become 'an instrument of economic guidance and a framework for investment programmes in metropolitan France and the overseas territories',[3] the executive feared that if submitted to the Assemblies it would lose the flexibility needed to adjust it to any variations in economic circumstances, and that if the Government were given a free hand they might defeat the purpose of the law by emptying it of all real substance. Besides, the Plan was already more than half fulfilled and things were proceeding smoothly, so the overburdened Parliament saw little point in embarking upon a debate that was likely to be thorny and inconclusive.

Instead of going thoroughly into the problem, those in charge were satisfied with overcoming the immediate difficulties. The general purpose of the credits to be voted by Parliament must be explained to Members, so that they would tacitly accept the Plan. To this end, and without entering upon fundamentals, two new features were introduced into the measure by which the Assembly voted the funds needed for the implementation of the Plan in 1950: the use to which those funds were to be put was described in greater detail than before, and an appended report by the Commissioner-

[3] Article I of the law of 27 March 1956 (No. 56–342), approving the second Plan.

General of the Plan, together with two 'Progress Reports on the operation of the Plan in Metropolitan France and the extra-metropolitan Territories of the French Union', gave Parliament a picture of the setting in which the money was to be spent.

THE SECOND PLAN

The problem of parliamentary approval was raised again in connection with the second Plan. By that time it had been recognized that the Plan was not an ordinary legislative document. The Bill relating to it was very short – only three articles – and conveyed approval of an appended document of over a hundred pages, setting forth the essential features of the Plan, with a description of the circumstances, a list of targets, a statement of the sums required to reach these, and an outline of legislation to be introduced. The Plan was like a programme announced by a parliamentary candidate, or a super-programme-law. Parliament was not asked to subscribe to the appended provisions, which together constituted the Plan and which would be the subject of decisions at a later stage, but to approve a general line of action.

This was a compromise between the rigidity of a law and the flexibility appropriate to the Plan: should the economic situation make it necessary, the targets mentioned in the appendix could be reviewed, on condition that the general trend of the Plan remained unchanged.

But this broad approval by the representatives of the nation was not a satisfactory guarantee of continuity for the four-year course of the Plan, for it might be called in question when the annual Budget was debated. Two sets of measures were therefore introduced by the Bill of 27 March 1956, approving the second Plan. Article 2 of that Bill made provision for programme-laws covering the different sectors of the Plan and extending over several years. Article 3 provided that each year, prior to the Budget debate, the Commissioner-General should submit a report to Parliament – and, for all matters relating to the overseas countries, to the Assembly of the French Union – a report on the steps taken to fulfil the Plan, the results achieved, the difficulties encountered and the adjustments required. This supplemented the annual report issued by the Governing Body of the F.D.E.S.

But owing to delays which supervened in the preparation of the document and its discussion in the Assembly, the vote on the second Plan was not taken until 27 March 1956, though the period covered by it was 1953–1957.

THE THIRD AND FOURTH PLANS

The form of the document remained unchanged, but now it was accompanied by programme-laws – still, as we have seen, too few in number – which extended its range.

Parliament was taking less and less hand in the matter, however. It was not consulted about the third Plan (Decree of 19 March 1959, published in the *Journal Officiel* of 11 April). Even the indirect control exercised through the annual vote of funds was diminishing. The sum earmarked for the programme-laws could not be rediscussed each year, and time-limits imposed by the Constitution of the Fifth Republic were too short to allow thorough scrutiny of the purposes to which they were to be put.

Did the interest shown in Parliament during the debate on the fourth Plan, approved on 23 July 1962 (*Journal Officiel*, 7 August 1962),[4] mean that the House had checked its slow retreat from economic questions in general and the Plan in particular? Experience will show.[5]

Meanwhile, Article 2 of the Bill approving the fourth Plan (No. 62–900, of 4 August 1962) introduced an important innovation. Before issuing its instructions for the fourth Plan to the Commissioner-General, the Government would put before Parliament a bill approving a report on the principal considerations guiding the preparation of the Plan in view of the need to develop the country: in particular economic expansion, the distribution of the gross domestic product between investment and consumption, the desirable pattern of final consumption, and the directions to be followed by social and regional policy respectively.

[4] Given in Appendix I (VI).

[5] There was considerable discussion, including 110 questions on a wide variety of problems, with special emphasis on the participation of local authorities and expenditure on social investment; but the debate was often pursued in a three-quarters empty Chamber and Senate.

II. OBSTACLES TO PARLIAMENTARY CONTROL

The fundamental requirements of planning seem to be incompatible with a parliamentary system in which power is divided between an elected legislative body and an executive which it controls.[6]

THE FLEXIBILITY OF THE PLAN AND THE RIGIDITY OF THE LAW

The flexibility of a Plan is hardly consistent with the rigidity of a law. Unforeseeable changes in the economic situation, political upheavals such as the accession of the overseas territories to independence, or new developments in international trade resulting, for example, from the institution of the Common Market, call for lightning adjustments which cannot be set forth in a legislative document. Approval of a general line of policy, rather than of a detailed text, is a solution which leaves the executive free to modify its aims. Moreover, the appended document omits reference to various points where changes will have to be made as the Plan proceeds, such as the dates of issue of government loans, which Parliament cannot be asked to establish by a single vote, because they will probably vary from year to year; the *Commission du Financement* makes recommendations for these in its submissions, as and when required, and this seems a satisfactory compromise.

THE COHESION OF THE PLAN AND THE DETAILED VOTE

The Plan is useful only in so far as it puts forward a group of consistent decisions. If any part of it is changed, the planned

[6] So far, that system has not been called in question. The Constitutional Law passed on 4 June 1958 declares that 'the Constitution shall be revised by the Government which took office on 1 June 1958, in the following manner: the Government of the Republic shall draft a Constitution embodying the principles set forth hereafter: 1. Universal suffrage shall be the only source of power. Legislative and executive power shall be conferred by universal suffrage or by the bodies elected by that method. 2. The executive and legislative powers shall be clearly separated, so that Government and Parliament may exercise their competence in full, each for itself and on its own responsibility. 3. The Government shall be responsible to Parliament . . .'

economic balance and growth may be endangered. According to the present system the National Assembly's Commission on Economic Affairs is supposed to debate the entire project first of all, and the specialized Commissions are not to give their opinions until this has been done. To prevent the fragmentation of the whole procedure, the Rapporteurs of the specialized Commissions and the Rapporteur of the Commission on Economic Affairs are obliged to come together while these bodies are deliberating, for they all do so simultaneously. This is a minor difficulty, but there are others, more serious.

The Plan is submitted in the form of an appendix to a parliamentary bill; like a treaty or a Prime Minister-designate's programme, it does not lend itself to being voted article by article. Yet Parliament cannot accept or reject it in its entirety. The means of fulfilling it may, of course, be refused at the appropriate moment, i.e. during the Budget debate. But apart from the necessity of a consistent policy, many of the means of fulfilment lie beyond parliamentary control, since they depend either on the executive or on the management of firms.

For a long time it was thought that it would be unconstitutional to alter certain parts of the Plan. Being submitted as an appendix, it cannot be changed by the ordinary procedure of amendment. When voting on it the Chamber of Deputies may put forward a draft resolution, but as the Senate has no cognizance of this the two Houses are liable to adopt conflicting decisions. There remains the possibility of interpolating, deleting or amending some provision of the appendix by specifically referring to it in an article of the Bill approving the Plan. But while this gets round the constitutional difficulty, it may easily produce a text incompatible with the conditions of economic balance. Parliament could eliminate this danger by giving the Government power to cut out automatically any proposal constituting a threat to equilibrium; but this would be tantamount to reducing the vote in Parliament to an expression of approval or rejection *en bloc*.

The fourth Plan indicated how matters might be arranged in a case where Parliament objects only to some minor point which does not throw the whole document out of gear. On 12 July 1962, the Prime Minister addressed a letter of rectification to the President of the Senate, amending the text on the lines advocated by that assembly. But if the discussion covers a wider field and the

Government takes a different view, the cohesion of the entire Plan is imperilled.

Hence, quite apart from questions of procedure, the difficulty still remains. Arguments on matters of substance have so far been avoided by Parliament's willingness to approve the general framework of the Plan without discussing its details. On future occasions Parliament is to undertake a preliminary scrutiny of the chief decisions in the Plan, and thus, in theory, acquaint itself with the broad lines of advance without causing disturbance by seeking to alter the finished document. Even so, the various possibilities will have to be clearly described in terms of the economy, and the politicians must have sufficient confidence in these studies to accept their findings. This, incidentally, is a problem affecting every form of supervision and thus more broadly the general relations between politics and economics.

THE CONTINUITY OF THE PLAN AND THE SOVEREIGNTY OF PARLIAMENT

The continuity of the Plan, which is the second indispensable condition of effectiveness, is incompatible with parliamentary control. It is useless to draw up a four-year Plan if its targets are to be called in question whenever the legislature chooses to discuss prices, subsidies and other economic matters, as it is likely to do, especially during the Budget debate. The Assemblies are at liberty to change their attitude – the more so because, to preserve the unity of the Plan, Parliament votes on the entire measure without arguing over any details of which it does not approve – and it seems intolerable that they should be committed to whatever decisions may be taken subsequently.

The present solution is a compromise. Parliament is in any case committed by its acceptance of the general trend of the Plan. But continuity is further ensured by two new legislative provisions, the programme-laws by which the investment programmes can be fully implemented, and the outline-laws (not necessarily dealing with finance) which embrace several legislative enactments with a common theme. Parliament retains its freedom of action in matters not affecting the progress of the Plan.

This compromise is not entirely satisfactory. It is inevitable that Parliament should give up some of its prerogatives, now that the necessity for planning takes precedence over outdated legal concepts. The fact remains that parliamentary control has been much diminished.

Has it been sufficiently so? Is not the fulfilment of the Plan endangered by the fact that the Chamber and the Senate are at liberty to take fresh decisions, though in fields of apparently minor importance, when the annual Budget is debated? The pressure of private interests may induce Parliament to make rules or adopt financial measures which, though considered singly they do not impede the growth forecast in the Plan, will jointly constitute a threat to its future.

THE CONSENT OF THOSE CONCERNED, AND PARLIAMENTARY REPRESENTATION

The final condition for the Plan's success is the consent of those concerned in the measures it foreshadows. The fulfilment of any non-compulsory Plan depends on voluntary action; it requires sacrifices which cannot be dictated but must be made willingly. As M. Rivero points out, however,[7] 'the consent of the parliamentary representatives is a legal fiction which has no psychological reality for those whom they represent: how many Frenchmen, when they pay the taxes voted by the members they elected, feel that they have consented to this sacrifice? But the fulfilment of a Plan which rejects outright the principle of success through constraint, requires from the workers and employers directly concerned something very different from the abstract, formal consent expressed in a parliamentary vote; it needs effective, personal support. . . . This result . . . depends upon the Plan being drawn up in terms different from those of a traditional legislative enactment.'

As parliamentary control diminished, group representation has increased.

III. THE INCREASE IN GROUP REPRESENTATION

The first sign of this is the now generally recognized importance of the Plan's Modernization Commissions.

[7] See article on 'Le problème juridique', already quoted, pp. 15 and 16.

In 1946 the legislature, rightly fearing that traditional forms of representation would prove ineffective, took steps to ensure that those on whom the fulfilment of the Plan would chiefly depend should help to prepare it and thus convince themselves that it was worth while. Experience has indeed shown that the Plans owe much of their success to the active co-operation of the Commissions, which provide an example of direct democratic action, supplementing the parliamentary system. The fact that the workers belonging to the C.G.T. were not represented between 1948 and 1959 did not prevent the system from working effectively.

This direct democratic action is a novelty. In theory, the members of the Commissions represent interested parties, not particular interests; these members are appointed in their individual capacity, not as representatives of a group – either because they belong to an outstandingly important firm or – though not necessarily – because they are members of a trade union. Their decisions are not put to the vote. Every effort has been made to avoid repeating the experience of the Vichy Government, by setting up a new system of corporative government, bringing together individuals who regard themselves solely as representatives of their respective groups, so that their discussions inevitably end in a deadlock.

The new policy at once encountered opposition from the industrial and agricultural unions, which often tend to equate membership of a Commission with the representation of their own interests. The way in which certain agricultural groups demanded that the then Secretary of State for Agriculture should submit the draft of a programme-law to the appropriate Commission of the Plan before carrying out his intention of presenting it in the National Assembly, shows that those groups intended to gain control of the Plan; and the opposition of a large proportion of the workers' representatives was prompted by the same reasoning. Thus, the direct democratic participation to which the Plan owes some of its success is liable to bring about the very developments that its promoters wished to avoid; but it is of great interest all the same.

Another aspect of the growing importance of group representation is the place now taken by the Economic Council. Though the present composition of this body is sometimes criticized, there are signs that a current of opinion is beginning to consider that it should have a greater share in preparing and carrying out the Plan.

A further increase in the power of the different groups may be noted at regional level, now that advisory functions have been conferred upon the recognized *comités d'expansion*, whose members include wage-earners, employers and Civil Servants.

Some people would like to go further, and advocate the revival, in association with the technical directorates of the various Ministries, of the equi-representative advisory bodies which took over from the *comités d'organisation* after the Liberation. These, it is said, should supervise the entire application of the Plan. The equi-representative method might also be extended to technological research centres, whose task would be to find means of improving the production of essential commodities.

But this group control, though increasingly successful, encounters the same difficulty as parliamentary control. Once the Plan has been drawn up, control comes to an end. All that can be done is to accept or reject it in full; to make a single change would reopen the whole issue. However, this difficulty is not so acutely felt by the Modernization Commissions, which take a hand in the actual planning.

IV. WHO SHOULD HAVE CONTROL?

There can be no real control of the Plan except at the earliest stage of its preparation, when the main hypotheses on which it is based are determined. True, the Economic Council was consulted before the preparation of the fourth Plan, but only on one specific point. It would in any case have been difficult to ask more of it, since the various directions or options the nation might choose had not yet been set forth in detail. This prior control relates to a limited number of basic options. It is impossible to pursue every aim simultaneously, a choice has to be made between increasing consumption and cutting down working hours, between the communal and the private provision of public services (such as transport), between different ways of distributing revenue (whether income shall or shall not depend on status, whether it shall take the form of payment for work or of assistance), between possible attitudes towards under-developed countries and regions, and so forth.

But if the political authorities are to make a considered choice, they must know what it will lead to. And alternative models of development, indicating all possibilities in full detail, are difficult to prepare and to present in simple terms. So far, as we shall see, the preliminary forecasts have only offered broad alternatives in the matter of growth.

Once this technical difficulty has been overcome, it will still remain for the bodies which are to take the decisions to show confidence in the prospects described. For they might challenge these. Their inclination to please the electorate – in other words, to try to eat their cake and have it – may prompt them to reject constraints which can never be one hundred per cent certain. During the parliamentary debate on the fourth Plan, some Members demanded enormous credits for every region; and the members of the Economic Council proposed unrealistic increases of income for all groups. This sort of thing would drive the technical experts and administrators to take upon themselves the decisions that the political authorities are unable to make.

However that may be, the question arises as to which of the authoritative bodies is to choose between the alternatives, to fix the objectives, before the Plan is put on paper. In economic matters the Civil Service and the executive have both taken liberties that went unquestioned either by the declining Parliament or by the organs of group representation, still in their infancy.

Up to now, parliamentary democracy has proved incapable of effective control or economic decision-making. Could it be replaced by an economic democracy, based on group representation instead of solely on election, acting by direct participation instead of through the ballot box, and seeking unanimity rather than a majority decision?

Group representation has played an important part at the level of the Commissions, in the Economic Council and in the *comités d'expansion*. There have been signs of genuine collaboration, giving fresh impetus to the Plan. There is a great temptation to push this development as far as possible by authorizing these bodies to make the fundamental decisions. Their familiarity with economic problems would surely prevent them from making flashy proposals? Two unfortunate debates in the Economic Council may damp this optimism; one was on the question of the most desirable rate of growth – and those present vied with one another in pushing it up – and the other dealt with the approval of the general report on the fourth Plan.

There is a danger in relying on organized groups. National and regional contacts between the various interests and the Administration lead to something resembling a corporative system, which may create a kind of mutual agreement to the sole benefit of the leaders of the different camps. Organized interests obtain privileges, at the expense of those which are not organized, and sometimes against the general interest. Problems are settled without reference to Parliament; they are removed from political control. The public, left in ignorance, loses interest and gradually accepts changes of policy by which the Civil Servants and the economic leaders, unsupervised, exceed the limits of their political responsibilities. Recent history has shown the threat of totalitarianism in the corporative system.

In all political circles the overriding tendency is to leave political control of the Plan to the two Chambers. We are even told that the Plan is to become the economic Charter of the legislature. According to the law of 23 July 1962, approving the fourth Plan, the essential options of the next Plan are to be submitted to Parliament. The Economic Council will, it is true, beconsulted before hand, but the Chambers will have the last word. It is a good thing for the needs of old people, the sick, and the non-organized in general, to be championed otherwise than by the groups. Besides, the nation's political representatives are aware of its immediate general interests, they are in closer touch with the population and its needs.

But there is a risk that the Chambers may fall under the sway of pressure groups and fail to take an impartial view.

CHAPTER V

Conclusion

A REALLY flexible Plan calls for unobtrusive but well co-ordinated organization, an overall view of the economic situation, rational and effective means of enforcement that will allow for certain automatic factors, and genuine political supervision. From this point of view the French Plan has provided interesting experience, but some rectifications are needed.

The organization has won general agreement; its flexibility, and the participation of the various groups in the Modernization Commissions, have kept official intervention from becoming too obtrusive. But everyone agrees that economic policy is not yet sufficiently co-ordinated, and everyone realizes that this cannot be remedied without revolutionizing the Civil Service.

There is no question as to the usefulness of general forecasts. The gradual progress of American economic policy in the direction of forecasting[1] confirms this, as does the increased reliance of the big French firms on the information published by the *Commissariat général*. Many firms now adjust their projects to this combined view of the future, which maximizes their profits and guarantees them a supply of materials and a market for their products. The State, learning by experience, now intervenes less frequently and to better effect. The steady progress displayed by the *Service des Etudes économiques et financières* in its analytical forecasting gives

[1] As already mentioned in the preliminary chapter, the United States prepares forecasts of various types. Those of the Council of Economic Advisers are among the most interesting.

It should be pointed out that for the big American firms to adopt such general forecasts would be a revolutionary development. The American economy is still based essentially on the principle that the individual firms grow by planning their own strategy, independently of one another. For wages, collective agreements are signed for each branch. The very idea of a combined forecast or general harmonization is still alien to the majority of businessmen.

reason to hope that present deficiencies will soon be made good.

Agreement about organization and forecasting leaves leisure for controversy about objectives and means of fulfilment. But the basic principles of French planning are no longer questioned.

Intervention is confined to the essential and the probable. Uncertainty still prevails in a few sectors where the consumer is involved; here it is not advisable to 'freeze' production-levels beforehand – these being sensitive to economic circumstances and of minor importance to development – or to antagonize the public, which dislikes interference with these sectors.

Furthermore, the fewer the decisions taken by a planning organization, the more effective they will prove. This axiom has been corroborated in the centralized socialist economic systems, and is truer still in our Western ones.[2]

Intervention is carried out indirectly, through financial measures, rather than by direct constraint, to which the French public is recalcitrant. Firms are offered incentives, but retain the right to select their methods of action; this avoids conflicting decisions by the authorities, and preserves the necessary flexibility. While constraint still has its value at times, it should be used as rarely as possible.

The undeniable effectiveness of the French system must not blind us to its imperfections.

Some sectors, such as oil, are hardly brought under the Plan at all. The rate at which oil production is to increase and its position in the scale of energy resources are decided almost without reference to the Plan, though oil research is financed by the public authorities. This state of things is an obstacle to the co-ordination of energy.

The pressure of national and international private interests is felt in other sectors too, now that frontiers have been thrown open to the Common Market. Motor-cars, shipbuilding and certain chemical industries tend to evade national requirements and the demands of the Plan, in order to fight against foreign competition.

While co-ordination at international level is urgently needed, firmer enforcement on the national scale seems equally desirable in many fields.

The nationalization of the banking system having been brought

[2] See Czeslaw Bobrowski, 'Le Modèle économique polonais', in *Les Temps modernes*, July 1957, p. 71.

to a halt, the guidance given to credit is still limited and is not well co-ordinated with taxation, budget policy and price-control. The pressure of large private interests meets little resistance here.

Co-ordination of the means of enforcement is timid and clumsy. They would be adequate if there were a genuine determination to make use of them. This difficulty cannot be solved by simply attaching the *Commissariat général* to the Finance Ministry and renaming the latter 'Ministry of Finance, Economic Affairs and the Plan', as was done under the Fourth Republic, or by handing it back to the immediate authority of the Prime Minister as the Fifth Republic has done.

The political control of the Plan is not well provided for.

Exceptional circumstances made it possible to establish the *Commissariat général* as a recognized official organ. Four successive Plans have been prepared without the principle of parliamentary control being questioned; but in practice it has been growing weaker all the time.

Thanks to a number of measures of adjustment, including the presentation of special government Bills, the adoption of programme-laws and outline-laws and the appointment of bodies to represent the interests concerned, the Plan has been admitted to our traditional system. Even so, the situation is not satisfactory, for the executive is neither sufficiently free nor properly supervised.

To place in an appendix to the Bill any measures that may need reconsideration does not bring them under government control: unless they are embodied in programme-laws or outline-laws, Parliament must eventually be asked to ratify or amend them. In any case the delegation of powers conveyed by such laws is not complete.

Parliament still has the power, in subsequent voting, to accept the provisions regarding taxation, for instance, and to destroy the harmony of the Plan. The economic interests wield a two-edged weapon; in the Commissions they agree to economic policies, the burden of which they evade at a later stage by bringing pressure to bear on Parliament to refuse the Government the means needed for applying them.

Though the legislature ties the hands of the executive, it exercises no effective control. In adopting the Plan it is only approving a general trend, and in voting for programme-laws and outline-laws it only acquaints itself with the programmes of individual sectors. Swamped in details, the Chambers cannot get a comprehensive view. But even the executive is not beyond the reach of manœuvres that endanger the unity and continuity of the Plan; experience has shown that the unco-operative attitude of Ministries and the pressure of private interests have a baneful influence, strengthened by the absence of real parliamentary control.

Parliamentary self-effacement has other consequences as well; it detracts from the interest of the electoral battle between different parties or within a particular party, and discourages participation at the lower levels in the taking of decisions, particularly for the fulfilment of the Plan.

For the last ten years there has been a spontaneous tendency to strengthen direct representation through the Commissions of the Plan, the Economic Council and the Expansion Committees. To carry this further would bring the interested parties into closer association and give more effective control to the executive, which could act as it thought fit for an agreed period.[3]

The tradition is that sovereignty passes from the nation to the Parliament, but no further. Why not consider that it extends to the executive? In that case the Assembly would merely retain control of certain basic aspects of legislation, such as the adoption of the Budget, and, without losing itself in details, carry out periodical investigations into the general manner in which the executive is using the sovereignty thus delegated to it.

Every scheme for overhauling the French Plan lays stress on one aspect or another, according to the political convictions of its author. Some of the workers' organizations, being suspicious of the authorities, would prefer the Plan to remain simply indicative and not to interfere too much with prices and self-financing – because if this led to intervention in the question of wages, the unions' hands would be tied. On the other hand, these unions would like to see more equi-representative supervisory bodies, even in the technical Ministries, and to obtain parity of representation in the Commissions of the Plan.

Others – belonging, paradoxical though it may seem, to traditionally conservative circles – think the Plan should take a stronger

[3] The constitution of the European Coal and Steel Community, with the High Authority and the Parliamentary Assembly, provides an interesting model.

line, particularly in the matter of wages, without being subjected to any closer control than hitherto.

A third group[4] rightly points out that there can be no real Plan and no real democracy until the public become aware that the Plan exists and begin to help it forward in two ways – by active participation on the part of the workers, or at least of their organizers, in the life of the individual firms, without which a necessarily collective operation cannot be successfully carried out; and by the election to Parliament of men determined to support economic planning and, by giving it their unremitting attention, to accept responsibility for its major trends.

[4] See Roger Jacques, 'Pour une approche syndicale du Plan', in *Esprit*, July 1961, pp. 16–39.

Part Two

PLANNING FOR AN OPTIMUM

PART TWO

Planning for an Optimum

THE METHODS of preparation of the Plan, like the procedure for its fulfilment, take clearer shape as time goes on, and those used for the last Plan are not final. The authors of the first Plan were working in an economy of scarcity, so they drew up programmes for the branches on which the revival of economic activity depended. In an atmosphere of comparative prosperity, it becomes less easy to fix targets.

Methods must be selected to fit the general concept of a Plan. In a socialist economy, based on collective ownership, the State has powers of compulsion which enable it, when fixing its objectives, to pay more attention to technical considerations than to spontaneous economic tendencies; whereas in a Western-style economy, the authorities make a careful study of the present behaviour of individuals, firms and groups, try to discover how the economy is developing on its own, and prepare a general framework. Then and only then do they draw up the Plan.

To prepare the framework and settle the details of the Plan involves choosing between a number of possibilities and trying to arrive at an optimum, even in the matter of localization.

CHAPTER I

The General Framework: The Forecasts

THE FORECASTS prepared in official circles – we shall not consider those undertaken by firms or private bodies[1] – are not to be confused with the actual Plans. The work of the Royal Commission of Enquiry into the economic prospects of Canada in 1980 (Ottawa 1956) and of the United States Council of Economic Advisers is not a preliminary to planning. It carries no suggestion of constraint requiring individuals to contribute to certain consistent aims.

Confusion arises because one phase leads up to the other. The Eastern countries, particularly Poland, went from planning to forecasting. In the West, on the contrary, forecasting has led governments to consider ways and means of controlling future developments.[2]

In spite of recourse to similar measures, appreciable differences still exist between the Eastern and Western methods. In France, forecasting is a *preliminary*, which decides what rates of growth are possible and in what *general framework* the Plan is to be drawn up. In Russia the overall rate of growth is fixed after the sectors have been explored individually, and does not seem to be a preliminary requirement; it is an integral feature of the preparation of the Plan.

This initial difference masks others, relating both to the aim pursued and to the line of reasoning adopted.

[1] See Gerard Colm, *The American Economy in 1960*, National Planning Association, Washington, December 1960. I do not wish to suggest that the forecasts made by private bodies are worthless, but official forecasts covering the whole field escape the danger that views on development may be distorted by the interests of a particular sector or by a firm's wish to rid itself of competition, and that different opinions may contradict one another.

[2] This applies to the forecasts made by the Council of Economic Advisers in the United States.

I. OBJECT AND CHARACTER OF THE FORECASTS

The forecasting at present undertaken in various countries comprises long-term forecasts (from 10 to 25 years) and medium-term forecasts (from 2 to 5 years).

THE LONG-TERM FORECASTS

For all their diversity, these have an underlying resemblance. Their object is to define the conditions required for economic development and the extreme rates of growth that can reasonably be envisaged.

The further a forecast extends into the future, the less reliable it will naturally be; far-reaching and unpredictable changes may take place on the national and international political scene.

The element of chance may, however, be somewhat reduced if a variety of working hypotheses is considered.

In any case, long-term exploration is essential. The economic structure cannot be disregarded; population movements and technical innovations have their unavoidable repercussions. Over a period of a few years, structures are by definition comparatively stable, so that economists tend to ignore their changeable nature. Changes become noticeable only over the long period within which economic policy must be adapted to changes in elements of the economic structure even before they occur. An increase in the population, especially if it is accompanied by the introduction of more complicated technological methods, leads to educational investment even before the child population reaches school age. Investment in sectors such as energy and coal and steel depends on the probable size of markets and supplies of raw materials twenty years hence.

Though they have a common purpose, the forecasts made in various countries differ from one another.

In Eastern countries, Poland for example,[3] where an overall long-term model exists, it is 'volitional'. It takes account, no doubt, of the structural determinisms revealed by studies which precede

[3] See Michal Kalecki, 'Le Plan à long terme pour les années 1961–1975' in *Perspectives polonaises*, No. 3, March 1959.

the Plan and cover population, technical changes, tensions in the producer and consumer markets, and trends in certain branches, such as energy.

But it rests on a policy determined and adapted by the public authorities, 'the formulation of a long-term programme of development to provide considered solutions for current problems.'[4] This forecast, known as the 'long-term plan', clarifies the prospects of the programme. It is not only 'volitional' but optimistic, since it rests on the assumption that policy will be adapted to circumstances and new measures introduced. It does not appear to be a preliminary to the Plan; the rates of economic growth are fixed during work on the Plan itself.

The long-term forecasts made in the West are more often 'spontaneous'. This is because economic developments are not entirely controlled by the authorities, who cannot be certain that decentralized or private agents will behave as they would like them to do, and must allow for spontaneous and unpredictable reactions. Thus, the definition of a policy in a Western country must be preceded by an analysis of spontaneous behaviour, which is not so necessary in the centralized, Communist States. If such forecasts are made entirely without reference to politics, they will be unrealistic; experience has given the lie to the predictions on growth formulated in the Report of the Royal Commission of Enquiry into the economic prospects of Canada in 1980, which were made in those circumstances. Forecasts usually assume that present policy will continue, or that only slight changes are to be made.

The Dutch forecasts, such as *An Exploration of the Economic Potentialities of the Netherlands 1950–1970*,[5] and those made in France are typical examples of 'spontaneity'.

Not being 'volitional', they are not binding upon future policy, which can always be adjusted, and they allow for the possibility of accidental obstacles to expansion – e.g. a disequilibrium of the trade balance due to fortuitous developments in other countries, or lack of dynamism in some quarters. Forecasting gives not merely one rate of growth but several, indicating the highest feasible limits.

The first long-term forecasts in France, which we shall consider at somewhat greater length, were made during the preparation of

[4] See Michal Kalecki, *art. cit.*

[5] Published in English at The Hague in 1961, by the Netherlands Planning Bureau.

the third Plan, and published with the title of *Perspectives de l'Economie française en 1965*.[6] When the fourth Plan was being prepared it was thought necessary to repeat this kind of exploration of the future for a period longer than that of the Plan (1965), carrying it forward to 1975.[7]

When preparations for the fifth Plan were launched, the *Commissariat général du Plan* carried its scrutiny as far as 1985.

This last study, which looks more than twenty years ahead, has a different purpose from its predecessors. It is not intended to specify a probable rate of growth, but to provide certain data which facilitate decision-making in such matters as town-planning, localization, and the choice between expenditure for social or economic purposes. It provides a group of views on selected subjects, rather than a comprehensive model of equilibrium.

In addition to these general analyses, various branches, such as energy, have carried out partial forecasts which are mentioned in the Commissions' reports.

THE MEDIUM-TERM FORECASTS

These are closely linked with the planning process.

In France, the Government issues general instructions for the preparation of the Plan on the basis of a wide range of information on technical and economic topics, with particular reference to economic forecasts of possible growth *during the period of the Plan*. For the third Plan the Government had before it forecasts covering 1961, and for the fourth Plan, forecasts going up to 1965 – both sets being included in observations drawn up for a longer period (1975 for the fourth Plan). These studies give the Government an idea of the rates of growth that can be achieved, and a choice of alternatives, together with a list of the chief obstacles to development that lie ahead.

Armed with these particulars, the authorities decide what the rate and nature of expansion shall be, and send their instructions to the Commissioner-General. The latter prepares a detailed medium-term forecast and distributes it to the working Commissions, to guide them in preparing the Plan.

After this, medium-term forecasting changes its character.

[6] Imprimerie nationale, Paris 1956.

[7] *Premières perspectives sur l'Economie française en 1975*; these were roneotyped and will not be published until later.

It becomes a working instrument within the Plan, a framework into which the Modernization Commissions must fit their efforts, so that the Plan shall hold together; specialists in a particular form of production cannot specify its possibilities of development without a bird's-eye view of the whole field – especially nowadays, when techniques change so quickly and different branches are so closely related in their growth. The general framework gives an overall idea of development and of the conditions required for it, which the Commissions accept as a working basis, though they argue about its bearing upon their respective fields.

At this stage the medium-term forecast must be worked out in detail, to provide accurate guidance for the many working parties, some of which deal with narrow segments.

And now it becomes 'volitional'. The political conditions which it is the essential purpose of the Plan to lay down are now established. The forecast has come to resemble the 'general directives' prepared by the Council of Ministers of the U.S.S.R prior to each Plan.[8] The choice between alternative policies having been made, it becomes necessary to discard all but one of the hypotheses of growth.

II. LINES OF REASONING

The lines of reasoning that may be followed in exploring the future vary enormously in exactness and in their frame of reference.

One may simply extrapolate past tendencies, carrying them forward into the future.

One may draw up a complete model of the economic structure, noting the largest possible number of constant relationships between productivity and production, production and investment, income and consumption, etc., and take these as the terms of a set of simultaneous equations on which a forecast can be based. But in their present stage of development, our information and procedures do not justify blind confidence in 'mathematical machinery' of the type used by the Dutch in their forecasts.

The French forecasts therefore made use of both methods. In dealing with *per capita* increases in income, extrapolation and

[8] See 'Les méthodes actuelles soviétiques de planification', in *Cahiers de l'I.S.E.A.*, Series G., No. 7, August 1959, p. 18.

constant relationships were used. When the relation between investment, foreign trade and production was to be analysed, the results obtained from the study of constant relationships were checked by the technicians and experts in the S.E.E.F. and the *Commissariat du Plan* in the light of their personal experience. No complete system of equations being available, the method of successive approximations was followed.

The prospect mapped out is simplified in various respects. As price fluctuations are not usually taken into account, it is expressed in constant prices.[9] Only the terminal year is analysed, no study of equilibrium being made for the intermediate period.

Even the frame of reference of the forecasts made for the fourth Plan was different from that of those which preceded the third Plan.

FORECASTS MADE FOR THE THIRD PLAN

The 1954–1965 forecasts[10] began by calculating the amount of the domestic product of the terminal year (dividing the domestic product of the year of reference into sectors and multiplying it by the index-figure of the active population per sector and by the index of productivity).[11]

The domestic product having thus been ascertained, the final demand was analysed by breaking up the gross domestic product into consumption, investment and export.

This procedure – the projection of the gross domestic product into the terminal year, followed by analysis of the final demand – has the undeniable advantage of making clear the actual mechanism of development; for growth is, indeed, determined by the increase in the population and in its efficiency. But it presents several difficulties from the standpoint of logic.

While it is possible to forecast the index-figure of the active population for each sector, the rate of increase in *per capita* productivity is an uncertain factor; and this is the more serious inasmuch as it constitutes the decisive element of the forecast. Past

[9] With the exception of rents and of a few goods whose price fluctuates widely and within fairly predictable limits.

[10] See *Perspectives de l'Economie française en 1965*, (Imprimerie nationale, 1956).

[11] Value added 1961, value added 1954, index of population 1961–1954, index of productivity in 1961–1954.

Table V

PROJECTION 1954–1965 (IN MILLIARDS OF NEW FRANCS) OF THE GROSS DOMESTIC PRODUCT

Variant II, the larger, taken as the framework of the third Plan

	Contribution to gross domestic product 1954	*Change in active population employed*	*Annual increase in productivity per active person*	*Increase in productivity per active person* 1954–64	*Index-figure of value added*	*Contribution to gross domestic product* 1965
Agriculture	20·30	81	4	154	125	25·30
Industry	67·60	115	4	154	177	119·70
Transport	9·50	110	4	154	169	16·00
Trade	25·90	107	3·2	141	151	39·00
Services	11·70	117	3·5	146	171	20·00
Contribution of firms	135·00	102·5	4·3	159	163	220·00
Contribution of households ..	5·20	92	3·4	145	133	6·90
Contribution of public offices	11·50	111	4	154	171	19·60
TOTAL..	151·70	103	4·2	158	163	246·50

tendencies are a guide to reasoning, but they are not enough; allowance must be made for elements which, though objective, are difficult to assess – the prospects revealed by technological progress, the advancement or backwardness of the national industries compared with those of other countries, the international economic situation – and others which are completely subjective, such as the dynamism of the entrepreneurs and the economic policy of governments.

It is also necessary to assess the growth of productivity in the neighbouring countries which are members of the Common Market, with which some degree of 'osmosis' will develop.

Theoretical studies which seek to elucidate the relations between increases in production, in productivity and in the active population, whether comprehensive or dealing with sectors, have proved to be of little use, if not entirely pointless.[12]

To arrive at a slightly more precise estimate of the growth of productivity, an indirect approach is adopted. Final demand and interim output are calculated for the different productivity rates

[12] See M. Fruit, 'La critique de la relation Cobb-Douglas', *Revue économique*, March 1962.

and gross domestic products of the terminal year. An estimate is made of private expenditure on consumer goods (based on the propensity to consume and on income changes proportionate to changes in production), of public and private investment – productive and unproductive – of intermediate output, and of imports. If final demand and intermediate output do not tally, the productivity rate must be too high or too low.

Incompatibility may be displayed in various ways. For example, the demand for certain forms of intermediate production (particularly energy) may be so high that to satisfy it by imports will create a deficit in the trade balance. Hence the decision that the annual increase in productivity for the third Plan should be 4·4 per cent and not the 7 per cent proposed in some quarters.

This indirect procedure makes it possible to fix a threshold and a ceiling for the target rates of expansion in productivity during the period under analysis. But in this case what is called the 'productivity rate' is merely a datum, a multiplier which yields a purely provisional estimate of the gross domestic product for the terminal year. The actual product, or the alternatives to which it is to be reduced, cannot be definitely ascertained until the final demand is analysed. In fact the figure which goes by the name of 'productivity' is no more than a resultant – for which reason the authors of the forecasts prepared for the fourth Plan decided that there was no point in wasting time on that datum and taking the roundabout path.

FORECASTS MADE FOR THE FOURTH PLAN

Hence, the long-term and medium-term forecasts prepared for the fourth Plan followed a different logical sequence. They began by establishing the probable upper and lower limits of expansion, went on to consider the elements of the final demand associated with that expansion, and ended by laying down the conditions of production.

1. *The limits of expansion*

These must necessarily be investigated, in order to determine the different elements of the final demand, including consumption. It would doubtless have been preferable to make a direct assessment of the needs of individuals and of the community, as desired by the trade unions and by the Economic Council.[13] But it is not possible to set an outright limit to requirements. It was therefore necessary to begin by making a rough analysis of growth, establishing certain facts and offering various hypotheses of development from which a selection could be made.

(a) The first fact is the increase in population (see Appendix V), which is calculated by a method familiar to demographers, using various ratios of natality and mortality, etc.

Here the outstanding features up to the year 1965 are a high rate of increase (·8 per cent per annum), with a total increase of nearly 50 per cent in the 15–19 age-group, an increase in the number of old people, and little change in the figure of the working population. The active population will show only a small increase (4 per cent, bringing the total to 20,480,000), owing to the raising of the school-leaving age to sixteen and the resulting increase in numbers voluntarily pursuing further education, which will not be offset by the probable increase in women's employment (caused by greater needs), and in immigration.

After 1965 the proportion of dependent persons (young and old) will revert to normal, while the active population will appreciably increase.

The other facts relate to investment and raw materials.

A certain number of reasonable hypotheses are added to complete the framework within which the anticipated expansion is to take place. These include the assumption that there will not be another world war, that France will be free from the localized conflicts that have been affecting her situation for years past, and that the extension of the Common Market will stimulate trade. It may also be assumed that there will be little change, in the next few years, in the means of intervention available to the authorities.

(b) The choice among the various hypotheses of expansion is guided, for lack of more precise theoretical data, by considerations based on the rates hitherto observed in countries where circumstances are similar to those in France. Without recourse to draconian measures, and without exhausting the possibilities of further productivity increases, the rate of growth of the French

[13] See J. Delors, *Evolution de la consommation des particuliers au cours des prochaines années*. Study submitted by the *Section des Investissements et du Plan*, 23 February 1960, *Conseil Economique et Social*.

economy over the last ten years has averaged 4·5 per cent; the forecasts made by national and international organizations[14] indicate – for France and for Europe – a future rate of between 3 per cent and 4 per cent. Except in the Eastern countries, Europe's rate of expansion has never risen above the neighbourhood of 5 per cent, nor is it expected to do so.

These points of reference are not decisive in the fixing of the rate; at best, they only yield a rough-and-ready model indicating the situation of the principal sectors of activity, according to the rate of growth chosen. Consequently, the French economic position in 1965 and 1967 was considered on the basis of three different hypotheses of growth:

1. A rate of 3 per cent, which was thought to be the minimum in view of the demographic situation, the nation's needs, etc. This rate could be attained easily, without particular effort.

2. A rate of 4·5 per cent, equivalent to the trend observed in the last few years.

3. Lastly, a rate of 6 per cent, which would entail new and more effective economic methods, and which France has never yet attained.

To estimate the most probable rate of growth, we must know what are the needs that might be satisfied, and what conditions of production would be required to achieve the various rates contemplated.

2. *The needs*

To discover these, we must assess individual consumption and analyse the needs of the community in consumption and in investment (see Table VI).

(a) Individual consumption depends on several factors:

The first of these is the population structure.

The second is the structure of incomes, which inevitably alters

[14] The O.E.E.C. reports forecast rates of between 2·75 and 3·1 per cent for Europe in 1955–1975, and 3·1 to 3·5 per cent for France.

The U.N. Economic Commission for Europe (*Europe in 1975*, Geneva 1957) suggests an average rate of 3 per cent for the period 1955–1975.

The E.C.S.C., in its *Rapport sur les perspectives de développement général des économies dans les pays de la Communauté*, forecasts 4·15 per cent for France and 4 per cent for the six countries as a group.

For the United States, forecasts agree in indicating approximately 3 per cent.

during a period of expansion, as a result of changes in the distribution of the active population, higher standards of education, and changes in the Government's tax policy. But it is only on the hypothesis that the rate of expansion will be a high one, and over a fairly long period, that certain effects of these changes are taken into consideration.

Nor are price changes considered – with certain exceptions, such as rents – partly for lack of sufficiently reliable information and partly because they seem unlikely to have any far-reaching effect on the forecasts.

Allowance is made for changes in consumption which may be encouraged and paid for by the authorities. Government initiative has very important repercussions on private consumption in such spheres as education (by raising the school-leaving age to sixteen), health, and housing (where the target set for 1975 is 400,000 dwellings per annum, of improved quality and larger size).

Once these factors have been determined, individual incomes are broken up into savings and consumption, in the light of the proportionate increase of these elements in the past or of the elasticity of expenditure, after which an analysis is made of the different categories of goods purchased, by considering propensities in relation to expenditure. This yields a picture of expenditure on the various categories of products which indicates the changes that may be anticipated at an annual rate of expansion of 3 per cent, 4·5 per cent or 6 per cent.

(b) Collective consumption

Expenditure, divided into current expenses and investment, is estimated separately for each item; general administrative expenses being found to increase less rapidly than production, whatever the hypothesis of expansion selected. Military expenditure, foreign aid and expenditure on research are also determined. It is noteworthy that, once a certain rate of expansion is exceeded, the importance of these items in the gross national product (G.N.P.) tends to diminish.

3. *Conditions of production*

Different conditions of production will be required in foreign trade, intermediate output, manpower and investment, according to whether the rate of expansion is to be 3, 4, 5, or 6 per cent.

(a) Foreign trade

This is estimated in two stages.

The first stage considers *quantities imported*, for large categories of products. An attempt is made to determine the ratio between the domestic output and the domestic demand for consumer and producer goods, such as steel and textiles, and then the volume of imported raw materials, such as coal, cotton and wool, required to meet the demand. Allowance is made for any frontier adjustments, changes in political status or new processes of manufacture, such as the substitution of artificial or synthetic yarns for natural ones.

In the second stage, the origin of these products is considered and preference given to those that come from the franc area. Naturally, the higher the rate of expansion, the larger the volume of imports and the quantity that will have to be sought outside that area.

The volume of exports is calculated in the light of the need to achieve a balance of payments at the end of the period under consideration. Exports have to pay for imports, for other foreign currency expenditure (repayment of loans, etc.) and for financial aid to the French overseas territories. This latter, which is to some extent set off against the transfer to France of the returns on capital invested in the newly independent countries, implies a surplus of goods and services. For the fourth Plan it will represent an annual figure of approximately 2 milliard francs.

The total volume of exports having been ascertained, the next step is to break them down into categories of products, first considering those in which trading is easiest, such as foodstuffs and textiles, and then distinguishing the more hazardous items. Exports to the different countries are checked by reference to the forecasts of the gross national product made for each of them by the international organizations.

This exploration shows that imports are likely to increase rapidly as production rises, and can only be covered, it would seem, by an appreciable increase in exports of machinery and of chemical and agricultural products. But such increases, particularly of agricultural exports, seem doubtful.

(b) Intermediate output

An attempt was already made during the preparation of the third

Plan[15] to determine the requirements of intermediate consumption, in addition to the value added per branch and the final demand for each large group. In the matter of energy, for instance, the forecasters not only studied the question of the respective shares of production to be used for domestic purposes and for lighting government buildings, but that required for industry, which is not included in the final demand. The purpose of this investigation was partly to discover, for the information of the Modernization Commissions, the probable levels of total – not merely final – consumption and production, and partly to give greater substance to the forecast.

Once needs, investment figures[16] and particulars of foreign trade have been discovered, intermediate output is investigated by either of two possible methods.

[15] The first French table differed in several respects from the Leontief tables. Taking the firm as its basis, it sought to ascertain the behaviour of the entrepreneur in its various aspects. It represented cross-sector relations in two tables, one showing the products and services bought by the sectors, and the other their sales of products and services. The well-known 'Leontief' table is based on the individual factory, and simply describes the technical relations between one branch and another.

Leontief Table

	sector I	sector II	
sector I			output
sector II			output
	input	input	

Table used in the French national accounting system

Table I

	product I	product II
Sector I		purchases
Sector II		purchases

Table II

	product I	product II
Sector I		output
Sector II		output

Statistical difficulties, and the complexity of the sector-product tables, for which an exaggeratedly detailed nomenclature had been adopted, have led the S.E.E.F. to revert to the principle of the single table, which it uses regularly at present with a 27-branch nomenclature.

The inter-industry table enables total production to be determined, once the final demand is known. A system of equations is used which balances employment, final demand and intermediate demand with resources, production and imports.

[16] We shall see later what way of escape was found from the vicious circle set up by the attempt to determine production in the light of final demand, including the investments which depend on that production.

The first makes use of certain correlations between the growth of the domestic product and that of total production which have been found in the past to be constant. But this method can only be applied to large-scale, clearly defined fields of production which stand in a known relationship to the expansion of a zone of the economy – e.g. energy production, steel production or chemical production as a whole.

The second method involves the use of tables showing inter-industrial relations, usually known as Leontief Tables, which plot the whole pattern of exchanges between the different zones of a given economy and the various items composing the final demand – the consumption of private individuals and public offices, investment and export. Assuming that the relations between the purchase and sale of goods and services remain unaltered throughout the period considered, or change only in conformity with the forecast, it is possible to work back from the final demand to the total production of various kinds, and the imports which will be needed in order to satisfy it.

This method provides a check on the breakdown of the projected domestic product. The table shows, for instance, whether the branches which specialize in the manufacture of capital goods will be able to cope with investment requirements.

The merit of this second method is that it offers the only valid means of arriving at the total production figures, which cannot be estimated by the first procedure; but at present it should only be used with caution. One reason for prudence is the imperfect nature of the reference table, which can never give an entirely accurate picture of inter-branch relations. Even if the table were flawless, one source of error would still remain to upset our calculations. For the factors governing inter-industrial relations – the ratio between total production in a branch such as iron and steel and the quantities of coal or iron ore consumed – change as time goes on. And the more detailed the analysis of the different branches and the longer the period it covers, the greater will be the changes.[17] But although we have become accustomed to various forms of technological change, such as the development of synthetic textiles, which

17 W. Leontief, 'On the Stability of Technical Coefficients', *The Structure of the American Economy 1919–1929*, Harvard University Press, 1941. P. Bauchet, *Les tableaux économiques: analyse de la région lorraine*, Editions Génin, Paris 1956.

ultimately alter the import pattern, it is difficult to assess their effect precisely, owing to variations in the yield of the use of energy and its sources, economies effected in the use of raw materials, and so forth.

Furthermore, technological changes are not determinative. Several hypotheses of branch growth may be envisaged within the framework of given overall expansion. But for lack of a clear picture of price fluctuations and relative costs, it has not been possible to develop each of these hypotheses in turn and calculate the optimum. The most that could be done was to reckon with a limited number of intentional changes, such as the development of atomic energy – though its profitability is not precisely known – and the go-slow policy adopted in closing down coalmines in order to avoid the social cost of finding new employment for the miners.

In any case, it is safe to say with respect to the indices of branch output in their relation to the rate of growth, that the higher the rate, the greater the inequality between the different branches.

Once these indices are known, it becomes possible to calculate labour and investment requirements.

(c) The demand for labour per branch and per region

Though, as we have already seen, it is comparatively easy to estimate the total active population, the question of its branch distribution is more awkward. Past trends may be usefully studied, but that is not enough; we also need to know what levels of activity and productivity may be anticipated, in the light of developments in foreign countries and as the result of investment. And this may lead to very different conclusions.

The most usual procedure in considering agriculture, however, had been to extrapolate historical developments, and the same has been done with regard to trade. In the public services, the increased school recruitment made it possible to assess the demand for teachers; the size of the armed forces was estimated on the hypothesis that current fighting would come to an end; and it was assumed that other personnel figures would show little change. Despite uncertainty on these points, the tables showing the distribution of the active population per branch of industry which were prepared for the third Plan have proved, in the light of experience, to be substantially correct.

Even if working hours have been appreciably reduced by 1975, it would appear that considerable expansion will be needed to ensure full employment of what will by that time be a large labour force. A 3-per-cent rate of growth would probably leave part of the manpower unemployed.

These forecasts are accompanied by an analysis of the skilled labour situation, which indicates a dearth of trained technicians and engineers (see Appendix VI), together with regional disequilibrium.

The study of regional disequilibrium supplements, from the geographical angle, the overall forecasts prepared in connection with the fourth Plan.

Wishing to form a definite idea as to the regions where the Government would need to intervene in order to ensure balanced employment, the *Commissariat du Plan* asked the various Commissions for particulars of their labour requirements in each region.

As it was feared that many of them would not possess the requisite information, they were given, at the outset of the work[18], a forecast of supply and demand on the labour market in each region, and asked to discuss this and amend it.

(a) Labour available in each region

The natural change in the active population is calculated per region in the light of the forecasts of total population; allowance is then made for changes of employment in the different age-groups, which are influenced by several factors.

The prolongation of school attendance – compulsory and voluntary – appreciably reduces the youngest section of the working population, between the ages of fourteen and twenty.

The earlier retirement age and the payment by the Social Security service of full pensions to workers on reaching that age, will help to reduce activity among the elderly.

Fluctuations in unemployment, which in France is close to the irreducible minimum, will affect the population in only a few regions.

It seems possible that the number of women in employment will increase, owing to the great differences between employment rates

[18] The Netherlands Planning Bureau (*Perspectives hollandaises pour 1970*, published at The Hague in 1956) made a similar study, as did M. Lenoan in a memorandum entitled 'Aperçu sur l'évolution régionale du marché du travail entre 1954 et 1965' (S.E.E.F., 1957). And by March 1960 the *Commissariat du Plan* had already prepared forecasts for 1965 and 1975.

in different regions, which result not so much from real unemployment as from lack of suitable work in the immediate neighbourhood.

The reduction in the numbers called up for National Service will make a great change in the employment figures for the 20–27 age group.

The estimate of the numbers employed in agriculture in each region is of particular importance, as it will indicate what surplus of the active population is likely to come from that sector and swell the demand for other forms of employment. This migration is steady enough to be assessed; it is determined, among other factors, by the low standard of living in agriculture, technological advances, and the offer of employment in other branches of activity.

Two separate investigations have given some idea of the scale of such migration.

1. In the first, the trends of employment in agriculture observed between 1921 and 1954 were projected to 1965. This forecast was prepared by M. Pressat[19] with allowance for changes in the age-structure of the population, for regional tendencies and for school attendance. By comparison with the position in 1954, he calculated the surplus agricultural population of working age for 1965.

This method, based on stability of migration, has the merit of being fairly precise.

But migration may not remain stable. There are some regions, such as Northern France, where productivity is already so high as to make any improvement in the standard of living of the agricultural worker dependent upon an acceleration of rural migration. In others, such as Brittany, incomes are still low, owing to overpopulation, and more rapid vocational migration is to be desired. At the other extreme, there are regions where the decline in population is such as to give grounds for anxiety. This has prompted a second method of approach.

2. The second method consists in estimating the manpower required for a rational farming system, covering the various types of crops.[20]

[19] See Report of the *Comité consultatif de la Population et de la Famille*, 'Les besoins en emplois nouveaux en France par département jusqu'en 1970' (Documentation française, 1961).

[20] This estimate, made by M. Coutin of the *Centre d'Etudes économiques*, is based on the following hypotheses: that the acreage under cultivation will remain the same as in 1954, and that it will be cultivated by the best technical methods known at the present day.

The increase in the numbers of the active population seeking non-agricultural employment in the labour market is ascertained by adding the natural increase and the changes in agricultural manpower.

(b) Employment trends

The demand for labour is more difficult to foresee than its supply.

It is impossible to predetermine the actual localization of industries, which is a matter for the Commissions of the Plan. The most that can be done is to forecast what the demand would be if regional development remained fairly constant. There are two ways of doing this.

The first assumes that employment in each sector in each region will increase in proportion to the expansion of that sector over the whole of France, as shown in the overall forecast. But this involves the assumption that the expansive energy of the industries in each branch is everywhere the same, and leads to over-estimating the offer of employment in depressed regions.

The second method simply assumes that total employment in every region will increase in a manner proportionate to its nation-wide increase.

Admittedly, there is something arbitrary about both procedures. But they lead to conclusions which stand the test of experience, for they have not been invalidated by later studies, based on the work done by the Commissions.

(c) Probable surpluses or shortages of labour

Comparison of supply and demand reveals discrepancies.

Some regions will have labour shortages – these include the Paris district and the Provence-Riviera area; while others, such as the Western parts of France, will have a surplus (see Appendix VI).

(d) Investment

As we have already seen, investment in housing, education and health is calculated strictly on the basis of needs.

Industrial investment is calculated according to the levels of output in those branches of industry which do not manufacture capital goods. For this purpose, forecasters may use the capital coefficients: the constant relation between the extra production in each sector and the investment required.[21] For lack of French

[21] This ratio is marginal if we consider investment rather than the capital already formed. It may be calculated on the basis of an average (taking a given

statistical tables, the *Service des Etudes économiques et financières* at the Finance Ministry has worked out coefficients based on studies made in other countries. The results have been compared with those obtained from direct surveys, and experts in the principal branches of industry – energy, iron and steel, transport – have calculated what amount of capital would be technically most suitable to a particular production level. These two methods have given much the same results, from which it would appear that if expansion is to be rapid, investment should increase more than production.

The forecast shows, in other words, that with a low rate of expansion – say 3 per cent – the necessary investment effort will tend to decline, whereas with a 6-per-cent rate of expansion it will have to increase (see Table VI). Views still differ on this point, it is true,

Table VI

RESOURCES AND USES OF GOODS AND SERVICES [1]

Resources	*Index* 1975/1956		
	1975 3%	1975 4·5%	1975 6%
Production	200	239	285
Intermediate consumption	198	232	274
Final production	201	244	291
Trade margins	179	218	253
Import duties and taxes	172	217	231
Gross domestic production	197	239	284
Imports	166	206	232
TOTAL RESOURCES	193	235	278
Use of Resources			
Domestic consumption	187	233	277
Net consumption by public offices	147	181	215
Gross fixed asset formation	203	250	312
Stocks and adjustments	226	248	272
Exports[2]	227	248	257
TOTAL USE OF RESOURCES	193	235	278

[1] Sources: Economic forecasts for 1965, based on the Government's directives and distributed in duplicated form to the Commissions for the fourth Plan.

[2] Calculated at domestic prices.

---

period for writing off the capital, and an annual increase in production), or on a direct survey, either comprehensive or partial.

The vague definition of the concept of capital and investment is a cause of considerable difficulty – for instance, are housing and land to be included under that head?

but studies carried out in France and elsewhere[22] show that it is generally accepted. The increased burden of investment is especially evident at the time when the speed accelerates, because of the changes which are then made in the productive system.

Investment raises difficult financial problems. Where development is rapid, a very high level of saving will be needed to cover investment, particularly in certain branches of production – in the engineering and electrical industries, taking 1956 as the base year, the index figure for 1975 is 700 – and it is not certain whether the managements are prepared to invest on such a scale or whether they would gain any financial advantage by doing so.

III. CONCLUSIONS

To sum up: the method of forecasting has remained the same, despite the changes made in the frame of reference between the preparation of the third Plan and that of the fourth. During the preliminary research for the third Plan, the extreme rates of expansion were not selected as a function of the increase in productivity – which was simply a multiplier chosen provisionally in the light of past experience in France and other countries – but were suggested by an analysis of the final demand compatible with those rates of expansion. Conversely, during the preparatory work for the fourth Plan, the analysis of final demand which prompted the selection of rates of expansion was based on a provisional hypothesis of growth already put forward. Any forecast must always be based on provisional hypotheses of development, followed by an analysis of final demand. In this sense there is no contrast between a plan devised by starting from consumption and one starting from production.

The merit of these forecasts is that they indicate the nature of developments in the distant future, so that a rational choice can be made between various rates of expansion – which is the purpose of planning. When the fourth Plan was prepared, three rates of growth were considered in the light of the long-term forecasts, i.e. 3 per cent, 4·5 per cent and 6 per cent.

Analysis showed that the lowest of these rates, while easy to

[22] See, for example, M. Kalecki, 'Le Plan à long terme pour les années 1961–1975', p. 8: 'The part played by investment in the national income may increase in proportion to the rate at which that incomes rises.'

achieve, would not be satisfactory. It would not make it possible to raise the standard of living to the extent desired by the population, to meet France's international commitments in aid to the underdeveloped countries, or to provide enough jobs for the young people who will be pouring into the labour market after 1965.

On the other hand, though the rate of 6 per cent was in itself very desirable – as unanimously pointed out by the members of the *Section des Investissements et du Plan* (The Investment and Plan Section) in the *Conseil Economique*[23] – it would be difficult to achieve. Not that any insurmountable obstacles stood in the way; but experience gained in 1957 and 1958, and borne out by the forecasts, indicated that tensions would arise in the energy and engineering branches, those with the highest rate of growth; lack of adequate productive capacity and shortage of skilled labour would lead to wage and price disturbances and to a deficit in the balance of payments.[24]

These difficulties could, no doubt, be overcome by strict constraints, such as the maintenance of long working hours, the emergency training of skilled workers, a strict tax system by which public savings could be increased, and firmer economic guidance. But would such measures be accepted? Moreover, international economic conditions would have to be sufficiently favourable not to hold back our exports. In view of all this, it seemed wiser to avoid the dangers involved in such a high rate of expansion. It was felt that something in the neighbourhood of 4·5 per cent would be more practicable, on the assumption that circumstances would remain unchanged.

However, the Government, not satisfied with following the most probable tendency, fixed a target for the Plan. Turning from the 'spontaneous' forecast to a 'volitional' point of view involving a change in policy, they chose a rate of 5·5 per cent for the fourth Plan, that of 6 per cent being too risky.

[23] They recommended 'that the target proposed to the Modernization Commissions should be the average annual rate of 6 per cent, to be attained progressively, beginning with a rate as close as possible to that achieved in 1961'.

[24] In his description of the Polish long-term Plan (*art. cit.*, p. 6) Michal Kalecki says that 'during work on the long-term plan, it has repeatedly been found that the Gordian knot of economic development is the foreign trade balance, that is to say the difficulty of balancing the indispensable rise in imports by a corresponding increase in exports.'

Though useful, are these forecasts of decisive value? Their analysis of growth has its defects, and is incomplete in many respects.

It does not review the entire course; in other words it does not show the successive phases of development or indicate in what way progress is liable to be impeded by irregularities in the timing of demand for investment.

Expansion is studied in the light of a combination of factors identical with that known in the past. Except in the case of energy production, no consideration is given to the possibility of any novel optimum combination of resources. We shall find this same omission when we come to consider the drafting of the actual Plan. Few social options are taken into consideration, except for those relating to agricultural migration, the decline in coal production and the reconversion of the naval shipyards.

Moreover, forecasts are apt to create illusions. A population of working age is not necessarily active, and if natural resources are to contribute to growth, they must be developed. To assume in forecasts that both these factors are elements of expansion, without considering whether the conditions for rendering them operative are present, may lead to exaggerated optimism.[25]

But despite these shortcomings, forecasting is the indispensable preliminary to any Plan.

[25] The most striking example of this is the forecast made in 1956 by the Royal Commission of Enquiry into the economic prospects of Canada in 1980, which postulated that there would be full employment for the active population – whereas in fact the unemployment rate has continued to fluctuate in the neighbourhood of 7 per cent. In the case of France, the forecast assumes that the proportion of women in employment will increase in many parts of the country; yet this depends on the existence, near their homes, of factories employing women workers. These methods of forecasting have been used without sufficient precaution in many under-developed countries, particularly in Africa. Possible rates of expansion have often been calculated on the basis of the population of working age and the country's natural resources, regardless of whether the circumstances were such that these factors could in fact be used. In other cases the equilibrium of the terminal year has been calculated on the basis of the technical factors existing in Europe (capital coefficients, consumption functions), whereas there can be no comparison between the industrial processes or the behaviour patterns of the two continents. This being so, it is not surprising that these 'models' have often proved disappointing and dangerous, giving the leaders of these countries the illusory belief that development will be automatic and rapid.

CHAPTER II

The Details of Planning

THE PLAN itself is prepared in several stages. To begin with, the Modernization Commissions work out the production targets and conditions of growth for each branch, in the framework of the expansion indicated in the forecasts. The information thus gathered is classified and the next stage is to coordinate the different aims and the means of attaining them.

I. DEVELOPMENT BY SECTOR

Each Modernization Commission is responsible for a certain number of products; together they cover the whole of the public and private sectors of production and distribution, with a few exceptions such as military supplies.

The Commissions conduct their explorations within a general framework of instructions and on the basis of the working documents supplied to them. The latter provide information regarding the base year of the Plan and forecasts of probable short-term developments (economic budgets). The Commissions are also given the forecasts for the terminal year – five years ahead – in a reduced nomenclature; the overall equilibrium of resources and their utilization, the levels of production in the appropriate branches, and the forecasts of consumption and investment are supplied as provisional data for them to amend and amplify.

The Commissions analyse the conditions of development for each branch of activity. In the course of this study they circulate among themselves the information for which they are asked in questionnaires accompanying the working papers.[1]

[1] The following outline of the method pursued is taken from a memorandum circulated to the Rapporteurs of the Commissions in June 1960:

The work is parcelled out among a number of working parties. The replies are then classified by the various Commissions, and it is at this stage that they make their first selection from among statements some of which are contradictory. They consider all aspects of the activity of each branch, including production, manpower and the conditions required for its fulfilment of the Plan.

PRODUCTION LEVELS

The forecasts do not give the Commissions a detailed picture, showing the development of individual products; they only deal with groups, so that – for instance – the future of wool in the textile industry still remains to be calculated.

One way of doing this is to base the calculation on a constant relation between the national product and the total production of a particular sector of the economy, such as iron and steel, energy or transport. This has the advantage of simplicity and is also fairly reliable, for unlike more subtle analyses, product by product, it overlooks none of them. But while it can be used in considering

---

The purpose of the questionnaire and the Tables [see Appendix V] is to summarize the information supplied by the Commissions in a standardized form. The Tables show the outlets available for the various branches, and give an estimate of the consumption, within each branch, of the principal intermediate products it uses. It is these elements, including those that determine the changes in technical factors resulting from the introduction of new manufacturing procedures or the substitution of one type of material for another, which form the basis for estimating the level and structure of production in each individual branch.

In studying the factors of production, the Commissions and Working Parties have to enter into details of the productivity trends to be anticipated, and therefore of the size and skills of the labour force which a branch will require if it is to reach its target. By studying the differences between the forecasts made when the third Plan was in preparation and the progress actually achieved during the period it covered, the Commissions should try to discover the connection between increased productivity and level of investment, and thus determine what amount of investment will be required at the level of productivity appropriate to the production targets. So far as possible, they should specify the nature of the goods invested (buildings, civil engineering works, plant, etc.) and the nature of the equipment (replacement and enlargement, heavy maintenance work).

(a) *Prices*

At the first stage it should be assumed:

(1) that the present methods of taxation and financing will continue.

energy or transport, it offers no means of ascertaining production in an isolated branch, such as one of the manufacturing industries, which stands in no constant relation to the national product.

The second possible method is based on market research, which varies according to whether the products to be considered relate to final demand – consumption, investment, export – or to intermediate demand.

1. *Family consumption*

With the forecasts as their general framework, the Commissions are guided by the investigations of the *Centre de recherche, d'études et de documentation sur la consommation* (Consumer Research, Study and Information Centre – C.R.E.D.O.C.), based on the study of differences in consumption in relation to income and of changes in needs, tastes and habits. The representatives of the different industries in the working parties also consider possible changes in the relative prices of competing goods.

---

(2) that the general level of prices of goods throughout the period will be the same as their 1959 average, and that the general increase in the rate of real wages required to make possible the increase in consumption envisaged by the Plan will be in the neighbourhood of 30 per cent over the years 1959–1965; which assumes that between now and 1965 the cost of services will have risen by approximately 15 per cent.

The prices of individual products are likely to vary in one way or another by comparison with this general level. The first forecast, now submitted to the Commissions, was based on the hypothesis that all prices would remain at their 1959 level. This is merely a conventional assumption, and calls for revision.

Steps should therefore be taken to determine the extent to which the Commissions anticipate that prices of products in their respective branches will depart from the average level. These changes should not be taken into account unless they are so considerable as to make the conventional assumption of constant prices appear excessively unrealistic.

(b) *Selection of technical methods*

A knowledge of the relative cost of labour, capital goods and raw materials is necessary for the comparison of the different technical possibilities available, and thus for the selection of the most economically favourable technical methods. As a general principle, preference should be given to the method least costly to the community.

(c) *Localization*

Commissions are asked to state where new factories in their respective branches of industry are likely to be set up. The only purpose of this information is to give an idea of the regions from which the different branches will

2. *Exports*

Except for the forecasts, the working parties have only piecemeal information on this subject. Up to now, E.E.C., E.C.S.C. and O.E.C.D. have not got very far in their general, co-ordinated studies of the development of the various countries, including that of their trade relations.[2] The Commissions and working parties are thus reduced to extrapolating the export trends observed in the past and correcting them by known changes in patterns of consumption and available resources in foreign countries. This has shown that there is an expanding market in food products, particularly fruit, vegetables and beef, and in the products of the engineering and electrical goods industries, but what the rate of expansion may be is quite unknown.

The present analyses of individual products are inadequate. Too often confined to value, rarely dealing with volume, they do not

---

be recruiting their employees. However, any Commissions which are in a position to do so should also give a regional breakdown of production in their branches.

(d) *Variants*

To assist the horizontal Commissions, which are responsible for amalgamating the individual reports, in making any rectifications required to produce a consistent overall forecast, the Commissions should strive to determine what amendments of their programmes would be necessary in certain eventualities, e.g.:

– Expansion of markets. Commissions should indicate the level beyond which a change in production targets would involve a disproportionate change in the quantities of raw materials and labour required by their respective branches. They should also estimate the probable effect on the volume of investment of a change in the rate of expansion of production.

– A change in the relative prices of raw materials and other factors of production. Commissions should make a particular effort to describe how some degree of modification of the comparative costs of labour and equipment might be expected to influence technical processes and production costs.

The study of these variants will also enable the horizontal Commissions to advise the Government as to the practical possibility of maintaining over the period of the fourth Plan the rate of expansion of 5·5 per cent suggested in the interim plan for 1960 and 1961.

[2] See the set of roneotyped documents in which these bodies discuss the future of their Member States. S. Svennilson, *Le développement économique de l'Europe entre les deux guerres*, O.E.E.C., Geneva 1956.

always specify the countries involved. Such information is particularly desirable now that dangerous uncertainties are resulting from the successive stages of the Common Market and France's changed relations with her former overseas territories.[3]

3. *Intermediate goods*

In the attempt to estimate probable activity, a Commission must have more than a knowledge of final demand (consumer and export) – unless its branch has no other main outlets. This applies to agriculture, the food industry, textiles, the wood and paper-making industries, and public utilities. But many branches also produce capital goods and, above all, intermediate goods.

Except where – as in the case of energy and transport – there is a constant relation between intermediate demand and gross domestic product, the former can only be discovered by studying the orders placed by one branch with another. In practice, the Commissions exchange information regarding the increase in activity which they expect to result from changes in final demand, and deduce from these the orders they are likely to receive.[4]

Thus divided among the Commissions, the calculation is liable

[3] No sooner had the fourth Plan been adopted by Parliament than it was discovered that the import and export forecasts for refrigerators were out by 50 per cent, largely owing to sudden competition from Italy.

[4] Even so, it must be emphasized that many elements of uncertainty persist in this method of calculation, particularly where the 'technical coefficients' are concerned.

Except in the large basic sectors, the demand for raw materials, energy and semi-finished products is not easy to determine.

This is calculated on the basis of the existing relationship between production and consumption in the branch concerned. But experience shows that such relationships or technical coefficients tend to alter as time goes by, and the managements themselves find it difficult to make sufficiently accurate forecasts for five years ahead. So extrapolation is apt to cause mistakes.

In the case of secondary products the basic data on which constant relationships could be worked out are lacking, since there are no precise statistics covering consumption per sector, or showing the domestic or foreign origin of those products. Consequently the domestic demand and the volume of imports cannot be forecast with certainty.

Again, the Commissions usually give their information in terms of quantity rather than value. This makes it more difficult to establish an average price and to determine the technical coefficients in terms of value.

to be misleading, however. For while each branch allows for an increase of activity resulting from the expansion of other branches, it ignores the 'boomerang' effect of its own development. For instance, the metal industries may base their forecasts on the activity of their customers, such as the engineering industries; but they cannot make allowance for the orders which will be placed with those industries as a result of their own expansion and of the increased activity of their suppliers. Inter-branch relations set up chain reactions which only a central authority can measure accurately.

The Commissions are decentralized agents, and to permit each of them to fix its own targets the branches of industry are classified in such a way that the dependence of one upon another is brought out more clearly than their mutual interdependence. Branches whose activity depends little or not at all upon those of the others, but is governed by final demand (consumption and export) announce their development to those from which they obtain their supplies, and so on down the scale, the most self-sufficient being the first to answer the questionnaire.

The possibility of classifying industries in a descending order of independence has been demonstrated by M. Aujac[5] in respect of current relations, but not of capital goods. In practice, the S.E.E.F. divides industries into only four groups: those which produce chiefly for consumption and export, those in which production prospects are linked by a constant relationship to gross national output, those which produce intermediate goods, and those which supply both consumer goods and capital goods (machine construction, building, civil engineering). Knowing the activities of the branches belonging to the first two categories, those in the third draw up their plans accordingly[6]. Lastly, as we shall see, the producers of investment goods rely on the information furnished by their customers, who include, by definition, all branches of activity and the general public.

In theory, the establishment of an order of priority enables the Commissions to make 'decentralized' forecasts for each branch,

[5] See H. Aujac, 'La hiérarchie des industries dans un tableau des échanges interindustriels', *Revue économique*, March 1960.

[6] This deduction is sometimes based on the constant ratio of the total production of a branch to the national product. Forecasts for the iron and steel industry take this ratio into account.

with no risk of error and with the full support of those employed in it.

Their detailed study of market prospects and customers' needs may lead the Commissions to question some of the preliminary forecasts, which were only meant as indications. But in the majority of cases it substantially confirms those forecasts. The last Plan also recognized the usefulness of the Commissions' market research. Their findings have not always been borne out by the facts, particularly in the branches most directly connected with the consumer market; but the responsibility for this rests not so much with the working parties and Commissions as in the difficulty – involved in any form of planning – of pinning down something so volatile as the behaviour of the general public. In any case, these mistakes occur chiefly in branches which are able to adjust themselves rapidly to economic circumstances, without serious repercussions on overall development.

4. *Capital goods*

The Commissions responsible for the branches which produce these goods have at their disposal not only the general estimate of final demand given in the forecasts, but certain particulars supplied by managements regarding volume of output and methods.

In the most concentrated branches, such as iron and steel, energy and transport, the work to be carried out is decided by technical experts in the light of the increase in production; specific programmes are drawn up, sometimes based on rational criteria. This leaves some elements of uncertainty connected with technological progress and with the energy resources which will be available in France; but alternative hypotheses are presented, based on the use of oil or gas, on the localization of firms to meet international competition, and on the industrialization of the underdeveloped regions.

In the branches of production which consist of smaller firms, such as the manufacturing industries, this forecasting is more difficult, and is usually undertaken on the assumption of a constant relationship between production and investment, the 'marginal coefficient'. The engineering and electrical industries are the most difficult to deal with, because they produce their own equipment, so that their activity is not a datum. In any case, investment in these branches is on a comparatively small scale, amounting to barely a quarter of the total.

The Commissions responsible for estimating the *amount of social investment* (education, sanitation, culture, urban development and housing) make their assessments direct. They take into account on the one hand the needs and on the other hand the amount of public money available – this being laid down in the Government's instructions – for needs cannot always be met in full, so that the only limit to investment is a financial one.

This complete (or, in the case of housing, partial) costlessness makes it difficult to decide the order of priority of equipment in the public services. Is street lighting to be put before schools? There are various criteria to provide guidance.

Sometimes the need is self-evident. Some services must be provided; in schools, for example, the number of classrooms will depend upon the number of pupils. In other cases an attempt is made to strike a balance between various types of expenditure undertaken to save lives in different ways (road-building, hospitals, etc.). The Plan's 'social' Commissions are only just beginning their study of these subjects.

Thus, the activity of the branches which produce capital goods is estimated by assessing the volume of productive and unproductive investment.

LABOUR REQUIREMENTS

These are calculated with due allowance for sex, skill, and regional distribution. The Manpower Commission takes the piecemeal estimates and brings them into line with the total available labour force. Any estimate of future labour requirements involves a somewhat speculative assessment of the growth of productivity in a particular branch. In most cases the needs are over-estimated, and the Manpower Commission has to correct the figures.

The study of skills and of regional distribution is still at the initial stage. To speak only of the latter, the Commissions, working within the framework of the preliminary forecasts, have given information about the localization of expansion and employment in their respective branches. But only the basic sectors have been able to give particulars facilitating correction of the preliminary forecasts – which, as already explained, are precarious – and indicating which regions are likely to have a labour surplus and thus require vigorous development policy.[7]

MEASURES OF REFORM

In their reports, the Commissions indicate the conditions required to ensure that the proposed targets will be reached. The complete list cannot be given here, despite their importance to the development of the French economic structure. They relate chiefly to:

– greater facilities for scientific and technical research, which is of particular importance to the expansion of the newest industries, such as chemicals and electronics;

– specialization and regrouping in certain firms and services, such as export services. This entails large-scale reconversion of the French firms, which have been too much inclined to neglect foreign markets;

– increased standardization and the preparation of long-term programmes to bring down costs, particularly in the building industry and in electrical engineering;

– the retraining of workers and the training of skilled technicians, of whom there is a disastrous shortage;

– measures of tax exemption and subsidies, lavishly employed by the Commissions, particularly to finance capital equipment.

VALUE OF THE COMMISSIONS' REPORTS

An effort is made to bring these reports into alignment while they are still being prepared, by comparing the information that goes into them. In their first attempt to establish an equilibrium the forecasts do not reach the general targets, so the Commissions make corrections. In agriculture, the meat target was raised in the light of domestic needs and export possibilities. In the engineering and electrical industries, a comparison of the forecasts with the customers' needs in capital goods, with export prospects and with the conditions required to ensure the balance of accounts led the planners to set higher targets for certain suppliers.

[7] The report of the Manpower Commission for the fourth Plan shows a marked improvement upon that of the third Plan; some figures quoted from it are given hereafter (Appendix VI).

Experience over the last few years shows the steadily improving quality of the reports drawn up since 1946, and their usefulness both to the public authorities and to the individual managements, to which they supply an invaluable body of information and statistics on future developments.

It cannot be denied, however, that they have their shortcomings. Some of these, relating to the consumption of a particular product by the general public, to investment by small firms, and to the value and volume of exports, are inevitable, for it will be a long time before even the best-equipped statisticians can predict changes in individual taste, fluctuations in comparative prices, technical innovations or the ups and downs of the international economic situation.

Other deficiencies will be made good in course of time, for with each successive Plan the Commissions provide fuller information. But they should do still more; in particular, they should offer alternative hypotheses on development, investment and export in the light of changes in the state of international trade, especially within the Common Market. However, they can only do this if they are themselves supplied with information about the structure of their respective sectors. The bodies responsible for technical supervision should make use of research units such as those already mentioned, in order to add to the knowledge they undoubtedly possess regarding the more concentrated branches. Above all, the many gaps in our statistics should be filled – by measures such as a periodical agricultural census (the industrial census to be held in 1963, which was recommended as long ago as the second Plan, will cover the whole range of economic activity, including the military sector and that of craftsmanship), a four-yearly population census – the indispensable basis for sample surveys[8] – and a more systematic use of the material accumulated during the preparation of the successive Plans.[9]

[8] A 'statistical' body responsible to the *Commission de l'Economie générale et du Financement* (Commission on Financing and the Economy in General) was set up in 1962, with M. Gruson, Director-General of the I.N.S.E.E., as its Chairman. It has drawn up a full programme for the development of statistics.

[9] Unfortunately the questionnaires are not always framed in the manner best adapted to the structure of the industries, nor do they always avoid changes of nomenclature, which are not conducive to accurate information. Moreover, they should ask for replies in terms of quantity, rather than value, because 'average prices' conceal and distort the facts of weight and volume. Comparison

In relation to the general equilibrium model required for the preparation of a Plan, the gaps in the information supplied by the Commissions are appreciable; mistakes are made in balancing resources and employment, owing to difficulties of nomenclature; the needs of the individual branches in raw materials, energy and semi-finished products are only described for the principal commodities, which makes it difficult to define technical coefficients in terms of value. And the reports give very few reliable particulars regarding income distribution, transfers, or general problems of finance and price policy.

Some of the reports concentrate on the conditions required for the fulfilment of the Plan. These thrust objective information into the background and are lavish with demands for price-increases, tax relief and subsidies. They turn into schedules of claims on behalf of the industry, or even of the employers. This distortion, which fortunately is not widespread, detracts from the value of the information and clearly indicates the danger of allowing 'interests' to be represented.

Another regrettable feature is the 'erosion' that accompanies the gradual amalgamation of the studies produced by the working parties into the Commissions' reports, and of these latter into the general Report. Unconventional proposals are lopped off at each stage, so that in its final form the Plan has sacrificed originality to cohesion.

II. THE GENERAL EQUILIBRIUM

The fourth Plan departed from precedent by effecting the synthesis of the Commissions' work in two successive phases.

At the first stage the Commissions' replies were compared and tested for consistency. The information thus obtained enabled the

---

of one product with another cannot, of course, be made in terms of quantity. But heads of private firms, and government officials, often base their decisions on quantities, without regard to prices. The example of Soviet planning shows the importance of analysis and forecasting in terms of quantity, when dealing with resources and employment in relation to prime commodities such as steel and coal, or to semi-finished and finished products such as certain capital goods. (See P. Bauchet, *Les tableaux économiques: Analyse de la région lorraine*.)

Government to reach a decision on the rate of expansion, which was fixed for the fourth Plan at 5·5 per cent, while the *Commissariat* notified the Commissions of certain incompatible proposals found in their reports and suggested compromises to help them in preparing their final forecasts.

The individual reports having been thus amended, a final synthesis was made and a table submitted, showing resources and uses in 1965. A typical example was the report of the Working Party on Equilibrium of the *Commission de l'economie générale et du financement du Plan* (Commission on the general Economy and Financing of the Plan).[10]

The equilibrium ultimately presented is not a mere summary of the Commissions' findings. It works those findings into a comprehensive scheme which takes account of the Government's instructions (rates of growth, targets for aid, for national defence and so forth) and of certain general hypotheses (the maintenance of a 'mixed' economic system with fairly stable income distribution, slow evolution of prices except in housing, and continued application of the Rome Treaty). It also indicates the financial and other conditions necessary for the maintenance of the equilibrium.

ESTABLISHING THE EQUILIBRIUM

In arriving at its figures for 1965, the Working Party on Equilibrium tried to steer a course between two dangers – that of simply extrapolating the past, and that of setting up targets which were unrealistic because they could not be reached without drastic political changes. It laid down a 'probable optimum'.

The study took as its starting-point the production targets regarded as feasible by the Commissions and the foreign trade forecasts, and proceeded to make sure that for each category of goods and services, resources (production and imports) would meet requirements (private and public consumption, investment and export).

In addition, an inter-industry table was drawn up to ensure

[10] This two-stage synthesis naturally complicates the task of the Commissions' Rapporteurs, who are obliged to make two sets of intricate calculations. Unless they can call on the assistance of research units attached, as I have already suggested, to each technical Directorate, they will be tempted to scamp one or the other of the syntheses.

consistency of both final and intermediate production. And lastly, the Working Party on Equilibrium investigated the labour situation to discover whether supply and demand would be equal at the desired level of production.

This study of physical equilibrium was accompanied by a financial study of the lines along which income, savings and public finance should develop to ensure that the distribution of income would coincide with that of the national product. Thus, the increase in private consumption must be paralleled by an increase in *per capita* income (allowing for savings and population trends). Similarly, the volume of private and public savings must increase in order to finance investment.

It remains to be seen whether the present machinery for steering the economy enables the desired targets to be attained, despite unforeseen developments in the economic situation and other, more permanent obstacles.

THE CONDITIONS OF FULFILMENT

At a time when customs barriers are being lowered, the first of these conditions is the co-ordination of the national economic policies of different countries. This seems particularly needful in regard to currency and investment.

Furthermore, if the Plan is to be fulfilled without inflation, domestic demand and production must both be regulated.

The first of these requirements in the domestic sphere calls for an incomes policy, with special reference to wages. Family purchasing power must increase steadily, but not too rapidly. At present, however, the Plan has no means of intervention at its disposal, except a limited power to manipulate taxation and credit. To avoid dangerous fluctuations, foreign demand should be more closely regulated within the framework of the Common Market. And public demand, though as yet a minor factor, is destined to expand rapidly and will require co-ordination.

In 1962, the regulation of production seems comparatively easy so far as the material and human factors of production are concerned. There are no bottlenecks, and except in a few parts of the country, unemployment and over-employment are not so marked as to call for exceptional measures.

On the other hand, the increasing investment will not be easy to finance. Firms will have to call upon outside help. It is questionable whether the present means of intervention are sufficient to overcome the reluctance of those managements unwilling to increase their indebtedness.

The present method of establishing a general equilibrium serves to reveal inconsistencies and clarifies the conditions required to ensure it. If the target of expansion is to be reached during the period 1961–1965, the increase in public expenditure and private consumption must not exceed 4·2 per cent per annum, a rate which will leave sufficient savings to finance the rapidly growing volume of investment.

But this study is incomplete. Hypothetical price trends are indicated for only a few of the most probable subjects of change, such as rents. The hypotheses advanced for income distribution are over-simplified. For the time being it seems impossible to draw up a picture allowing for all price and income changes,[11] though an effort is being made in that direction.

Lastly, one may wonder whether it is sufficient to make a study of equilibrium for the final year of the Plan alone.

III. ANNUAL DEVELOPMENTS

That there will be an equilibrium for the terminal year does not mean that it will be achieved in each of the intermediate years, because rates of growth are variable. Progress was slow in 1952 and 1953, then it speeded up, seemed to lag again in 1958–1959, and has now resumed its rapid advance. Though economic 'cycles' in the strict sense of the term are becoming less marked, fluctuations seem to be inherent in economic life; they contrast with the simplified picture of regular expansion which is given in the Plan.

The rate of growth of investment does not remain constant throughout the period of a Plan. In particular, new work undertaken in the basic industries varies as a result of technical inventions, increased demand, and the number of the active population for whom employment has to be found. These factors can only be

[11] The S.E.E.F. is attempting to perfect a monetary model with variable prices, so that the Commission can allow for price changes in their schemes for production and the financing of investment.

foreseen in part. And changes in the growth of investment, in their turn, affect the expansion of production.

Unexpected events occur. The Korean war and the nationalization of the Suez Canal had repercussions on our supplies of raw materials and energy, and hence on our foreign balances and on our production. The fluctuations in prices and output which arise in the international economic field serve to speed up or slow down our economic development by affecting the volume of our imports and exports, and only an out-and-out policy of self-sufficiency could preserve us from this result. And after all, manufacturers and government officials are not proof against the collective waves of optimism or pessimism which sweep periodically over the business world.

THE LIMITATIONS OF FORECASTING

Changes in the rate of expansion can be foreseen: several Commissions, especially those which deal with the basic sectors, already describe their development year by year. The Working Party on Equilibrium stresses the predictable changes in the chief factors: investment, energy resources, and above all manpower, which will increase considerably from 1964 onwards, owing to the arrival of great numbers of young people on the labour market.

This information is of more help than an unrealistic picture of regular growth in preparing business leaders in the private sector – whose importance to the fulfilment of the Plan has already been emphasized – to deal with these changes in tempo. More important still, the public authorities, thus forewarned, can take steps to prevent the unemployment or stagnation which might result, for instance, from a sudden flood of new labour or from a falling off in some types of investment. The annual economic policy is thus laid down in advance.

It would be a good thing if this form of analysis were generally adopted. At present, while the branches concerned with the supply of energy and with transport – electricity, the atomic industry, the coalmines, rail and air transport, airports – provide a fairly detailed picture of the developments they anticipate, the other basic industries are culpably secretive about their timetables of investment, employment and foreign trade. The overall studies carried out by the 'horizontal' Commissions, such as the Manpower and Finance

Commission (Working Party on Equilibrium), do not have enough specialized investigation to build on, and are sometimes unduly vague.[12]

Though undeniably useful, the preparation of equilibrium accounts for each of the five intermediate years is hampered by difficulties more serious than the mere dearth of information. Lacking the forecasts prepared for the Plan, the equilibrium account for the terminal year is based on certain data, such as the figures of consumption and foreign trade. The fundamental variable is the level of production chosen on the basis of these data.[13] But once this main target has been fixed, it becomes a datum for the calculation of the equilibrium in the intermediate years, which depends upon a certain adaptability of consumption and foreign trade to the requirements of investment.[14] It would no doubt be possible to construct theoretical models possessing that adaptability. But in practice this would be tantamount to a denial of the constraints imposed by fluctuations in exports and incomes, which cannot be foreseen.

Exports to foreign countries depend not only upon the situation of the exporting country, but also, and even more, upon that of the international market, the development of which is difficult to anticipate. Similarly, private consumption does not follow the dictates of the authorities; the most they can do is, in certain circumstances, to slow down the growth of certain types of income. Consumer trends cannot be predicted accurately from year to year, because the looseness of the measures of intervention admissible in a liberal economic structure makes it impossible to place constraint upon the behaviour of private individuals.

The same uncertainties naturally impede the definition of equilibrium in the terminal year. But it is permissible to assume the existence of cycles, lasting five years or so, in which the economy rejoins the trend at regular intervals, so that medium-term forecasts

[12] In particular, the general report of the Manpower Commission suffers from the inadequacy of the forecasts supplied by managements with regard to the number and levels of skill of the workers they will require.

[13] See J. Bénard, 'Problèmes et instruments de synthèse d'un plan indicatif', *Cahiers de l'I.S.E.A.*, Series *D.*, No. 10 May 1958, p. 37.

[14] These requirements might be made less rigid by drawing up optional programmes for the nationalized industries and for the State. Certain forms of expenditure which are not directly productive could be accelerated or retarded to meet the economic circumstances.

are likely to be more accurate than short-term ones.[15] Moreover, if equilibrium is disrupted at any point during the five-year period, a policy can be devised to restore it in the meantime.

ANNUAL RECTIFICATION AND CONTINUITY

Thus, if development is to be forecast for each year of the Plan, targets will have to be rectified every year – if, as is probable, they are jeopardized by trends in consumption and in foreign trade.

Procedure for doing this is already in force. When the Budget is drawn up the Commissioner for the Plan makes proposals regarding certain investments, in particular those to be undertaken by public corporations,[16] and suggests means of financing them, embodying these recommendations in a memorandum he prepares in agreement with the Economic and Social Development Fund (F.D.E.S.). Once the Budget has been adopted, the Fund's committees work out the details of the transactions and the means of financing to be used.

The annual progress reports of the Plan, of the Council of the F.D.E.S. and of the national accounting system take stock of the situation and give short-term forecasts.

The slowing down of expansion in 1958 and 1959 disrupted the equilibrium forecast for 1962; this was amended by a general enactment, and an interim plan for 1960 and 1961 was drawn up while the third Plan (1957–1961) was in progress.

This method is to be carried further;[17] by the terms of Article 3 of

[15] It will be noted that expansion slowed down in 1952 and in 1957, which suggests a tendency to periodical slackening in the pace of growth, though this no longer constitutes a recession. The five-year forecasts are not fundamentally affected by it, because the trend remains constant (4·5 per cent increase in the national income); the fulfilment of the first Plan was delayed by a year, that of the second Plan was a year ahead of schedule, and that of the third Plan again came a year late.

[16] This procedure has not yet been completely worked out. See P. Bauchet, *Propriété publique et planification*, pp. 298, 299, 300.

[17] There is no lack of earlier legislative enactments. Article 3 of the Decree of 16 January 1947 states that should the Commissioner-General 'responsible for ensuring the fulfilment of the Plan . . . deem that such fulfilment is for any reason endangered, he shall inform the appropriate Ministers and, if need be, bring the matter before the Prime Minister or the Inter-ministerial Committee. Decisions relating to the fulfilment of the Plan or to its adjustment in the course of the year shall be prepared by the competent administrative departments and

the Bill approving the fourth Plan (No. 62–900, of 4 August 1962), the Government is required to present to Parliament a report on the fulfilment of the Plan, showing what its financial implications will be during the coming year. After this they are to submit a set of measures and to fix, in agreement with the Budget Directorate, the amount of public money to be invested in the coming year. In conjunction with the Finance Bill, this report will ensure a close relationship between the Plan and the Budget. It is to be discussed by restricted permanent commissions, to ensure that the advisory bodies which helped to draw up the Plan shall not be 'by-passed' during these annual proceedings.

But if the Plan's targets are revised, and a new forecast prepared, when each new Budget is presented, the situation may ultimately change as it has done in the Soviet Union, where planning is now annual rather than multi-annual. The latter form is no more than a statement of intentions, practical policy being framed on a yearly basis. France, with its decentralized economy, has more reason than the U.S.S.R. to apprehend that practical developments may not conform to the forecast, and to favour periodical adjustment. But care must be taken to prevent the medium-term Plans from fading away, as that would destroy continuity of policy.

The attempt to arrive at a general equilibrium constitutes the final stage of the Plan. But a provisional general equilibrium is worked out for each hypothesis of expansion at the very beginning, when the forecasts are prepared. A second synthesis is made when the Commissions are half-way through their task, in order to discover any inconsistencies and fix the definitive rate of expansion, in the vicinity of the one originally chosen. The equilibrium of resources and employment established by the working party on equilibrium and inserted in the Plan differs from those which preceded it only inasmuch as, being based on the work of the Commissions and on the Government's arbitration of controversial

---

other bodies in agreement with the agencies of the Commissioner-General for the Plan.'

The Decree of 19 March 1959 (No. 59.443), approving the third Plan, likewise stipulates that each year, before the presentation of the Budget, the Commissioner-General for the Plan, in agreement with the Ministries concerned, shall prepare a report describing the measures adopted in fulfilment of the Plan, the results obtained, the difficulties encountered and the adjustments found necessary.

points, it is final; it is not appreciably different. The bodies which work out the Plan do not question the general framework laid down by the earliest forecasts.

But is it realistic? Does it represent an optimum? We shall answer these questions in the next two chapters.

APPENDIX TO CHAPTER II

How the General Equilibrium is Obtained[1]

The Working Party on Equilibrium of the *Commission de l'Economie générale et du Financement* is responsible for ensuring that the Commissions' proposals are consistent and that they conform to the Government's instructions. It checks the equality of supply (home production and imports) and demand (final private consumption, investment, consumption by public offices, exports), the balance of final and intermediate resources (shown in a table of inter-industrial relations), the co-ordination of demand to available labour, and the adequacy of the flow of money to real equilibrium. The Working Party bases its calculations on an annual rate of growth of 5·5 per cent in the national Product.

I. BALANCE BETWEEN SUPPLY AND DEMAND

First the production targets are specified, and then the uses for the resulting output.

PRODUCTION TARGETS

It proved impossible to make a direct comparison of the information provided in the different reports, for these vary too much

[1] This is described in full in the Report of the Working Party on Equilibrium for the fourth Plan, a roneotyped document issued by the *Commissariat général du Plan d'Equipement et de la Productivité*.

Table VII

INDEX OF PRODUCTION AND DISTRIBUTION OF THE ACTIVE POPULATION PER BRANCH[1]

	Branch	Index of Production 1965 1959 = 100	Annual increase in productivity %	Number of active population (in 1000s) 1959	1965	Difference	Index 1965 1959 = 100
01	Agriculture and forestry	130·5	6·3	4,540	4,100	− 440	90
	Total	—	—	4,540	4,100	− 440	90
02	Agricultural food industries	128·8	3·9	665	680	+ 15	102
03 A	Solid mineral fuels	90·0	2·2	222	175	− 47	79
03 B	Gas	151·7	7·2	23	23	0	100
04	Electricity and various	181·5	7·6	90	105	+ 15	117
05	Oil, natural gases, fuels	149·5	7·2	61	60	− 1	98
06 A	Building materials	136·8	5·1	192	195	+ 3	102
06 B	Glass	147·2	6·0	53	55	+ 2	104
07	Iron ore, steel	144·4	4·3	209	235	+ 26	112
08	Non-ferrous ores and metals	156·4	7·1	26	27	+ 1	104
09 A	Semi-manufacture and processing of metals	139·7	4·7	444	470	+ 26	106
09 B	Machinery and apparatus (non-electrical)	150·0	5·1	611	680	+ 69	111
09 C	Machinery and apparatus (electrical)	180·0	5·6	293	380	+ 87	130
09 D	Motor vehicles and cycles	140·0	4·8	274	290	+ 16	106
09 E	Naval and aircraft construction and armaments	104·4	2·4	182	165	− 17	91

10	Chemical industries and rubber	157·4	6·4	355	385	+ 30	108
11 A	Textiles	130·9	5·2	554	535	− 19	96
11 B	Clothing	137·2	5·4	500	500	0	100
11 C	Leather	122·8	4·3	220	210	− 10	95
12 A	Wood	132·9	5·2	300	295	− 5	98
12 B	Wood-pulp, paper, cardboard..	148·7	5·2	123	135	+ 12	110
12 C	Press, publishing	142·8	4·6	183	200	+ 17	109
12 D	Processing of plastics and miscellaneous industries	167·9	5·2	162	200	+ 38	123
13	Building and public works	146·1	5·1	1,350	1,460	+ 110	108
	Total for industrial branches (02 to 13)	—	—	7,092	7,460	+ 368	105
14 A	Transport	129·6	3·2	680	730	+ 50	107
14 B	Telecommunications	152·1	5·3	256	285	+ 29	111
15 & 16	Services	142·0	2·8	2,209	2,655	+ 446	120
17	Trade (retail)	133·6	3·7	1,618	1,740	+ 122	108
	Financial institutions	—	—	185	210	+ 25	114
	Public offices, including education	—	—	*283*	*390*	+ *107*	*138*
	Domestic service	—	—	570	570	0	100
	Total for the tertiary sector....	—	—	7,208	8,060	+ 852	111
	Total active population in employment			18,840	19,620	+ 780	104

[1] Source: Proceedings of the working party on equilibrium; figures prepared in consultation with the Manpower Commission (see General Report of that Commission, pp. 44 and 45).

in their form and leave some fields completely unexplored (services, output for the armed forces) and others insufficiently investigated (information being supplied in terms of quantity rather than of value, etc.). The comparison is therefore effected with the help of supplementary statistics and of a classification of all the particulars given in the economic table of the Finance Ministry's Bureau of Economic and Financial Studies.

This table includes the information provided by the Commission regarding the rates of expansion of the activities of the industrial branches and the indices for the output of the different products. It sheds light on the changes in intermediate consumption, on which the Commissions give little information, and provides a means of verifying the forecasts of the Commissions which analyse the different branches from the angle of purchasers and sellers of goods.

The result is a threefold picture of the terminal year of the Plan, showing the domestic production totals, the value added in each sector – i.e. total domestic production less intermediate consumption – and the expansion of the various products and services.

It will be noted that during the period covered by the fourth Plan the most rapid expansion is evidenced in electricity, the heavy electrical, engineering and chemical industries, steel production and iron mines, while that of agriculture and services is less marked (see Table VII).

The Working Party on Equilibrium, in collaboration with the Manpower Commission, decides whether the employment trends foreseen by the Commissions to deal with increased branch production according to sector are concordant, whether the total demand for labour is consistent with the available active population and whether, in each branch, the increased productivity arrived at by correlating the increase in production with the increase in personnel is convincing – investment figures being taken into account in this connection (see Table VII).

USES: INVESTMENT, CONSUMPTION, FOREIGN TRADE

Once the firms' intermediate consumption has been deducted from total production, the output remaining, or gross domestic product, should be sufficient to cover the uses proposed: though the estimate of these which is made by the Commissions does not cover the whole ground.

1. *Gross investment* is reclassified in the first place under the following heads: Entrepreneur, Investment by firms, Investment by public offices and Housing, and subsequently per type of product.

In assessing the firms' investments, the first step, here again, is to bring the Commissions' estimates of the investment made in the base year into line with those of the *Commissariat du Plan* and the S.E.E.F. (*Service des Etudes économiques et financières*). The Commissions' forecasts of investment increases are then adjusted to a definition of the concept of investment which is the same for all branches, and completed by adding the other sectors – craftsmanship, public offices, services, etc. – for which no assessment had been made. These new estimates are based either upon direct inquiry from those concerned or upon a corrected extrapolation of the past relationship between investment and production in the branch under consideration. The Commissions having provided no assessment of stocks, this had to be undertaken as well.

During the period 1961–1965, investment is to increase more rapidly than gross national production (28 per cent as against 24 per cent). Investment in housing shows only a small increase (25 per cent), because housing construction has now been stabilized at an annual figure of approximately three hundred and fifty thousand dwellings. Administrative investment shows a greater increase than any other, the chief item being social equipment (+ 50 per cent). Productive investment rises steeply (28 per cent), but is uneven; some branches show much more than the average rate of expansion – these include telecommunications (110 per cent over the base year, 1959) and chemicals (72 per cent) – even though the first estimates made by certain Commissions were, with their consent, amended to a lower figure at the request of the *Commissariat du Plan*; whereas in other branches growth is set much lower (see Tables VIII and IX).

For lack of the necessary elements of information[2] it has been impossible to confirm these estimates by precise theoretical

[2] See Part II, Ch. IV for comments on the comparison between a few foreign capital coefficients and the inquiries made in the principal French branches. When a more searching analysis is undertaken, the absence of sufficient data renders this comparison impossible.

Table VIII

SHARE OF INVESTMENT IN GROSS NATIONAL PRODUCTION[1]
(in % at constant prices)

	1949–51	1952–55	1956	1957	1958	1959	1961	1965
Total of gross fixed asset formation	19·5	18·2	19·9	20·6	20·7	20	20·2	21·9
Gross fixed productive capital formation (exclusive of administrative investment and housing)	14·5	11·6	12.6	13·3	13·4	12·7	13·0	13·6

[1] See report of the Working Party on Equilibrium for the fourth Plan.

Table IX

INDEX FIGURES SHOWING TRENDS IN THE DIFFERENT BRANCHES[1]

	Sales made by the branch to private consumers 1965–1959	*Investment in the firms composing the branch* 1965–1959
Agriculture, forestry	119·0	142
Production of the agricultural and food industries	121·5	138
Solid mineral fuels	104·5	85
Gas	141·0	141
Electricity, water and various	183·5	205
Petroleum, natural gas and fuels	183·0	142
Building materials	133·0	128
Glass	140·0	153
Iron ore, iron and steel products........	—	187
Non-ferrous metals and ores	—	69
Semi-manufactured products	127·5	151
Machinery and mechanical apparatus ..	181·0	171
Electrical goods	211·5	186
Motor vehicles and cycles..............	169·0	163
Naval and aircraft construction and armaments	—	110
Products of the chemical industries	164·0	172
Textiles	133·5	148
Clothing	138·0	150
Leather	128·0	205
Products of the timber industry	134·5	145
Wood-pulp, paper and cardboard	147·0	146
Press and publishing	145·5	180
Products of miscellaneous industries	145·5	190
Building and public works	146·0	156
Transport	122·0	123
Telecommunications	140·7	210
Housing service	134·5	—
Other services	143·5	166
TOGETHER....	135·8	147·2

[1] Bill approving the economic and social development plan. Documents of the *Assemblée Nationale* No. 1573, 1st ordinary session 1961–1962 (No. 117).

calculations in terms of the relationship between production increase and investment.

Investment was subsequently calculated per product by the S.E.E.F. and the *Commissariat du Plan*, on the basis of the few particulars given in the Commission's reports.

2. *Family consumption* was estimated by the competent agencies (prominent among them the C.R.E.D.O.C.), and the result of their investigations transmitted to the Commissions – no Commission being responsible, strictly speaking, for this particular study.

The analysis of consumption begins with observations relating to the *total population* and its division into large social and vocational categories. These observations, which are based on the findings of the Manpower Commission, indicate certain changes in the composition of the social and vocational categories to which the heads of families belong, such as the decline of the agricultural population, the growing number of senior managerial staff and the greater number of inactive persons.

Once the distribution of the population among the large categories is known, it remains to determine consumption. This is done in a manner similar to the study of the preliminary forecasts, but in greater detail, by drawing upon variations of consumption deduced from the study of family budgets and from the observation of relative changes in consumption which have occurred in the past and in foreign countries. The result suggests that family consumption will increase by 23 per cent in four years, i.e. slightly less than supply (25 per cent). Progress is particularly marked in transport, hygiene, health and housing.

This study of private consumer trends is completed by a breakdown in terms of products and services.

3. *Administrative expenditure* was again estimated by the competent agencies, the Plan's Commissions dealing with only a few of its aspects, such as transport and social, educational and health investment. Overall forecasts of receipts and expenditure and of those of the State, the local authorities, the Social Welfare Service and private international administrative bodies were drawn up.

This expenditure was calculated on the bases of various hypotheses: in the case of defence expenditure, the hypothesis that the military operations in North Africa would be concluded, etc.; in that of expenditure on education, hypotheses relating to school enrolment and to the duration of school attendance.

Expenditure on road maintenance and the infrastructure of transport was calculated on the basis of receipts from certain special funds and from the local authorities, and in the light of the needs created by the development of methods of transport, particularly air and sea transport.

4. *Foreign trade*. The figure submitted by the Commissions were reclassified in the framework of the S.E.E.F. nomenclature. In the light of the hypotheses advanced for the overseas *Départements*, the Commissions' estimates were corrected to ensure a satisfactory balance of payments. It is anticipated that during the fourth Plan exports will rise by more than 21 per cent and imports by more than 23 per cent. Within the franc area, imports are expected to increase more than exports, whereas it is thought that with foreign countries the reverse will apply (see Table X). But it is not impossible that imports from the Common Market countries by the engineering and heavy electrical industries may increase, while agricultural exports to those countries may decline.

Table X

TRADING TRENDS[1]

(*In milliards of New Francs, 1961*)

	1961			1965		
	Foreign Countries	*Overseas Territories*	*Total*	*Foreign Countries*	*Overseas Territories*	*Total*
Exports[2]	27·5	11·5	39	34·8	12·3	47·1
Imports[2]	25	7·5	32·4	31·2	8·7	39·9
BALANCE....	2·5	4	6·6	3·6	3·6	7·2

[1] See Bill approving the Economic and Social Development Plan. Documents of the *Assemblée Nationale* No. 1573. First ordinary session 1961–1962, p. 30.

[2] Including services.

With regard to the Overseas Territories, the amount of aid granted and the assessment of their industrial development indicated the probable trend of relations with them during the next few years.

COMPARISON BETWEEN DOMESTIC PRODUCT AND CONSUMPTION

Once they have been reduced to homologous terms and completed, the Commissions' estimates of gross domestic product, imports and final demand are compared in a table of 'Resources and their Use', so that they can be brought into equilibrium (see Table XI).

Table XI

RESOURCES AND THEIR USE[1]

Resources	*In milliards of NF. at 1961 prices*		*At 1965 indices*	
	1961	1965	1959=100	1961=100
Gross domestic product ..	271	336	138	124
+ Imports	33	40	153	123
− Exports[2]	39	47	144	120
= Gross resources available for use at home	265	329	140	124

Use of resources	1961 *Milliards of NF. at 1961 prices*	%	1965 *Milliards of NF. at 1961 prices*	*Indices* 1961=100	%
Consumption	206	77·9	252	123	76·8
Investment............	59	22·1	78	130	23·2
(of which stock variations amount to)	(4)	(1·4)	(6)	(138)	(1·6)
'Productive' investment	36		46	128	
'Administrative' investment	7		11	150	
Housing............	12		15	125	
TOTAL....	265	100	330	125	100

[1] See Bill approving the Economic and Social Development Plan. Documents of the *Assemblée Nationale* No. 1573. First ordinary session 1961–1962, pp. 118–119.

[2] Including the balance of use of services and advantages in kind.

This general framework uses constant prices. But a number of the forecasts of markets and activities prepared by entrepreneurs whose position gives them a near view of final demand were arrived at intuitively and with allowance for elements which their authors cannot dissociate, including price changes. Similarly, the forecasts of investment and of energy consumption are inseparably connected with the anticipated price changes. If the forecasts are fitted into a general model which ignores these elements, mistakes will be inevitable. Therefore the estimates have to be adjusted. This raises the problem of introducing prices into a comprehensive model.

II. MONETARY EQUILIBRIUM AND THE ACCOUNTS OF THE ECONOMIC AGENTS

A comprehensive economic table, based on accounts covering firms, public offices, families and foreign trade, sets forth the principal monetary relations, income, expenditure, loans and borrowing, and shows whether, in money terms, equilibrium can be achieved in 1961, whether savings will be sufficient to finance the investment required to achieve equilibrium, and whether family incomes will be adequate for the purchase of consumer goods.

Families

Family consumption having been determined in terms of physical equilibrium, the next step is to ascertain the corresponding gross income, allowing for other uses (savings, taxation, investment).

Average *per capita* income increases at the rate of 5 per cent per annum (with an annual increase in population of 0·9 per cent).

Table XII shows income trends, on the assumption that the income of all the main social categories will observe an identical rate of growth, and allowing only for changes in the active population.

Table XII

TREND OF FAMILY INCOMES[1]

	Milliards of Frs	*At 1965/1961 indices*
Net wages	104·9	128
Gross income of self-employed persons	67·9	118
Interest and dividends	7·1	134·1
Social services and welfare contributions	46·2	133
Subsidies for investment and war damage reparation	1·3	70·6
Miscellaneous	14·5	110
TOTAL NET INCOME	241·9	125

[1] See report of the *Commission de l'Equilibre général et du Financement* for the fourth Plan, p. 48.

Increased saving, which might well result from financial stability and the reduced proportion of expenditure on building, would make it easier for firms to finance their investment.

Firms

If the firms maintain a high level of production to meet large export demands, their savings would rise more rapidly than their investment figures. In view of uncertainty regarding the effects of the Common Market, it was decided to assume that the rate of growth would remain unchanged at 34 per cent.

Public finance

Equilibrium here is not so well assured as at present; because expenditure will increase more rapidly than receipts – particularly expenditure on investment, salaries of staff in the State educational system, agricultural subsidies and social transfers.

It was therefore necessary to find a means of ensuring equilibrium, and the method selected was the transfer of funds from households to firms and public offices (see Table XIII).

Table XIII

BALANCE OF RESOURCES AND THEIR USE[1]

Resources	*Millions of Frs*	*Indices* (1961 = 100)	Use of resources	*Millions of Frs*	*Indices* (1961 = 100)
Firms' savings	39,500	135	Firms' investments........	56,400	134
Family savings	29,600	137	Family investments........	9,500	105
Surplus of current income over expenditure in public offices	7,600	100	Investment by public offices	10,500	150
			Balance of transactions with foreign countries	+ 300	
TOTAL......	76,700	131		76,700	

[1] Report of the *Commission de l'Equilibre général et du Financement* for the fourth Plan, p. 53.

CHAPTER III

Are the Plans Effective?

IS THE French economic expansion attributable to the existence of a Plan? There can be no definite answer to that question, but we may note that growth has been particularly vigorous since planning was introduced. As pointed out by Mr Dow,[1] 'France has had three successive four-year plans since the war, and is soon to enter on a fourth. During this time it has achieved a rate of economic growth at least double that of the United Kingdom. Opinions will differ as to how far one has been the cause of the other: other countries which do not organize economic planning have also grown rapidly. It is my impression that many of those who attended the conference came to the conclusion that the French joint planning procedure must have contributed something to France's rapid economic development.'

Broadly speaking, the effectiveness of a Plan may be assessed by the speed of economic expansion. As we have seen, the French economy is now expanding more rapidly and more smoothly than before the second world war. It is often pointed out that this also applies to the U.S.S.R., Germany and Italy, but all such comparisons are dangerous for many reasons, not only statistical ones; age of development, natural wealth and other factors play their part, alongside the Plan, in slowing down progress or accelerating it. And it is most important not to equate the growth of the economy with the well-being of the population. Since we are not in a position to assess the latter, we shall restrict ourselves to quantitative criteria.

Comparison of the French Plans with the results they have achieved will show us how far they have been realistic, and by

[1] 'Economic Planning in France', *Planning* (P.E.P.), Vol. XXVII, No. 454, August 1961, p. 208: record of a conference organized by the Institute of Economic and Social Research.

comparing them with foreign rates of expansion we can gauge their ambitions.

I. OBJECTIVES AND ACHIEVEMENTS

It is not always possible to make a precise comparison between the Plan's objectives and its achievements, particularly in respect of the aggregates, resources and uses. This holds good for most countries, however.

The nomenclatures used in the forecasts are not always identical with those employed in recording the results. Reference prices are liable to change. For instance, the targets for the third Plan were based on the 1954 prices and classified under 183 heads. The results were recorded on the basis of the 1956 prices, using a nomenclature with only 28 heads.

However, the errors caused by these differences appear to be comparatively trifling.

THE FIRST PLAN, 1946–1952

The analysis of the first Plan was impaired by the fact that national accounting was still elementary and that the expressions 'national production' and 'national income' were used somewhat vaguely; this led the authors of the Plan to fix its targets in real quantities per product rather than in terms of aggregates.

The table of resources (No. XIV) shows the results achieved.[2]

It will be seen from this that national production is 39 per cent higher than in 1946, 19 per cent higher than in 1938 and 3 per cent higher than in 1929 (Table XV).

The authors of the Plan had announced that industrial production would be 25 per cent higher than in 1929, but in point of fact the increase was barely 12 per cent, because of the slowing down of economic activity in 1952, which was accompanied by an appreciable deficit in the balance of payments (see Table XX).

[2] See the report on the fulfilment of the Plan (1951), entitled *Cinq ans d'exécution du Plan de Modernisation et d'Equipement de l'Union française*, p. 378. Owing to changes in nomenclature and to the increasing precision of the terminology adopted, the erroneous results are not entirely identical with those given in *Comptes de la Nation*, 1960, Vol. I (*Les comptes récapitulatifs 1949–1959*). We give them nevertheless, because they use a nomenclature very similar to that in which the targets were expressed.

Table

TARGETS AND FULFILMENT

Primary industrial products	Units[2]	First Plan: Fulfilment 1929	1938	1946	1950	1951	1952	Target 1952–53	% of fulfil-ment o target
Coal	Mt	55	47·6	49·3	52·5	55	57	60	96
Electricity	GkW	15·6	20·8	23	33·1	37·9	40·6	43	95
inc. hydro-electricity	GkW	—	—	—	—	—	—	—	—
Gas	Mm³	—	—	—	—	—	—	—	—
—	Mth consumed	—	—	—	—	—	—	—	—
inc. natural gas	Mth	—	—	—	—	—	—	—	—
Fuel oils	Mt of crude processed	0	7	2·8	14·5	18·4	21·5	18·7	115
Steel	Mt	9·7	6·2	4·4	8·7	9·8	10·9	12·5	87
Aluminium	kt	—	—	—	—	—	—	—	—
Chemicals	Index figure	—	—	—	—	—	—	—	—
Cement	Mt	6·2	3·6	3·4	7·2	8·1	8·9	8·5	105
Primary agricultural products									
Wheat	Mq	9·2	8·1	68	77	70	84·2	95	88
Meat	kt	1,750	1,700	1,250	2,015	2,000	2,065	2,200	94
Milk	Mhl	138	146	95	150	160	150	170	88
Sugar	kt	825	769	415	1,250	1,150	900	1,300	70
Housing	Units completed				68,050		74,920		

[1] See *Rapports d'exécution du Plan de modernisation:* 1952, pp. 9, 133; 1958, p. 6; 1961, p. 30. *Deuxième Plan de modernisation et d'équipement*, p. 14. *Troisième Plan de modernisation et d'équipement*, p. 14.

[2] k = 1000 units (e.g. kt = 1000 tons), M = one million units, G = one milliard units; th is the abbreviation of *therms*; q is the abbreviation of *quintals*; hl = hectolitres.

The same thing happened with agricultural production, which was to have been 16 per cent higher than the average for the period 1934–1938, but showed an increase of only 8 per cent.

There was a year's delay in the fulfilment of the first Plan.

Production in the basic sectors reflects this delay (see Table XIV).

Nevertheless, the results were brilliant by comparison with 1938. The quantity of energy per head of the population rose to 2·35 tons of coal-equivalent, as against 2 in 1938. Production and return on capital in the coalmines showed a sharp increase at the same time. Steel production was more than 150 per cent of the 1938 figure, while that of cement showed a 200 per cent rise. The total number

XIV

OF THE FIRST THREE PLANS[1]

Second Plan Fulfilment 1957	Target 1957	% of fulfilment of target	*Third Plan* Fulfilment 1958	1959	1960	1961[7]	Target 1961 Third Plan	Interim Plan	% of fulfilment of target
59·1	61[3]	97	60	59·8	58	56	62	56	100
57·5	55	105	62·2	64·5	72	76	76	76	100
24·9	29·2	85	32·2	32·8	40	38	38[8]	38[8]	100
3·6	3·8	95	—	—	—	—	—	—	—
—	—	—	30·5[9]	37·4[9]	50[9]	60[9]	60[9]	60[9]	100
—	—	—	5·2	12·5	20	36	36	36	100
25[4]	30[5]	84	30	30·8	33	43	42[10]	42[10]	102
14·1	14	100	14·6	15·2	17·3	18	17·5[11]	17·5[11]	103
—	—	—	169	173	235	280	230	260	108
184[6]	130[6]	142	128[12]	146[12]	160[12]	188[12]	145[12]	164[12]	115
12·5	—	—	13·4	14	14·2	14·6	14·7	14·9	99
110	95	116			110·1	96	110		88
2,500	2,500	100			2,780	3,000	3,100		97
200	200	100			226	236	265		88
1,350	1,500	90			2,509	1,810	1,550		118
70,000	240,000	111	290,100	320,400	313,800	320,000	300,000		106

3 Productive capacity.
4 Consequence of the Suez events in 1956: 26·8.
5 Refining capacity.
6 Index-figure 100 in 1962. These two index-figures are not strictly comparable.
7 Provisional estimate.
8 Productive capacity at average hydraulic level.
9 Exclusive of gas used in blast furnaces and domestic consumption.
10 Refining capacity.
11 Maximum capacity.
12 Index-figure (1956 = 100).

of tractors had risen from 30,000 in 1938 to 150,000. Consumption of potassium fertilizers showed a 40 per cent increase.

But Table XIV also shows appreciable backwardness, particularly in the case of steel, and this was even more marked in the manufacturing industries, which were intentionally neglected.

The policy of giving priority to the basic sectors came in for its full share of criticism. But experience has shown that unless these

Table XV

FIRST PLAN: INCREASE IN NORMAL PRODUCTION

	1929	1938	1946	1947	1948	1949	1950	1951	1952
Gross national product (in milliards of 1938 francs). . . .	460	397	330	358	400	427·5	441	463	470
Index-figure (Base 100 in 1938) . .	115·8	100	83·1	90·2	100·7	107·7	111·1	116·6	119
Annual rate of increase	—	—	—	+8·5%	+11·7%	+6·9%	+3·1%	+5%	+2%

branches expand the others will not do so – for they cannot progress without energy and transport – and moreover, that as the basic sectors expand, they draw the others in their wake. This policy has been accused of causing inflation. If inflation occurred, it was because the appropriate fiscal and other measures which should have absorbed surplus income were not taken. Besides, the first Plan had proposed a series of reforms, including that of the tax system, and the creation of special funds.

THE SECOND PLAN, 1952–1957

This was fulfilled a year ahead of schedule, thus making up for the delay in the first Plan.

Table No. XVI (resources and their use) shows this advance.

In 1957 national output was 29 per cent higher than in 1952, though an increase of only 25 per cent had been anticipated.

This growth was due to the fact that investment had increased more rapidly than consumption. But this development was accompanied by a new disturbance in the balance of payments in 1956 and 1957.

Industrial production stood at an index-figure of 145 instead of the expected figure of 130 (base year 1952), whereas agricultural production had only reached 117 instead of 120.

The targets for basic outputs were exceeded in many cases (see Table XIV), including chemicals and building; the time-lag in fuel oils is explained by the Suez events. Among manufacturing industries, motor cars, electrical engineering, paper and textiles were

Table XVI

SECOND PLAN: GROSS NATIONAL PRODUCT AND ITS USE
in milliards of NF. 1954[1]

	1952	1957	*Index* 1957 1952=100
National production[2]	129·00	166·70	129
Other elements of the national product	17·00	20·20	119
GROSS NATIONAL PRODUCT	146·00	186·90	128
Use of the national product:			
Private consumption	98·80	127·50	129
Consumption by public offices	23·80	27·10	114
Gross asset formation (including stock changes)	25·70	36·30	141
Export surplus	−2·30	−4·00	
TOTAL	146·00	186·90	128

[1] *Rapport annuel sur l'exécution du Plan de modernisation et d'équipement* 1958, p. 16.

[2] The concept of national production is peculiar to French national accounting. It includes a smaller number of outputs than the national product as understood by international organizations. Such items as the pay of management or domestic servants must be added to national production to obtain the gross national product.

advancing rapidly. In agriculture the balance was disrupted by cereal production, which was increasing too quickly.

Investment targets (see Table XVII) were exceeded by an average of 10 per cent, particularly in fuel oil and nuclear activities. The industries producing capital goods were still backward, despite the special attention devoted to them, while the production of consumer goods was proportionately flourishing. Social investment, housing and school building exceeded the forecasts.

Table XVII

INVESTMENT DURING THE SECOND PLAN
in milliards of NF. 1954[1]

Branches	*Total for 1954–1957* *Forecast*	*Fulfilment*
Agriculture	11·35	11·70
Energy production and mines	12·62	13·15
Steel production and iron mines	2·67	2·65
Chemicals	1·65	1·95
Manufacturing industries	7·75	7·30
Transport, communications and tourism	8·70	8·05
Housing	18·96	24·35
Educational and health investment	3·52	4·50
TOTAL	67·22	73·65

[1] Source: Third *Plan de modernisation et d'équipement*. Decree No. 59–443, of 19 March 1959, p. 16.

THE THIRD PLAN, 1957–1961

Disequilibrium in various branches of foreign trade and tension in the labour force led the authorities to take steps which appreciably reduced the rate of expansion in 1958 and 1959. Hence the interim Plan, drawn up in 1960 to correct the targets of the third Plan and introduce new measures to re-activate it.

1. *The development and use of resources* (see Table XVIII) showed that the increase in gross national production was not quite equal to that laid down in the original target. Its expansion had, however, been marked by the restoration of the foreign trade balance, exports having risen more rapidly than imports.

2. *Investment* had increased at a notably higher rate (29 per cent) than consumption (20 per cent for families, 8 per cent for public offices).

Table XVIII

DEVELOPMENT AND USE OF RESOURCES DURING THE THIRD PLAN[1]
1956 = 100

	1961 *Forecasts third Plan*	1961 *Interim Plan*	1961 *Fulfilment*
1. *Resources*			
Gross domestic production	127	123·5	123·6
Imports	110	118·2	126
TOTAL RESOURCES	125	122·7	124
2. *Use of resources*			
Private consumption	124	117·6	120
Net consumption by public offices	112	117·2	108
Investment	128	126·5	129
Exports	135	160·0	160
TOTAL USE	125	122·7	124

[1] Source: Bill approving the fourth *Plan de développement économique et social*, No. 1573, Paris 1961, p. 70.

Industrial output stood at an index-figure of 131 as against a target figure of 133, while agricultural output had reached the anticipated index-figure of 120.

These views were corroborated by the development of the basic products. The original targets had been reached, except for coal; the abundant supply of hydrocarbons had led inevitably to the stabilization of production. Chemicals and aluminium production had increased more rapidly than was anticipated (see Table XIV).

Most of the manufacturing industries lagged behind the forecasts, but it should be remembered that these were not intended as fixed targets (the index-figure was 133 instead of 136).

Agricultural output had fallen short of targets in some respects, but this gave no cause for alarm because, with the exception of meat, the goods were in surplus and not easy to dispose of.

Housing construction, too, had exceeded its target.

Investment had reached the target figure for the third Plan (see Table XIX), as had social investment; health investment, however, was backward.

Table XIX

INVESTMENT PER BRANCH[1]

	Third Plan 1957–61/1957	*Fulfilment* 1957–61/1957
Agriculture. Forestry	5·5	4·8
Agricultural and food industries	3·9	4·7
Energy	6·5	5·8
Iron and steel, non-ferrous ores and metals	5·5	5·6
Engineering and electrical industries	5·1	5·0
Chemical industry	5·8	6·1
Textiles, clothing, leather, wood, paper, miscellaneous industries	5·5	4·7
Building, public works, building materials	5·3	4·5
Transport and telecommunications	5·8	5·7
Services	5·0	5·0
including retail trade	4·7	4·9

[1] The figures given in this table show the ratio of the sums invested from 1957 to 1961 to the total invested during the single year 1957. This is the only valid method of comparison, in view of the changes made meanwhile in the method of calculating investment.

Source: Bill approving the *Plan de développement économique et social*, p. 73.

To sum up, expansion during the last fifteen years has conformed fairly closely to the forecasts given in the Plans. In 1952–1953 and again in 1958–1959 it was somewhat slowed down as a result of localized labour shortages and deficits in the balance of payments (see Table XX), but there was no recession. Delays or advances on the forecasts were slight, and partial disturbances, such as inflation, foreign trade deficits and regional disequilibrium never brought expansion to a halt or caused serious unemployment.

Table XX indicates a creditable degree of expansion, though allowance should be made for the continued inadequacy of

Table XX

THE NATIONAL PRODUCT AND ITS USE 1949–1961[1]

			1950	1951	1952	1953	1954	1955	1956	1957	1958	1959	1960	1961
Change in gross national product at market prices (volume)	Compared with previous year		107·6	106·0	102·6	102·9	104·8	105·8	105·0	105·9	101·8	102·4	106·4	104·4
	Expressed as index-figure (1949=100) ..	100·0	107·6	114·1	117·1	120·5	126·3	133·6	140·3	148·6	151·3	154·8	164·2	172·1
	In value (milliards of NF. 1956)	134·2	144·1	153·1	157·1	161·7	169·5	179·3	188·3	199·5	203·1	207·9	221·2	231·0
Percentage of use of gross national product in current francs	Private consumption ..	67·8	67·2	68·2	67·3	67·5	67·0	66·9	67·1	66·6	66·0	65·3	65·0	65·6
	Consumption by public offices	12·0	12·9	13·6	15·4	15·7	13·9	13·0	14·6	14·8	14·3	15·0	14·6	14·6
	Asset formation......	20·0	19·2	18·9	18·5	16·9	17·8	18·6	20·1	20·7	20·7	18·6	19·3	18·7
	Gross national expenditure	99·8	99·3	100·7	101·2	100·1	98·7	98·5	101·8	102·1	101·0	98·9	98·9	98·9
	Exports and income payments from foreign sources	15·5	16·4	17·3	15·1	14·6	16·0	15·8	13·8	13·4	13·6	15·1	16·0	16·0
	Imports and income payments to other countries	−15·3	−15·7	−18·0	−16·3	−14·7	−14·7	−14·3	−15·6	−15·5	−14·6	−14·0	−14·9	−14·9
	Gross national product	100·0	100·0	100·0	100·0	100·0	100·0	100·0	100·0	100·0	100·0	100·0	100·0	100·0

[1] *Rapport sur les comptes de la Nation de l'année 1961*, Imprimerie nationale, 1962, pp. 274–275.

statistics on certain points, including distribution of income among the different classes and occupational categories and the quality of products and services, etc., which are not shown. A 70 per cent increase in the national product in twelve years gives France a very satisfactory position in the field of peaceful international competition.

II. COMPARISON WITH RATES OF GROWTH IN OTHER COUNTRIES

Compared with expansion in the iron curtain countries, our own rate seems modest. In the Soviet Union, the national product increased from 1950 to 1958 at a speed of approximately 10 per cent per annum, and is expected to exceed 7 per cent per annum in the years 1959–1965 (Seven-Year Plan)[2]. One non-Communist country, Japan, attained an annual rate of 11·5 per cent from 1947 to 1952 and of 8·3 per cent from 1953 to 1958.[3]

To speak only of the Western capitalist countries, Table XXI shows that France is only third among the Common Market countries – though Italian and German expansion was no doubt favoured by exceptional factors, including an abundant labour supply which did not exist in France (see Appendix V).

Table XXI

GROWTH OF THE GROSS NATIONAL PRODUCT PER EMPLOYED PERSON IN DIFFERENT COUNTRIES (1959–1961)[4]

	Annual rate
Germany	5·1
Italy	4·4
France	4
United States	2
United Kingdom	1·9

These figures show that a Plan is no guarantee of exceptional expansion. They give rise to speculation about the value of the objectives proposed. Are these satisfactory? Do they constitute an optimum?

[2] See J. M. Colette, 'Le taux de croissance du revenu national soviétique', *Cahiers de l'I.S.E.A.* Series *G.*, No. 12, November 1961, p. 121.

[3] See introduction to the document already mentioned: *Doubling the national Income*, Japanese Planning Agency, Tokyo 1961.

[4] See O.E.E.C. Economic Studies, July 1962.

CHAPTER IV

Optimum and Alternatives

THE PLAN is essentially concerned with consistency. Without interfering in the management of the individual firms, the *Commissariat* assembles their projects, as set forth in the branch balance-sheets, and makes sure that they fit into the general framework already indicated by the comprehensive forecasts. If any incompatibility is found, the position is discussed with the branch or branches concerned, and various inducements offered so that equilibrium may be achieved.

But except in the principal basic sectors, the firms' plans are not disputed or their technical and financial decisions questioned: no *optimum* is worked out.

The preliminary choice of a rate of expansion[1] is in itself tantamount to the search for an optimum, of course. But that rate is fixed in the light of the firms' policy, which guides rather than conforms to the Plan.

It is true that for the last few years the public corporations concerned with energy production and transport have selected the factors most conducive to the fulfilment of the aims suggested in the Plan. These branches even pursue their co-ordinating efforts within the Commissions. But they are more or less alone in doing so. The question now arises as to whether the search for economy of means, for an optimum, can be extended to the whole system, whether there is a logical method of choosing between the alternatives confronting nations, branches and individual firms.

[1] The choice between a rate of 5 per cent and a rate of 5·5 per cent which was made while the fourth Plan was being prepared involves no fundamental difference in growth.

I. LOGIC OF THE OPTIMUM

The general features of an optimal situation in a given community, with its techniques, individual preferences and income distribution, have been described by Pareto and a number of later writers. An optimum is achieved when the system of production is operating in such a way that production in every industry has reached its highest possible level, so that no factor can be shifted without causing a general decline in production. Conversely, so long as any change in the productive pattern can lead to increased output, the optimum has not been achieved.

Consumption, too, is at its most satisfactory when private consumers cannot alter their choice of goods without diminishing the pleasure they receive from them, the ratios of marginal utilities being then the same for all.

Definition of the aim to be achieved is difficult, and insufficient; that of the means of achieving it is still more necessary and even more difficult.

Prices play an essential part. As M. Massé points out,[2] they have a dual function: 'a distributive function, by which they determine income, and a selective function, by which they steer the economy towards the most useful forms of production and investment.' Prices are indispensable signals for the guidance of the agents of production, irrespective of whether they are fixed, together with quantities, by a central authority or reflect the trends of a free market.

If prices are fixed at a rational level, i.e. if they are equal to marginal costs, the community as a whole will achieve a social optimum without being confronted with the difficult task of defining the optimum. The general interest must make due allowance for particular interests, but it cannot be a 'function' of these, in the mathematical sense of the term. Particular interests, being subjective, do not lend themselves to expression in figures; they cannot be compared or added. This difficulty can be avoided by making sure that agents pursuing their own interest shall conform their behaviour to the general interest, which is then served without the need to calculate it in advance. Individual behaviour is to be guided by the search for maximum profit. When prices are fixed at a

[2] See P. Massé, 'La pensée moderne et l'action économique', in the *Bulletin du ministère des Finances*, April-May 1961, p. 12.

level conducive to production at the lowest social cost, general and particular interests are satisfied simultaneously. Prices have this quality when they are equal to marginal costs.[3]

The rule of equality to marginal costs has the further advantage of facilitating the decentralization of decision-making.

DECENTRALIZED CHOICES AND COMPREHENSIVE APPROACHES

In theory, all that is necessary is for the producer to know the normal price. At a given marginal cost of production, a demand is expressed. Any increase in production beyond the point at which demand and cost are balanced entails a loss for the entrepreneur and for the community, since the factors could be better utilized elsewhere, in producing goods more useful to the consumer. The optimum is arrived at by a process of gradual adaptation.

Without dwelling on the practical difficulties, we may note that the obstacles in the way of entirely decentralized calculation include the lack of a competitive context – which makes it impossible to fix prices spontaneously at the level of marginal costs – difficulties of calculation and other, more fundamental hindrances.

– The first of these is that the fixing of prices equal to costs includes development costs, i.e. investment costs. But the cost of capital goods varies according to the volume of demand, which is itself influenced by price. This difficulty could be overcome by successive approximations if capital goods were infinitely divisible. However, they are often discontinuous, and are responsible for decreasing costs.

– The second difficulty is that the authorities are obliged to intervene in order to establish a measure of equality among individuals and groups in the community, since at the initial stage some of these may be unable – for lack of the necessary resources, for example – to make a free choice as producers, and still more as consumers. The result of this is that the State proceeds to redistribute income by a variety of means – subsidies, transfers, tax adjustments. This redistribution does not follow Pareto's logic; it inevitably involves a comprehensive approach, and distorts the allocation of resources.

[3] This idea, and those which follow, are discussed at length in my book *Propriété publique et planification*, pp. 53–100.

– Thirdly, great restrictions are inevitably placed on the consumer's freedom of choice. Producers influence his preferences by a variety of means, such as advertising, technical research concentrated on certain products, and prices. The Government prohibits dangerous forms of consumption (alcohol) and opposes any lopsided development of the productive machinery which might hamper the development of capital goods; it takes a comprehensive decision.

– Lastly, ignorance regarding the future compels the State to intervene in order to predetermine development to some extent and to guard against rash and ill-informed decisions which might lead to irremediable disaster.

All this makes up a comprehensive framework into which decentralized decisions based on marginal calculations have to be fitted.

The fixing of a collective optimum allowing for spontaneous tendencies and guiding them also entails a difficult choice between various alternatives.

THE ALTERNATIVES

The search for an economic optimum is conditioned by *fundamental choices* in such matters as hours of work, aid to under-developed countries, transfers of income for the benefit of certain social categories, and even the system of ownership and methods of economic management. These choices cannot be left to individual preference, which is not unanimous, so they have to be made by the authorities who, in theory, represent the general will. Several variants of the Plan may be prepared in conformity with these *optional aims*. The political authorities are then able to give informed consideration to the effect of whatever course they select upon the factor they wish to increase to the maximum – the national product, for instance. The length of the working week, the amount of aid given to under-developed countries, and so forth, have consequences which can in theory be ascertained.

Other alternatives relate to the *structure of production*, the activities to be developed: the growth of one branch in preference to others – of agriculture rather than the engineering industries or the tourist trade, for instance – results from fundamental options regarding national policy, such as the choice between economic nationalism and common markets. But if the decision is in favour of international trade, each of the activities contemplated can contribute to the development of exports: the choice of the branch or branches to receive official encouragement will depend upon comparative prices, development costs, means of financing, the economy of raw materials, social dynamism or the stimulus provided by the development of an atomic industry, for example.

Further alternatives relating to the structure of production have been discussed in the Commissions of the Plan without so far receiving any logical and consistent reply. What form of financing should be encouraged – self-financing or loans, i.e. price-raising or increased fiscal pressure and public subsidies? There is also a choice in each branch, between overall economic progress and the intensive modernization of certain integrated firms. And the localization of activities remains to be decided.

These questions arise, though usually only by implication, at all stages of the Plan's preparation and fulfilment. It was the first syntheses prepared for the fourth Plan that prompted the choice of industries on which the export effort was to be based.

Lastly, is a particular output to be obtained by using manpower in preference to machines, or the contrary? Are traditional techniques to be followed, or a high degree of automation employed? It is easy nowadays to decide these questions at branch or firm level, but they have overall repercussions that cannot be ascertained because at present we do not possess sufficiently comprehensive or detailed models.

Progress is nevertheless being made in the formulation of these alternatives.[4] The models express the technical and political constraints by which the economy is affected – such as full employment, situation regarding the balance of trade, availability of means of financing and the satisfaction of fiscal demands – in the form of equations or inequalities. It is possible to choose, from several alternatives relating, for instance, to techniques of production or branch development, the one which maximizes the objective function.

[4] See Hollis B. Chenery and Kenneth S. Cretschmer, 'Resource Allocation for Economic Development', in *Econometrica*, October 1956, pp. 365–399. See also P. Massé, '*Suggestions préliminaires pour un essai de programmation mathématique*', multigraphed memorandum issued by the *Commissariat Général du Plan d'équipement et de la Productivité*, Paris, October 1960.

So far, these models do not cover an entire community, for they fail to reflect its full complexity. Yet, as we have seen, they are a necessary means of clarifying the choice to be made by the political organs of control.

The Western countries, being largely decentralized, are faced by a two-fold problem when aiming at an optimum. Logical considerations, together with the dearth of free markets, oblige them to construct a *comprehensive framework* for the activities of the firms; they have to define this and explain how it is to be built up. The programmes prepared by the central body never enter into the details of the activity of the firms, for they are independent centres. Yet there must be an attempt to determine an optimum for them, because our political and economic system rests on the assumption that *decision-making is decentralized.*

The definition of the collective optimum affects both the Plan and the individual firms and, among other things, influences the choice of investments.

II. THE CHOICE OF INVESTMENTS IN THE FRENCH PLANS

This clearly reflects the dual intention pursued by our economic system: at the national level comprehensive decisions are to be made, fixing the total figure of investment and distributing it among the different sections; while the individual branches and firms are to make decisions on their own behalf.

The Plan is supposed to ensure that all these choices are rational.

COMPREHENSIVE CHOICES

The nation's capital investment programme cannot be determined simply by taking the firms' decisions as to their own investment and adding them together. Security, welfare, development and other considerations demand that a certain amount of social and economic investment shall be undertaken and that the available capital goods shall be distributed among the different sections of the economy.

– In France, strictly speaking, there is no choice in the matter of the *total volume of investment in relation to consumption*. The preliminary forecasts include an estimate of the amount of productive and unproductive investment[5] required for each hypothetical rate of growth of the gross domestic product. Once the rate has been definitely selected, the investment figure follows automatically. Unproductive investment is planned to meet various needs with the public money that is expected to be available. Aggregate productive investment is determined with the help of average and marginal capital coefficients projected from the past or corrected in the light of observation of foreign countries. There is thus no attempt to arrive at an optimum, and no choice.

– *The volume of unproductive capital investment* is influenced, naturally, by its usefulness, but the resources and credit available to the authorities for financing such investment are other determining factors. If industrial investment increases while the national product remains unchanged, unproductive investment diminishes. There is a kind of mutual relationship between productive and unproductive investment.

That relationship is all the more manifest because unproductive investment, as its name suggests, is determined not by considerations of profit-making capacity but in the light of the needs it is to satisfy or in the interest of equilibrium. So far as housing, education and research, town-planning and health investment are concerned, the assessment of how much an individual costs and how much he brings in in different conditions of capital equipment is only just beginning. Even the assessment of needs is, of course, an improvement on the completely arbitrary methods that obtained until recently. But the approach is still subjective and the 'necessary' expenditure is not ascertained.[6]

When a choice has to be made between building a hospital, a barracks, a bridge and an electric power-station, there has to be an estimate of the relative yield of productive and unproductive

[5] Productive investments are those intended 'to create goods and services habitually dealt in on the market' (See *Les Comptes de la Nation*, 1960, Vol. II, p. 1607).

[6] The fact that the assessment of needs is made by technicians does not – as is too readily assumed nowadays – render it more reliable. These services being to some extent gratuitous, there is no scale of prices to reflect the preferences of those who receive them; so the political bodies would be in the best position to express the wishes of the community if they could resist the temptation to make this an opportunity for vote-catching.

services. In the national accounting system it is possible to make arbitrary assessments: the product contributed to the nation by a civil servant is assumed to be equal to his salary. But it would be dangerous to take such estimates as the sole basis of choice, for their apparent objectiveness is misleading.

A method sometimes adopted is to present alternatives with a certain number of social investments, when showing the economic differences resulting from the varying amount of productive capital investment available. But this systematically perverts the calculation and leads back to the old mistake of ignoring the results of so-called unproductive investments, just as, at times when the economy is out of balance, changes are made in those investments as though in themselves they were of no value to development.

Economists tend to thrust into the background anything they are unable to express in figures. In calculating a true optimum, the yield of social investment must be taken into account.

We have seen that there is no real choice involved in determining the total volume of productive investment, and the same applies to *its distribution among the different branches*. As we noted when considering the analyses prepared by the Modernization Commissions, investment in each branch is fixed on the basis of technical information in the case of the heavy sectors, on capital coefficients drawn in most cases from foreign sources,[7] and even on projections of past relations between business turnover and capital equipment.

It is true that, thanks to the information supplied by the firms, the analysis of the relationship between current outflow and investment as shown in the inter-industry tables is becoming more widespread, as is the attempt to establish an equilibrium. But equilibrium is no guarantee that an optimum will be attained. Quite apart from the problems involved in allowing for 'uncertainties', the construction of a comprehensive model is hampered by the difficulty of defining what is meant by profitability.

In considering the turnover criterion of an investment or the possibility of economizing capital, the economist is apt to overlook the external economies and 'pump-priming' quality of certain modern forms of capital investment, such as atomic equipment, and give preference to investment in the textile or motor-car

[7] So far there has been little progress in the study of capital coefficients in France. No general, systematic investigation has been made of their stability or of the influence of technological progress on their value.

industries, where the immediate yield will be higher. This has led to mistakes in the localization of industries, which tend to be established in areas where supplies and markets are readily available at present, without allowing for future changes.

There is an obvious need for more comprehensive and dynamic criteria, taking into account the existence of points of growth and foreign economies; but these are not in operation for the time being, and in their absence no free choice is possible.

THE CALCULATIONS MADE BY THE BRANCHES AND FIRMS

Within the framework of the Plan – to whose design they thus contribute – the individual firms, and sometimes even the branches, formulate their own investment policy without reference to the central authority. But with a few exceptions, such as Energy and Transport, there has so far been no attempt to arrive at a rational solution. We will now consider the accepted criterion of profitability, and then the elements taken as the basis for calculating it.

1. *The criterion of profitability*

The fourth Plan undoubtedly made better use of this. The instructions given to the Rapporteurs recommended, among other things, recourse to the method of the *bilan actualisé* (discounted balance-sheet), or gross profit (the difference between total product and total cost) discounted to the present. The only investments included in the Plan are those showing a profit at a 7 per cent rate of discount.[8] Capital investment which reduces total cost to the lowest possible level for a given production is regarded as constituting an optimum for the branch or firm concerned.

The application of this criterion leads to a number of difficulties.

– The first is that of breaking out of the vicious circle we mentioned earlier – caused by the fact that investment is calculated on the basis of marginal prices which vary with the volume of capital goods required. To get round this difficulty, it is assumed at the

[8] Special report of the Transport and Waterways Commission for the fourth Plan, Imprimerie nationale, Paris 1961, p. 77. Taking A_n as the yield for year n and I_p as the investment expenditure for year p, the balance-sheet B discounted to the present would be worked out as follows:

$$B = \Sigma \quad \frac{A_n}{(1 + i)^n} - \Sigma \frac{I_p}{(1 + i)^p} \qquad 1 + i = 1{\cdot}07$$

first stage of the calculation that costs, and therefore prices, will remain at their present level. The trend of resources and their use is considered on this basis. Prices are subsequently adjusted with due allowance for the necessary level of investment and the various constraints which make themselves felt, such as the need to ensure supplies and to deal with bottlenecks.

– The second difficulty relates to the estimate of costs. If the firm's optimum is to correspond to that of the community, the costs taken into account must not be only those which appear in the firm's books. For instance, in addition to wages they must include the cost of providing transport for the workers, which devolves upon the community, but results from the firm's policy. To individual costs must be added the social costs occasioned by the firm's development. Some future costs cannot be exactly predicted, and must be arrived at by the calculation of probability: technical progress not only affects the price of machinery or the introduction of new methods, such as atomic energy; it also creates uncertainty as to the length of life of plant, and hence as to the rate at which it should be written off; obsolescence is a more frequent cause of replacement than wear and tear.

Uncertainty regarding future prices is a universal impediment to the calculation of profitability, for goods and services do not come on the market until a year, or even several years, after the calculations are made. Is there any hope that 'generalized markets' will be set up, with deferred delivery prices on which manufacturers could base their plans?[9] But consumers, who are ignorant enough about present conditions, could never form a rational judgement about future prices. We must simply hope that one day the Plan will be able to predict prices more accurately than at present, and thus enable manufacturers to make rational calculations.

2. *The factors of the calculation*

The attempt to determine minimum total cost is made in the light of decisions taken by the authorities and of market reactions

[9] See G. Debreu, *La théorie de la valeur* (published in English as *Theory of Value*, Wiley, New York 1959), a thesis, Paris 1956; and 'Une économie de l'incertain', *Economie appliquée*. No. 1, 1960.
P. Massé, 'La pensée moderne et l'action économique', in *Bulletin du ministère des Finances*, April-May 1961, p. 12.

which govern the 'prices' established by the branch or the firm as the basis of its policy. That policy will be consonant with the general interest only if these 'signals' satisfy the logic of marginal costs. So if the attempt to ensure profitability is not to conflict with the public interest, the prices of the products and services of labour (wages) and of money (interest and exchange rates) must conform to this standard.[10]

Only in exceptional cases is the price of the products and services bought by a firm established on a rational basis.[11] In most cases it is governed by empirical decisions. Competition no doubt creates situations which may be acknowledged to have at least a slight bearing on marginal costs. But it would be extremely optimistic to assume that prices are near to marginal cost, particularly in oligopolistic sectors. This type of price-fixing at present prevails in France only in the supply of electricity and in railway transport. Its extension to other sectors and to less homogeneous productions is difficult even in theory and would lead to generalized price-control. The most that could be done would be to prevent conspicuously monopolistic practices.

However, for the time being at least, the opening up of frontiers does not militate in favour of more rational policies. Rivalry for the conquest of new markets is leading to over-capitalization and cut-throat prices. Unless matters are regulated on a European scale, national standardization is doomed to ineffectiveness.

Wages, too, should conform to the marginal standard; in other words a given quantity of work should be remunerated on the same scale everywhere, in proportion to its productivity. We are far from having reached this point, and the difficulties that stand in the way are innumerable. But in theoretical calculations, at any rate, it should be possible to follow the example of the Energy Commission for the fourth Plan, which adopted a uniform method of calculating the wage and salary structure for all firms in its field.[12]

Interest should, in principle, be equal to the marginal productivity of capital. In this respect, theory is somewhat vague. Are we

[10] Future prices as well as current prices should in fact conform to this logic, but I will not labour the point.

[11] When prices are fixed at the level of marginal costs, the purchaser is paying the current expenses and development costs of the product purchased.

[12] See *Rapport général de la Commission de l'Energie du Quatrième Plan* p. 36.

to consider productivity in each sector separately, which means taking several different rates? However that may be, a great many calculations have been made without regard to productivity or any other standard, including rate of growth.[13]

It is permissible to use a theoretical rate of interest in such calculations. The Soviet planners – though they do not use the word – take several of these; but the third French Plan proposed a single rate of 8 per cent, and the fourth Plan suggested 7 per cent. Is this figure meant to be related to the rate of expansion, or is it a kind of average between the 4·5 per cent interest payable on public loans made by the F.D.E.S. and that charged for private lending, in the neighbourhood of 10 per cent? In any event, the adoption of a single rate has the advantage of enabling a comparison to be made between the yield of investment in different sections of the economy. For the time being, however, only two Commissions – Energy and Transport – use this rate.

Pricing is also distorted by other factors, such as exchange rates, which can be unified for the purpose of theoretical calculation by using the official rate of some foreign currency, such as the dollar, at some chosen date. Fiscal policy has a marked influence on the relative prices of the different products and services. In the absence of *neutral* taxation, the imposition of a general system of indirect taxation with an equal incidence in all sectors would have the advantage of avoiding the distortion of production costs and hence of the firm's choice. Despite the improvements brought about by the institution and gradual extension of the value-added tax, much still remains to be done.

If the elements of the calculation do not all conform to the desirable standards, the firms, in pursuing their individual interest, will not serve the general interest. And such is indeed the case at present. In a decentralized economy like that of France, this leaves the planners the choice of two methods of preventing irrational behaviour on the part of the firms.

It might be possible to ask the firms to supply detailed information regarding their conditions of production, their investment programmes and methods of financing these, their localization, their labour force and the variable aspects of their behaviour. Their attitude would then be studied in the framework of a price system

[13] In any case, history provides no evidence of a connection between interest rates and rate of growth.

conforming to the theoretical standards, making it possible to lay down a programme of production and optimum investment. But there is a fundamental difficulty here: the firms will shape their policy to fit real prices, not the prices worked out by the planners. An attempt should therefore be made to establish prices closer to the standard levels, or else to impose some form of constraint, compelling firms to act in conformity with the Plan. This involves the danger of close control of the economy, which would deprive planning of much of its present flexibility.

The tendency appears to be to pursue more limited objectives. The public authorities would thus make an effort to adjust certain prices, while the example of the Energy Commission might be followed for purposes of calculation, by adopting a few theoretical prices – in the matter of interest and exchange-rates, for instance – and instituting a more homogeneous system of wages and salaries. Investigation of future price-trends would clarify the conditions of financing and of the return on capital equipment. Lastly, the firms – or at any rate the largest of them – should be required to supply particulars of alternative policies which would enable the public authorities to select the course most conducive to the general interest.

The branches and firms have a criterion of profit-making capacity. It is, however, not likely to guarantee at the same time an optimum for the firm and a social optimum, inasmuch as the distribution of social costs and of present and future collective returns is still uncertain.

Very little concern for the optimum is in fact shown. The Energy Commission makes calculations at branch level, but oil development largely escapes analysis, which affects the overall study.[14] The Transport Commission, in agreement with the Bureau of Economic Studies of the Ministry of Public Works, makes studies of profitability, though these deal with sub-sections (railway, water or air transport) rather than with the branch as a whole. The co-ordination of transport – i.e. the distribution of investment among the different services in the light of their profit-making capacity – is still at the initial stage and is hampered by rivalry not

[14] The report of the General Commission on Energy for the fourth Plan (Rapporteur, M. Gouni) represents an important step forward in the attempt to measure profitability within a branch.

only between the public and private sectors, but even within the public sector – for the S.N.C.F. has to compete not only with road transport but with Air-France as well. This competition is only natural, but it is to be regretted that the context of prices, fiscal policy, wages and public aid within which it takes place cannot, save in exceptional cases, be established in standardized conditions. Now that customs barriers are being lowered, co-ordination would be a matter for Brussels and not for Paris alone, however.

At the level of the firms, the transport and energy sections, and more especially the public corporations in these fields, undertake most of the calculations made to determine the return on investment. Some private firms also do this nowadays, it is true; but such attempts to arrive at an optimum are still exceptional.

III. OPTIMUM AND GEOGRAPHY

Although the Plans are characterized by increasing attention to geographical considerations – as is evidenced by the development of the regional Plans and the *tranches opératoires* – a number of decisions are still taken regardless of localization. Up to now, research has been conducted along two parallel lines and its results have seldom been combined. One form of research is concerned with national consistency and is based on forecasts of production, consumption and investment prepared per sector and not rationally broken down per region, except in the case of nationalized energy production and certain forms of transport. The other deals with regional programmes which enumerate the desirable sites for public utilities (schools, town-planning, health and social equipment) on the basis of estimates of local needs, but seldom in the light of their economic efficiency. Collective investment, the direct return on which seems to be lower in Paris than in the big provincial cities, is not discussed at all;[15] nor is the localization of heavy industry. It is the exception for expenditure on utilities and industrial equipment to be based on considerations of optimum localization.

[15] The fourth Plan upholds, without giving reasons, the view that Paris is a growth-point with a magnetic attraction for French expansion; but it does not state the cost of its development compared with that of other towns, nor does it mention the impetus given to expansion by unused margins of productivity, which are negligible in Paris and considerable in the provinces.

This forgetfulness of geography and its constraints has been fostered by the centralization of the administrative structure. But blind spots in economic thinking have been a still greater hindrance to research.

There can be no research without information; and this is very inadequate. Little is so far known about the geographical migration of men and capital, production relationships, the flow of goods and services within a region and from one region to another, or the relative circumstances of different regions.[16] The centralization of decision-making has intensified that of information, to the detriment of regional statistics.

Looking deeper, we find that in this sphere there is a complete separation between political and economic theory. The theory of localization, which was developed to its culminating point by August Lösch in Germany, seeks to account for what is regarded as a satisfactory situation, rather than to modify it. It does not proffer any guide to intervention. Moreover, the firm's choice is all-important according to this theory, the criteria of localization being the lowest possible costs for the firm, in transport and other respects, combined with the highest possible revenue. This theory ignores the cost to the community of housing, transport and the provision of utilities.

But it is no longer sufficient to consider only the need to reduce a firm's costs to the minimum. The most prominent of these – transport costs – has lost much of its importance owing to technological changes. More important still are the other reasons which nowadays impel governments and inter-governmental organizations such as the E.E.C. to intervene in the choice of sites.

The need to provide employment for the population makes it desirable for the individual regions to avoid unbalance between the supply of labour and the demand for it, since the disruption of that balance results in large-scale migration. Efforts must also be made to prevent an excessive disparity between incomes in different regions.

The public authorities are confronted with a variety of tasks in which economic theory is of no great help to them. The localization of firms and towns is bound up with the question of regional development, and the difficulty of choosing between alternatives

[16] A permanent working party on regional statistics was set up by the *Commission du Financement* (Finance Commission) of the fourth Plan.

is all the greater because they are frequently interdependent. They have to be considered in such an order that the dependence of one upon another becomes evident. We will deal first with the localization of certain firms, then with town-planning and, finally, with regional organization.

THE LOCALIZATION OF CERTAIN FIRMS

Observance of the constraints which determine the geographical position of some branches of production is a fundamental requisite of economic development. These are no doubt of less importance than formerly, and a good many firms are indifferent as to where they set up. But to produce 'no matter what, no matter where' leads to artificially high costs, is wasteful and slows down expansion.

1. *Classification of industries*

A. Lösch[17] classifies industries according to whether their localization is 'determinate' or 'indeterminate'.

The *former* are subject to natural constraints which indicate one or more particularly favourable sites for them. Some of these constraints derive from their production technique, and take the form of high transport, supply or delivery costs. Iron and steel production and the non-ferrous metal industries must be situated in the vicinity of mines, well-equipped harbours and sources of energy; oil refineries and petroleum chemistry must be near to the places where petroleum is delivered or consumed; carbon chemistry must be near coalmines etc. Others, though 'determinate', have a more fortuitous localization. The proximity of an iron and steel works leads to the establishment of industries for the semi-manufacture of metals. The decline of activities such as textile production and leather goods manufacture has the effect of confining them to the traditional centres of output.

The second group – that of the 'indeterminate' industries – is the larger of the two. Even with them localization is not a matter of complete indifference; but they can flourish in so many places that it need not be a guiding consideration. Activities attract one another owing to the advantages derived from concentration,

[17] See August Lösch, *Die Räumliche Ordnung der Wirtschaft*, G. Fischer, Jena 1940, Part I.

making it very difficult to study the interdependence of the different firms in the matter of localization. We must therefore confine ourselves to the 'determinate' branches. As their localization determines the provision of utilities in a particular region, and its subsequent development, it is the first matter to be decided.

2. *Localization*

In principle a site is chosen where conditions will be most advantageous; in other words, where maximum receipts will be combined with minimum costs. But it is difficult to discover the influence of localization upon receipts. All we can do here is to consider a few aspects of costs.

The search for minimum transport costs led to the now familiar construction of 'isocost' lines round the supply-points and of 'isodapanes' as combinations of isocost graphs. The geographical distortion caused by political frontiers, points of junction of routes of communication and differences between transport surfaces (land or water) is also clearly recognized.

Energy and manpower costs also help to decide localization. Though none of these costs considered separately is enough to settle the choice of a site, they play a great part in the development of industrial concentrations in places where their combined aspect is favourable.

But it is important for costs to be kept down not only for the firms but for the community as well. This is impossible unless services are everywhere sold to the economic agents at their real cost.

The price of energy and transport does not always correspond to their cost. The introduction of the 'green tariff' in the supply of electricity has, of course, put an end to some illogical aspects of the earlier situation. But the price of coal and fuel oil, which is a prominent feature of the expenditure of industrial firms, varies from one region to another in a manner that is not always rational. In 1962, Western France seemed to be handicapped not only by having no coalmines, but by the existing scale of charges (which made little difference between the cost of imported coal and the delivery price of the domestic output). Prices are affected by the existence of harbours suitable for foreign coalers (such as Brest) and by arrivals of low-price foreign coal.

Nor do transport rates correspond to costs, as is shown by the well-known example of Paris suburban traffic. The latest schemes have rectified some of the mistakes previously made in railway charges, but the rates charged for other methods of transport are not equally logical.[18] Improved co-ordination and the alignment of charges would make a considerable difference to the relative circumstances of the various regions.

Lastly, manpower prices fail to reflect their cost to the community. For instance, the authorities – albeit to a very varying degree – cover the general expenses involved in daily life under the heading of hospitals, education and housing. The State does not pass the cost of these services to the firms in the form of taxes proportionate to its outlay. The present national system of taxation does not lend itself to regional differentiations, whether in the form of indirect taxation or of direct taxation such as a tax on wages and salaries. The situation is further aggravated by the trend towards the nationalization of local expenditure and the increasing weakness of local finances. The result is that in the regions where services are chiefly financed by the nation, firms are to all intents and purposes subsidized. Licensing is less stringent and tax evasion easier in Paris than in the suburbs or the provinces, and this draws many firms to establish their head offices there.

Again, real costs are camouflaged by the subsidies and grants with which the authorities strive to encourage regional development. There lies the great danger of subsidies. If they give an immediate and lasting stimulus to activity, they are justified. But they are liable to attract industries whose uneconomic character is concealed while the aid continues, and which find themselves grappling with increased difficulties once it is withdrawn.

If public utilities are spread over the country in an irrational manner, regardless of regional differences in their profitability, individual and collective costs are likely to be different. Roads, the modernization of railways, grants for education, have not always been logically distributed; local political pressure has played its part. An unsystematic distribution of public works affects relative

[18] See P. Bauchet, *Propriété publique et planification*, p. 170 *et seq*. The attempt to establish a rational price-system is constantly upset by interference, especially from Parliament. Members bring pressure to bear in order to obtain the lowest rates for their own constituents, and thus prevent rational geographical exploitation. The debate on the fourth Plan (10–22 June 1962) was brought to a standstill by demands of this nature.

prices in the different regions and has an adverse influence on the decisions made by manufacturers.[19]

If attention were paid to ensuring that collective equipment would pay its way, it would become easier to choose suitable localities for certain groups of industries and to decide between alternative sites for new towns.

TOWN-PLANNING

Towns are born and grow because they offer advantages to those who gather there. Each one has an area where goods are produced and marketed, and their relative importance depends on the value of the services they provide.

Hitherto, their number and size have been determined by the individual calculations of the agents who settle where they can make the highest profits. But official intervention should now begin to play a greater part in urban development. Considerations of sanitation and health, or merely the need to ensure the satisfactory operation of public services such as transport and education, should prompt the State to decree the shape (ribbon development, concentration or cluster), amenities, number and size of towns, so that the necessary services shall be available to every member of the population.

Though it is to be hoped that progress will be made in assessing the profitability of urban investment, it is important that the economic agents should remain free to follow their preferences in the choice of locality. But they cannot choose freely unless the population of each economic area is meeting the expenditure incurred on its behalf. This is a somewhat vague concept, but France should have a rating system resembling that of Britain or America, which helps to regulate the size of towns. This weighs so heavily in big cities like New York and San Francisco that it limits their growth – contrary to what happens in Paris.

REGIONAL ORGANIZATION

This is not simply a matter of choosing sites for industries and laying down regulations for the size of towns; too many activities

[19] The inadequacies of the State school system in Northern France drove industries away from that region, at a time when there was local unemployment among unskilled workers.

and public utilities are 'indeterminate' in location. Since it is not possible to analyse all the factors that make for geographical interpendence between firms or between utility projects, we must change our angle of approach and turn from a micro-economic study to a macro-economic one.

This means considering each region as a single unit, with its own industries and towns. Into this frame of reference we have to fit the most appropriate activities. A theoretical choice can be made in the light of the available quantity and quality of manpower – which is determined by the Plan – of the resources and markets available for each product – which are shown in the regional and cross-regional inter-industry tables – and of real costs. But in actual fact this analysis cannot be carried very far, because the necessary calculations are extremely complicated, particularly where inter-industry relations are concerned.[20] Moreover, the activities and utilities of the individual regions cannot be properly covered by a purely regional study; they need to be considered on a national and European scale.[21]

It is somewhat hazardous to try to arrive, through the Plans, at an optimum geographical development. Even when simple criteria are available there is a risk of error. Ill-considered economic calculations may lead to investment in parts of the country where development is already proceeding rapidly, even if better returns could be obtained elsewhere, simply because the future looks more secure in places where suppliers and customers are already numerous.[22] Unless calculation is based on a clear view of the future, it may even aggravate regional disequilibrium.

Furthermore, this kind of planning restricts freedom because its tendency is to tell workers where they are to go. It is thus important to decentralize decision-making, so that interference will not be carried too far. National or international bodies must no doubt be allowed to decide the position of firms which have a 'determinate' localization, and of towns and large-scale public works. But

[20] For inter-industry tables, see my book *Les tableaux économiques: analyse de la région lorraine*, Génin, Paris 1956.

[21] The policy of the *Nord* Region of France is dictated by its position at the intersection of the axes Antwerp–Paris and London–Liége–Aix-la-Chapelle.

[22] It is a remarkable fact that in the most strictly-planned economies, such as that of Soviet Russia, concentration is such that drastic steps, like bans on the recruitment of labour, are taken to protect some districts from congestion and others from being deserted.

considerable initiative will have to be left to regional bodies, and private business, too, should be permitted to choose the localities most convenient to the firms themselves and to the community in general. This means that the prices paid for services at any given point of the territory must correspond to real costs; and that requires a revision of charges and of local taxation.

IV. CONCLUSION

Faulty though it may be, the theory of the optimum is now logical enough to guide the decisions of firms and of the public authorities, though only if all alternative possibilities are clearly presented.

At the level of firms, particularly in private industry, there remains much to be done to ensure the rational study of the choices open to them in technical and economic matters, for these are too often overlooked. Analysis of this kind, as well as clarifying the views of the firm concerned, would enlighten the State as to the consequences of its decisions.

At the level of the State, a wider range of possibilities should be examined. In addition to the alternatives presented at the initial stage, which relate to the rate of growth, collective investment, individual consumption and certain production-levels, there should be others, in such matters as foreign-exchange policy, decentralization of industry and, most of all, in financial policy – on points such as the choice between self-financing and loans, different types of taxation, and above all, income-distribution.

To make sure that the models will give the public authorities a picture of the consequences of their actions, they should be simple in form and present only a few straightforward, realistic alternatives.

But W. Leontief[23] and many other authors have shown that it is difficult to discover the relationship between price changes, fluctuations in the income of the different groups in the community, and production levels, without putting forward a number of abstract hypotheses; we are no longer in the day of the classical economists, when the main trends in population, incomes and prices could be explained by a few elementary laws.

This will be seen from one simple, topical example. Owing to the

[23] See Wassily Leontief, *Studies in the structure of the American Economy*, Oxford University Press, New York, 1953, Chs. III and XII.

stability of the social forces involved, it is reasonable to assume that for the next few years income-distribution will be based on a stable long-term relation between wages and profits. But this simple formula tells us nothing about medium-term price trends. Will inflation result from the pressure simultaneously exercised by the different groups in order to secure higher incomes? If so, in what branches of industry or in which regions? Will it be moderate, or uncontrollable? What effect would it have on prices and consumption? There is no definite reply to any of these questions, and this leads to uncertainty about the relationship between distribution and consumption.[24]

Uncertainty persists even in those countries which supposed that it could be dispelled by a scientific analysis of the economic situation and by extensive socialization. Experience in the Eastern countries shows that decisions based on the impartial laws of sociology and modern economics, however sound in scientific theory, have sometimes proved fallible in application. The same is true in France – even more so, because our economy is not sufficiently centralized to be firmly controlled by the hand of officialdom. For instance, when considering how to increase exports, the authorities may feel doubtful whether to subsidize a branch of industry in which the ratio between the extra capital equipment needed and the export figure to be obtained is comparatively low, but whose leaders are lacking in drive.

Even as it stands, the Plan gives some protection against the erratic behaviour of individuals, by showing them that they have economic interests in common. Every effort should now be made to associate them still more closely with its preparation and fulfilment.

But whatever is done in this direction, periodical revision of the Plan will remain necessary; especially as, by throwing open her economic frontiers, France has exposed herself to the consequences of events beyond her own control.

The mere existence of the Common Market means that sooner or later the basic structure of the French Plan and of the national accounting system will have to be thoroughly overhauled. Hitherto, the foreign account had been regarded as something adventitious and under control; now it is to be fundamental and indeterminate. Unless this uncertainty is to pervade the whole model – which

[24] For distribution models, see *La répartition du revenu national*, by J. Marchal and J. Lecaillon, Ed. Génin, 1958.

would destroy the Plan – a new analysis of the French economic machinery will have to be made, treating the Plan as a regional section of the European planning system.

But we know from experience that the theory of regional development is extremely vague, and we should be well advised to elaborate it more fully.

In short, while it is undoubtedly necessary to devise means of coming closer to optimum conditions, uncertain factors must be handled with caution; though the task of adapting the machinery of analysis to meet structural changes – of which the Common Market is not the least important – calls for a certain boldness.

Part Three

THE PLAN, THE FIRMS AND THE SOCIAL CLASSES

PART THREE

The Plan, the Firms and the Social Classes

APPEARANCES suggest that years of war and political revolution have made no change in the French economic system. Those who were hoping for a complete transformation are again disappointed, while the conservatives are relieved; both sides declare that nothing has altered, that the Plan has had no effect.

It is true that the capitalist structure and institutions have not been overthrown; a few rifts have appeared in the political structure, the private ownership of the means of production and the private financing of capital equipment, but without causing radical changes. Behind the old façade, however, the whole working of the system has been transformed.

The inception of planning in Europe coincides with the development of an economic life more regular in pattern than before the Second World War. Recent years have not been marked by the violent reconversion crisis that has traditionally followed the conclusion of hostilities, and about which Malthus said a number of interesting things as long ago as 1820.[1] The West has not passed through any economic depression comparable to that of 1929, though the established flows of foreign trade have been disturbed by political changes. Expansion has been halted now and again, but disequilibrium and unemployment have never reached catastrophic proportions. Growth has not only been more regular, but more rapid.

This has led to extensive changes in the economic machinery, and the Alsop brothers were right in saying that one of the reasons for these changes is to be sought in the investment programmes

[1] See T. R. Malthus, *Principles of Political Economy*, section X.

drawn up by Jean Monnet. They carry us far from the established concepts (still taught in our schools), for those resemble the picture Malthus draws of his own day, with a touch of the popular broadsheet which always seems to be a hundred years old. While we are still in the throes of this transformation it is impossible to describe all its aspects; but it is of the utmost importance – particularly for industrialists and political leaders – to be aware of some of them.

An employer, at any rate if he is at the head of a large firm, does not behave nowadays exactly as he would have done in the past; his decisions regarding production and investment are not reached in the same way. I hinted at the underlying reasons for this in my preliminary chapter, and I now propose to analyse the economic mechanism by which the changes have come about.

On the other hand, class reactions have become more complex. The nation's growth has taken a new turn.

CHAPTER I

The Plan in the Light of Managerial Decisions

THE PLAN is radically altering the attitude of many industrial managers who take part in the Commissions and read their publications. Nevertheless, cases of incompatibility between private interests and general objectives are not unknown, and though these cannot jeopardize the existence of the Plan they may distort its application.

I. FIXING THE PRODUCTION AND INVESTMENT PROGRAMMES

Unlike Soviet planning, the French system leaves the entrepreneur to decide the volume and methods of his production. Exceptions to this rule are found in part of the public sector and even extend to a few private firms; but they are not important enough to invalidate the principle. Nevertheless, decisions are not guided by the same criteria as in the past.

It would, of course, be absurd to deny that profit still plays a part in determining production levels. Changes in the quantity and quality of the goods put on the market are still influenced by considerations of costs and of the prices at which they can be sold, since these decide the margin of profit. Companies are prompted by their immediate financial and commercial interest to restrict their sales when costs rise or prices and demand decline, and *vice versa*. But managements take other factors into account as well; the concept of profit has altered.

PROFIT HAS ALTERED

The head of a firm no longer has the same interests as in the old days. The advantages he anticipates from its development are no longer the same.

The late nineteenth-century capitalist was always the entrepreneur; since he had the money needed to pay wages, purchase current goods and – above all – cover investment, he could manage a firm. The possession of money being rare at that time, the fact of possessing it was more important than managerial ability. This state of things is clearly reflected in the outlook of the classical economists and of Karl Marx.

Nowadays, however, salaried employees or managers control productive capital which does not belong to them. There are several reasons for this division between the ownership and the management of a firm.

A great proportion of French capital is now owned by the State.

In the private sector, many people are not in a financial position to hold vast capital sums; Rockefeller, Ford and Wendel were exceptions, and even so, their heirs were obliged to form limited companies with their property. The national capital is divided among family groups, small shareholders, the public corporations which produce energy and organize transport and communications, and the large banks.

Lastly, the entrepreneur who can frame new policies is becoming more important than the shareholder. Countries with a progressive capitalist system prefer to give their business leadership to energetic men rather than to rich capitalists. True, these men do acquire some of the capital, but often at a later stage, as a reward for their sound management. The National Industrial Conference Board found that technical know-how was more important than capital when seeking a managerial appointment, and that 80 per cent of business executives had obtained their posts on the strength of their qualifications and not through the influence of financial groups.

But, it may be objected, the financial interests represented by the banks or holding companies have a controlling influence in the firms' boards of directors. Surely they will compel the entrepreneur to fall in with their views and conform to the behaviour typical of the traditional capitalist?

I will not deny that financial groups do exist, or that they bring pressure to bear on the economic conduct of companies. But they do not enforce their views unilaterally, and they are often opposed by the entrepreneurs, who have means of resistance through which they can get their own way.

In the public sector the managers have no owners over their heads. And the capital they control is very large; Graf von Schmoller's vision of a community where all the principal industries were nationalized seemed utopian at the end of the nineteenth century, but it is no longer so. Under the pressure of public opinion this sector is beginning to follow a policy guided by the general interest, which the technicians responsible for it are expected to apply.

In the private sector, there is often a clash of opinions between the management and the members of the board of directors or the representatives of the financial interests involved.

The managers are often in a strong position. They constitute the essential factor in the smooth working of the firm, and its progress might be jeopardized by too much outside interference. They are the dynamic and permanent feature of the business, the function of the board of directors being confined to periodical inspection, and experience shows that their importance is increasing.

Not being the proprietors of the company, the managers do not look to it for quite the same advantages as though they were. They aim at making the firm yield a profit on business rather than on capitalist lines.

The traditional capitalist's idea of profit is an immediate financial return, whereas the entrepreneur is more interested in the long-term development of his firm; the former is more concerned with preserving and augmenting the owners' personal fortune, the latter with increasing the power of the firm; and nowadays this entails taking risks and looking far ahead. Now that production processes take so long to mature, the entrepreneur has to make forecasts and draw up plans which will not yield immediate results and cannot be judged on their day-to-day effects. The calculation of profits has to take all the circumstances into account and covers longer and longer periods.

Unlike the capitalist, the entrepreneur recognizes that a firm's profits are tied to the healthy condition of the nation's economy. The management of a big business is aware of the vast scale and increasing interdependence of different industries, and avoids taking decisions which are incompatible with what it believes to be the national interest.

Those firms which have been nationalized so that they shall better serve the community, and are bound by the rules of public service, have a particularly close connection with national development. Many private entrepreneurs also realize that the prosperity of their firm both depends upon and conditions that of their suppliers and customers, and that the larger the firm, the closer the connection. The few, large managements at the head of the French iron and steel and chemical industries are well aware that a return to the pre-war policy of 'playing for safety' by limiting the increase of their output would slow down national economic expansion and consequently their own growth.

But when an entrepreneur is trying to earn a profit which depends upon the long-term development of his firm and of the nation, is it possible for him to predict that profit in advance and take it as a guide in determining his level of activity?

Certainly not; for he cannot foresee, at a distance of five years or so, the changes in prices, costs, interest-rates and wages upon which his profit depends. He can no doubt form a general idea of whether a particular transaction will end in a profit or a loss, but he cannot be absolutely certain and precise. Moreover, in a situation affected by the interdependence of a number of sectors, the quantity of goods to be produced is a determining factor of profit, rather than *vice versa*.

Nowadays many entrepreneurs follow the Plan's indications with close attention, because they feel the need of some more reliable reference-mark than that of profit.

When the aims of the directors conflict with those of the entrepreneurs, the latter are prevented from doing exactly as they would like; but they often get their own way, especially as their arguments carry a certain weight in financial circles. It is safe to say that the new concept of profit is gaining ground on the old one, and that the Plan is playing an ever-greater part in helping to determine production levels.

THE PLAN AND THE PRODUCTION SCHEDULES

The level of production proposed in the Plan for the different branches is not only a useful point of reference in fixing production levels far ahead; it is also, in theory, the most desirable level, because it ensures harmonious development.

The objectives are established in such a way that each branch will be able to obtain the products and services it needs, and to sell a maximum quantity of goods. Since optimum income growth is associated with full employment, the consumers should have a purchasing power sufficient to absorb this output, and a market is thus assured. This state of things can come about, of course, only if every sector, and in particular every key sector, observes the production levels indicated in the Plan. If the coalmines refuse to provide sufficient coal, on the (perfectly reasonable) excuse that in the distant future they will have to cut down their activity and meet heavy social expenditure, there will be a power shortage which will compel every firm to slow down its development.

The State has several means of intervention with which to avert this danger. In the public sector, there is the financing of investment; in the private sector, measures such as loans, tax policy, price-control, orders placed with the engineering and heavy electrical industries by the nationalized firms, and general economic policy. True, these means of enforcement are not well co-ordinated, and leave loopholes for those unwilling to fulfil the Plan. But if entrepreneurs feel sure that their own prosperity depends on national expansion, and that this is reciprocally influenced by their behaviour, they will follow the Plan's instructions – so long as the production targets selected by the planners in the light of the general interest are consonant with maximum profits for industrial firms.

PLANS AND INVESTMENT PROGRAMMES

In the old days an entrepreneur decided the level of his investments in the light of three factors: market fluctuations, new inventions, and the money at his disposal.

The influence of changes in consumer demand in prompting the seller to revise his capital investment programmes was pointed out by Professor Aftalion in his well-known theory of the 'accelerator' – an accurate description of a state of things that now belongs to the past. It was one in which profit-seeking motives would induce an entrepreneur to make sudden changes in his orders for capital goods, which fluctuated more widely than consumer demand itself. If the demand for a particular commodity rose by 10 per cent, investment in that branch of industry might increase by 100 per cent; if demand remained constant, investment might fall to nothing. Activity in the manufacture of capital goods was thus very irregular. According to Aftalion, this relationship between investment and production was responsible for the periodical depressions that used to occur before the war. Analysis of the pattern of their recurrence does, indeed, show that the activity of the branches producing capital goods used to fluctuate widely and more noticeably than that of other sections.

The invention of a new manufacturing process may either diminish investment or increase it. If it occurs in a sector where the demand for manufactured goods is small, or under unfavourable economic circumstances, the consequent surplus production may lead the entrepreneurs to reduce their total capital investment and indirectly bring about a crisis. Whereas in other circumstances, by reducing overheads it may lead to increased demand and thus, indirectly, to increased investment. Here again, any abrupt change is likely to cause disturbance.[1]

Lastly, as we said just now, investment depends upon the funds available to the entrepreneur, and indirectly upon the reserves created by national and branch savings. Now that those who save money are not necessarily identical with those who invest it – as they were in the old days when the principal investor was the farmer, who saved money in order to buy a plough – it sometimes happens that private individuals do not save enough, or that they invest their savings in ways that are not of interest to the manufacturers.

The latter must then limit their investment to what the credit they can obtain will allow.

The Plan now plays a decisive part in the elaboration of investment programmes.

We have already enumerated the reasons for this. Investment has to be planned and prepared far ahead; a hand-to-mouth policy is no longer feasible, owing to the scale of the expenditure required and the length of the period it covers. Production schedules, too, are drawn up for a long period and on a national scale, and since investment and production are interdependent, the former must fit into the overall pattern which is only to be found in the Plan. The yield on investment also has to be calculated on a long-term

[1] Malthus had already foreseen this problem; see his *Principles of Political Economy*, Section V.

basis, and this, too, requires a knowledge of the general conditions affecting expansion and sales prospects.

In the Plan, the general level of investment depends on the use made of the national product. Roughly speaking, this is divided between consumption and investment. Consumption varies under the influence of a number of factors, some of them economic (growth of resources), others psychological (the desire for comforts) or political (the Government's decision to guide the general expenditure). Investment is tied to the needs of the productive sector, and thus to expansion. If the demands of 'spontaneous' consumption and investment were added together, their sum would of course exceed the utmost possible figure of national product, even allowing for foreign aid and for a trade deficit. Hence, in determining the respective shares of consumption and investment, a balance must be struck between the growing demand for consumer goods and the necessity of increasing the nation's capital in order to produce more goods.

Investment is then divided between the different branches, according to their needs. The State cannot, of course, dictate to the firms about their investment. But it does supervise the financing of investment programmes in the public sector and those of the iron and steel and building industries, for example, which are considerably dependent on low-interest government loans.

Within this framework, the entrepreneur is at liberty to decide the level of his firm's investment, with an eye to its profit-earning capacity. Does his behaviour conform to the Plan's forecasts?

In the nationalized branches, the entrepreneur must comply with official decisions in order to obtain funds for investment. In the other heavy industries the State can in principle control certain factors affecting the long-term profitability of an investment; the market is partly dependent upon its policy of income-distribution, and costs are affected by State loans and other forms of aid. An entrepreneur who complies with the requirements of the Plan will demand, in return, that the State shall guarantee him a return on his investment. If, during the period of the Plan, a change in his profit-making prospects prompts him to reduce or increase the agreed volume of investment, the State, too, is entitled to reconsider its policy.

In the sectors which are composed of smaller firms, investment is less onerous and therefore more subject to the influence of short-term factors, such as the level of demand and the cost of materials. Changes in prices and in profit-making capacity cause rapid variations in investment figures. Nevertheless, entrepreneurs do take into consideration the general expansion forecast in the Plan. In some branches, such as agriculture, building and electrical engineering, they are encouraged to fall in with the Plan's investment programmes by more direct forms of market manipulation – by price-regulation, housing subsidies, orders from the nationalized firms, or a reduction of investment costs through some form of assistance, such as grants for the purchase of agricultural machinery. But the State does not intervene unless the investment is large enough to have a definite influence on general economic development.

CONSEQUENCES

In all countries, investment is more regular than before the war; statistics show that the tendency to 'zigzag' is now much less marked.[2]

Long-term forecasting and planning are prominent among the steadying factors. The 'accelerator', the entrepreneur's abrupt reaction to fluctuations in demand, which used to cause irregularity in orders for capital goods, was a purely automatic response to market trends. If a management ignores these temporary fluctuations and fixes investment as part of a long-term programme, the changes made subsequently will be slight. The management must of course adjust its forecasts to meet any lasting change in the market, but such adjustment will be gradual and moderate, and will not disrupt economic balance. Entrepreneurs used to vary their investment in the manner described by the accelerator because in those days they acted blindly; such fluctuations are less likely now that entrepreneurs act deliberately, with foresight, and have a Plan to guide them.

The second steadying factor is that invention and innovation have to a certain extent been brought under control. They used to be considered rather as chance developments or acts of God – helped on, of course, by human effort, but occurring unpredictably. The lead recently taken by the Russians in inter-planetary rockets

[2] See *Etudes et Conjonctures*, October 1955, p. 857 *et seq.*

shows that inventions can be prepared far in advance, and many countries, in making long-term forecasts for a plan, have now realized how much can be gained by invention and research. They are making intellectual investments on a tremendous scale, in the form of technical and psychotechnical laboratories, market studies and organizational research. Inventions and innovations, prepared far ahead, are now as much the source as the result of new investment; they form an integral part of investment, and the sums spent on them are no longer determined fortuitously.[3] The date by which a particular technical discovery will be perfected, and the capital required, are predicted approximately; the introduction of the turbine engine in motor-car manufacture will not come as a surprise, nor will the use of atomic energy on the railways or in shipbuilding. A plan's long-term forecasts show managements that intellectual research is a paying proposition and thus diminish the risk of recurrent stagnation entailed when invention proceeds by fits and starts.

Profit-seeking still plays a great part. In deciding its volume of investment, every firm is guided by monetary considerations at least as much as by the Plan's forecasts, which are only made per sector. Financial considerations are preponderant in small companies, retail trade, the crafts and agriculture, where the cost of capital equipment is not heavy and can be covered within a short period.

However, profit-making is no longer the result of fortuitous developments; the State guides it, too, to induce the entrepreneur to act in conformity with the Plan's forecasts while leaving him free to make his own decisions within the firm itself. In the old days, the supply of and demand for savings did not always tally. Nowadays, the effect of self-financing is to level up savings and investment in the big companies. Wishing to encourage this balance in the interests of the Plan, the Government can do so through its tax policy, through the use of public money, and by controlling credit. Adjustment to economic circumstances can be ensured to a certain extent by preparing expectational economic budgets, and by liaison between the Directorate of the Budget, the Treasury, the *Fonds d'Equipement* and the *Commissariat du Plan*. Thus, the

[3] It is true that the speed with which new inventions appear increases the rate of 'obsolescence', making it more difficult to predict the profitability of capital goods.

financial factors by which managements are guided also reflect the trends of the Plan.

Now that the entrepreneurs' decisions relate to a longer period, are made in the light of the Plan and are less influenced than formerly by sudden temporary disruptions of the financial balance, they have become more regular than in the past and no longer provoke violent periodical crises.

This rational guidance involves only a minimum of direct constraint for the managements, since production and investment programmes are usually drawn up for the whole sector, not for the individual firms. A management decides the amount and type of its investment in the light of the Plan's general forecasts, but is also influenced by commercial and financial considerations – in small firms, indeed, almost exclusively so. The nationalized firms are necessary exceptions to this rule, since they rely on public money to finance their investments.

The entrepreneurs' reference to the Plan when reaching their decisions indicates that we are moving out of a community which acts blindly, into one with a forward-looking organization.

The transfer will not be completed, however, unless the conditions upon which a plan's success depends are satisfied by the agents of economic development, and particularly by the managements, which have a comparatively free hand when planning is flexible. The harmonious development of the different types of production and the growth of the firms and of the national economy are contingent upon respect for the relations underlying the Plan; the entrepreneurs, in carrying out their production and investment programmes, must not bring pressure to bear on the legislature or the executive in order to obtain exorbitant financial conditions or induce the authorities to make changes, for their benefit, in the structure of prices, credit and costs round which the Plan was built up. Experience has shown that such pressure disrupts the balance between investment and purchasing power, to the detriment of some sectors; the State can adjust this unbalance in some cases, but only if it is kept within bounds.

Since the State does not control private credit and self-financing, its intervention is only marginal, as it were, and some sectors may ignore the Plan if they find it incompatible with the programmes of their component firms.

II. HOW THE PLAN MAY CONFLICT WITH THE PROGRAMMES OF THE FIRMS

If the Plan forecasts a rate of development corresponding to what is thought to be normal growth, the sector concerned will work to that forecast. But if the Plan advocates an appreciable change, it will usually run into difficulties. Let us consider some of these.

BEHAVIOUR

Growth may be slowed down by 'conservative' behaviour. The credit policy of some large financial groups which cling to the precepts of Malthus, and fidelity to old-fashioned manufacturing processes or to the family structure of a firm, are factors which impede development or reconversion in the engineering electrical and textile industries, for example. Investment may fall off at times under the influence of a wave of pessimism. Matters have sometimes been righted by the normal methods of intervention, such as financial assistance or the placing of orders by the public sector. But so far there have been no recurrent depressions of a serious nature. If one of these should again occur, the existing means of intervention would not be sufficient to cope with them, especially where credit is concerned.

The same type of behaviour sometimes prevents the shrinkage or reconversion of activities for which the market is narrowing. In such cases the sectional interests bring pressure to bear through their parliamentary representatives – or, if the latters' influence is declining, make a direct approach to the administration or the executive – to secure aid and protection for its market. Examples of this have occurred in the milling trade, in shipbuilding and in certain branches of agriculture. The producers of wheat, sugar-beet and alcohol, whose exports and surpluses are subsidized, have made repeated attempts to obtain still more favourable conditions for their output, though it already exceeds the levels laid down in the Plan.

THE PROFIT-MAKING CAPACITY OF THE FIRMS

When the production schedules and investment programmes set forth in the Plan do not ensure maximum profits for the firms in the sector concerned, opposition makes itself felt from the moment the Commissions set to work. The example of the steel industry shows that the subsequent discussions lead to a kind of unwritten quasi-contract; the section promises to fulfil the objectives of the Plan in return for various advantages in the matter of loans and sometimes of prices. The public authorities adjust the financial factors so as to make them conducive to what the firms regard as a level of profit compatible with the general interest. The requirements of the Plan may be said to dominate the financial situation, with the exception of the firms' profit-making calculations, to which we have already referred.

This is not always the case, of course. The State is disarmed when considering production in a sector where the individual firms have to face oligopolistic competition and sometimes even to deal with foreign competitors.

COMPETITION AT HOME AND ABROAD

There are instances of keen competition among a small number of producers all acting independently. Rejecting the discipline of a common policy, they fight for a monopoly of the market and systematically over-invest in their firms. When determining their strategy they no doubt reckon with the increased purchasing power and expanding sales predicted in the Plan. But each of them tries to grab the lion's share of the market and to push his investment beyond the desirable figure.

Matters have been made worse by the lowering of customs barriers, which has encouraged producers in the different countries to hope for a share of foreign markets. The motor-car industry offers a particularly striking example of this. Motor-car firms all over Europe have launched into a policy of over-investment, justified solely by the hope of defeating their rivals and driving them off the market. The oil firms, the airlines and the shipbuilding industries, backed up by subsidies from their governments or local authorities (such as the German *Länder*), are locked in a similar struggle, which is beginning to spread to other branches, including chemical production.

Once gripped by this strategy, a sector is lost to the national planning system; whatever the Government's means of intervention, market constraints will be too strong for them. This situation can only be brought under control by a supranational authority.

UNPREDICTABLE CHANGES

Happy accidents occur now and then. Costs are brought down by some important innovation, by the discovery of natural wealth such as oil, or by a particularly vigorous national effort. Production becomes more profitable and increases at a greater rate.

But it more frequently happens that partial distortion increases costs and slows down expansion. Certain firms are stagnant; they fail to supply the other sectors on the one hand with goods, and on the other with customers holding adequate purchasing power. Large companies, farmers' associations and groups of wage-earners often exert pressure in order to obtain credit, raise their prices or increase their income; this taps any surplus purchasing power, so that it is no longer available for other forms of financing or other customers.

GROUP PRESSURE

The programmes of the industrial firms cannot be brought into line with the Plan unless the general conditions required for fulfilling the Plan itself are ensured. The most important of these conditions is that current production shall be properly divided between capital goods and consumer goods. If an unforeseen and expensive dispute breaks out, or if large-scale pressure is exerted by groups of farmers, wage-earners or manufacturers in order to raise incomes and consumption to inflated proportions, the mass of savings and goods available for investment will be reduced. This puts a strain on credit and on capital goods, leading to higher prices and a lower return on investment, whereupon the volume of investment declines in its turn. The consequent disruption of balance is reflected in the financial situation, which influences the managements' decisions. If inflation is only temporary, the State can intervene to adjust the financial conditions of investment and halt the increase in consumption, if only by allowing prices to rise more rapidly than the consumers' incomes; this will encourage capital investment and bring it back to the lines laid down in the Plan. But if inflation is deep-seated and lasting, the Plan itself will have to be adjusted to meet the greater demand for consumer goods by raising the production targets, as Khrushchev has done in the U.S.S.R. Up to now, the action of the pressure groups in France has not caused any permanent disturbance of the financial situation and thus of investment and expansion.

Thus it is that all social circles share the responsibility for growth. An unduly rapid increase either in industrial profits or in wages may lead to excessive consumption and ultimately to the revision of the Plan.

But is there not a possibility that the class struggle, like the behaviour of the managements, will be modified as a result of the Plan?

CHAPTER II

The Class Struggle, the Plan, and Long-term Development

EVERYONE nowadays realizes that the class struggle influences economic development. The different groups accuse one another of restricting expansion.

The theme of class warfare, already a favourite topic with the classical economists, including Adam Smith and Malthus, was of course taken up again by Marx, who gave it a harsher aspect by declaring that the struggle must end in the collapse of the capitalist system, since it could find no solution while that system endured. Although Marx's views have been confirmed in other respects, recent developments in France contradict this particular theory. So far, the class struggle has not brought about the downfall of the capitalist system. On the contrary, it may be said to have enabled capitalism to construct instruments such as the Plan, which have consolidated it and may perhaps, in their turn, change the nature of the struggle itself.

I. THE CLASS STRUGGLE AND THE COLLAPSE OF CAPITALISM

THE MARXIST ANALYSIS

The Marxist analysis is so well known that its main features need be recalled here only to show how they have been transformed in present-day France.

Marx's theory assumed a perpetual conflict between two classes of the community – the owners of the means of production, or capitalists, and those who had no share in their ownership. The capitalist hires the worker, pays him a wage just sufficient to keep him in working condition, and sells the product of his labour at a higher price. The difference between wages and prices is surplus value. This theory is based on a situation in which the capitalist is both an employer of labour and a lender of money, drawing the entire profit of the transaction. So far, this seems to be the old theory of the classical economists, unchanged except for a certain hardening of attitude which is reflected in Marx's terminology; he speaks of classes and capital where Adam Smith used the words 'groups' and 'advances'.[1] This comparison indicates the part played in Marx's description by the facts of nineteenth-century economic life.

Marx goes further. The capitalists, he says – as Ricardo had pointed out before him – try to increase their profits by buying new machinery. For a time they are successful; but new owners enter the field and try to make greater progress, so the temporary extra profit vanishes. Moreover, the gain on a given quantity of goods is reduced, because the proportion of fixed capital (plant) that enters into the cost of production increases, while the proportion of variable capital (labour) diminishes, and it is the latter alone which produces surplus value. The tendency for the rate of profit to decline, coupled with the attempt to achieve maximum gains, thus launches the capitalists into a scramble to accumulate.

Marx predicts that this process will result in concentration, owing to the disappearance of the weaker firms. The consequent permanent disruption of equilibrium will take the form of underconsumption among the workers, and of technological unemployment; technical advances, together with the closing down of many firms, will throw the workers on the street, provide a permanent surplus of labour – thus perpetuating the minimum living wage – and hold down purchasing power below the value of the goods produced. Violent economic crises will temporarily restore the balance just when a breakdown seems inevitable; increasing concentration will accentuate the disequilibrium, until a day comes when the dominant system, reduced by now to a few units of production, is overthrown and makes way for a Socialist society.

[1] Marx's theory was based on the labour theory of value, borrowed from Ricardo, but he carried it much further. For him, the value of labour is not a mere working hypothesis; labour constitutes the sole value; price and value are separated in the capitalist system because it is a system of exploitation.

Hence, the development of capitalism amid conditions of instability and accumulation gives birth to a completely different type of organization.

THE REAL SITUATION TODAY

The current situation in France does not fit in with this picture. Even if today's comparative prosperity is only temporary, our country does not present the aspect of a capitalist system in its death-throes. Marx's portrait of capitalism is not borne out by events. Even the recent discussions in the French Communist Party have produced no evidence of increasing pauperization, either absolute or relative. The threat of unemployment is diminishing and making way for a shortage of labour in all categories. And as the Soviet leaders have pointed out more than once, modern capitalism does not lead inevitably to crises and stagnation; since 1946, national output has risen by about 5 per cent per annum.

To account for this state of things without falling into the errors declared by Marx to be characteristic of bourgeois thought on the subject of capitalism – the refusal to analyse the situation in terms of class and the division of the elements of distribution into more than two groups – we will resume our consideration of the class structure in present-day society.

In our economy, the wage-earners are becoming less like a proletariat and displaying more middle-class characteristics; they are losing their sense of insecurity and isolation and their impression of being occupied in degrading manual labour. Incidentally, Marx, unlike his disciples, foresaw that trade union pressure would bring about an absolute rise in the standard of living. Large sections of the working class are benefiting from higher wages, shorter working hours, guaranteed employment and improved working conditions, even if these have been offset by higher output quotas. Anxiety about the future has diminished in many homes. Moreover, many of the best-paid workers save money and invest it, so that their reactions are no longer those of the unskilled labourer with no capital but his two hands.

The tendency for the workers to be crowded into slum districts is not increasing. Town-planning and increased transport facilities are already reducing it, and will do so still more as time goes on.

Above all, the structure of the non-capitalist class is changing.

If we consider the relative size of the groups composing the active population, we find that the number of persons employed in services – taking the word in its widest sense – is increasing more rapidly than the number of those employed in manual labour. In the factories the occupational pattern has changed; the number of clerical and technical staff is rising more quickly than that of unskilled workers.

It is true that the increase in the numbers of technicians and of persons working in public services is accompanied by a fall in the number of self-employed persons and of independent 'centres of decision'. But in a dynamic capitalist economy, the son of a worker in a large factory, or of a peasant in a poor district, feels that he has come up in the world if, instead of being a blue-overalled apprentice, he is a student at a technical school, with the prospect of becoming a technician or a white-collar worker. A man who is doing active but not strictly manual work will hesitate to throw himself into an ideological struggle and thus damage his prospects of promotion. Without forgetting the millions of unskilled workers whose situation is still tragic in many respects, we may say that the majority of the working class can now count on increasing security and is less physically involved in the productive process.

On the other hand, the capitalist class, too, is changing. It is turning into a new class of entrepreneurs. We have already looked at the causes of this transformation – they include changes in the techniques of production, in the concept of ownership and in the structure of business firms. The entrepreneur is not so much a money-lender as a manager, responsible for combining the different factors of production.

This twofold development, by changing the proletariat into a middle class and the capitalist into an entrepreneur, has transformed the behaviour of the two groups in their struggle and given the lie to Marx's prophecy about the development of capitalist society.

In the matter of wages, the theory of exploitation drew its revolutionary force from the fact that the capitalist was both an employer and a money-lender who took the entire profits of the business. The present-day employer is not necessarily the owner; he may be merely the manager of a private or nationalized firm; this may spread exploitation more widely, but it becomes proportionately weaker. Even if we admit that the non-capitalist entrepreneur behaves in exactly the same way as a capitalist, the fact remains that, since he does not own the business, he will receive only a share of the profits. Exploitation exists, but it is widely diffused; it reflects the situation in every community, where those in power exploit their subordinates. The rapidly increasing information which reaches us from the completely socialized countries, together with our experience of how nationalized firms work, suggests that this kind of exploitation is perhaps not confined to the capitalist countries. However that may be, the clash of interests is far less bitter now than when it took place between a class of owners and one which owned nothing except its capacity for labour.

Furthermore, when the son of a worker or peasant has achieved some degree of material security and has risen to be a technician or an office worker, he will be inclined to think that the system to which he belongs is a progressive one. He will hesitate to join a group whose aim is to destroy that system, particularly when the factory offers to improve his standard of living appreciably if he will 'keep away from politics'.

He may even hope for 'collective' promotion; for though this is a slow process it does take place, in a dynamic capitalist system with an ever-growing demand for technicians and high-grade staff. There are undoubtedly grounds for complaint about the inadequacy of individual promotion regarded as a sign of social mobility. But property is no longer, as it was until recently, an essential condition of accession to certain posts. A sociological analysis of French business leaders would show that some of them have risen within two generations from worker to technician and from technician to manager. The latter change, effected in one generation, gives a truer picture of the leading class in France than any over-simplified talk about the 'two hundred families'.

Finally, the wage-earner feels less cut off from the management now that his work is no longer purely manual and his life is no longer cramped by poverty.

It is true that France still has a fringe of unskilled workers who sell their labour by the day, with no security as to the future, and feel united to their kind by the bond of wretchedness. Most of them are foreigners – Poles, Italians, and above all North Africans. But they are in a minority.

Subject to a lesser degree of 'alienation', dealing with managers who are either salaried employees or part-owners, the French wage-earner of the twentieth century is less tempted to become a militant than were his nineteenth-century forerunners – the more so because their struggle has led to a change in the behaviour of the employers, a change in institutions and the introduction of planning. This may be regrettable, but there is no point in looking at today's world from the angle of the nineteenth century, as so many Socialists do. We shall do better to consider what it has to teach us.

II. THE CLASS STRUGGLE AND THE SOCIAL BALANCE IN FRANCE

There can be no doubt that it was the very violent pressure exerted by the trade unions even before the end of the nineteenth century which brought home to employers and to government circles the urgent need for radical changes. That pressure is still effective, particularly in conjunction with the resolve not to add fuel to the fire of Communist propaganda, and this must be remembered, though without denying that technological changes have played their part in hastening and consolidating reform.

The struggle against low wages and pauperization originated with the workers. Nowadays it has the approval of the most dynamic managements. A sense of economic solidarity has led them to regard the wage-earner as their first customer, and to agree to higher wages, as the textile industry recently showed. Social Security, too, has finally been accepted as a means of regularizing purchasing power and keeping the nation in good health; poor and unhealthy people cannot be active producers and consumers.

Every election programme is now based on the fight to eliminate unemployment and crises, initiated by the workers' organizations. For although unemployment keeps wages down, its victims consume very little and therefore make bad customers. A crisis has repercussions on industry, and entails losses. In advocating a high level of production, the dynamic industrialist is automatically advocating regular prosperity and growth.

Growth has become the overriding concern of the French leaders. The will to progress is gradually replacing the caution of an earlier period, when it was felt that one should not go too fast. The comparison with the Soviet economy also points to the necessity for peaceful competition.

Planning owes its inception to concern for full employment and expansion. It became clear at an early date that there could be no hope of an improvement in the economic situation without specific development projects, co-ordinated by official intervention. The United States Employment Act of 1946, which set up the Council of Economic Advisers to supervise economic activity and prepare stringent measures to be applied by the Government in the event of a crisis, makes it clear, as do the various publications issued by the *Commissariat du Plan* in France, that expansion without crises could only be achieved by a partial surrender of sacrosanct liberalism.

Even the French employers who came to accept planning only after it had begun, now agree without hesitation that it has done a great deal to stabilize the economic situation.

The Plan puts business men in a better position to prepare and apply balanced long-term programmes of investment and production; the actual forecasts of expansion it provides are a guide to them. Again, thanks to the Plan, consumers can anticipate what new needs they will be able to satisfy, can demand higher incomes and spend enough to absorb output. State intervention, too, becomes more effective.

Thus, by facilitating the creation of a number of institutions, first and foremost the *Commissariat du Plan*, the class struggle has contributed to the country's growth and stability. Far from hastening the destruction of the capitalist system, it has so far helped to reinforce it.

However, it cannot be denied that in other ways the class struggle is a danger to growth; it entails risks that planning should be able to avert.

III. THE CLASS STRUGGLE AS A FACTOR RETARDING GROWTH: ROLE OF THE PLANS

Unless the capitalist system expands smoothly and rapidly, it cannot survive in the world of today. In peaceful competition between their growth-objectives, the Soviet and Western world are fighting for the survival of their respective systems just as definitely as in an atomic war. A comparative falling-off in the rate of French expansion would mean that we could no longer ensure the development of the overseas territories, and they would thus feel more strongly drawn towards the Soviet-style totalitarian systems. The converse applies in the case of those systems.

If the class struggle were to slow down expansion, it would lead to the downfall of our institutions as inexorably as the process of self-destruction predicted by Marx.

What are the factors by which the rate of growth of the Western economies is at present determined?

FACTORS OF GROWTH

Apart from natural wealth and a dynamic atmosphere, the principal condition of growth is a general harmony between the rates of development of the population, of production and of investment of the product of growth. The existence of the Plan, with a consistent government policy to offset short-period monetary disturbances, helps managements to establish that harmony.

The groups concerned must all abide by the rules, however, and it is essential, in particular, to make full provision for the investment on which future output directly depends. This becomes impossible if private consumption exceeds the share of production allocated to it, and thus encroaches upon the share which should be used for investment.

But, it will be asked, cannot the State regulate income distribution through taxation and budgetary measures, in such a way that the general public will consume enough to absorb output but not more? This over-simplified view of political economy is based on the mistaken and old-fashioned belief that consumption depends upon, and is governed by, the income distributed.

CONSUMPTION AND SOCIAL GROUPS

This belief was propagated by Keynes and all the analyses which tie consumption to real income by elasticity coefficients. But if we read the classical economists or observe the present situation in France, we discover that to argue in this way is to ignore the stimulus provided by variations in individual needs and the pressure exercised by the different groups in order to satisfy them.

Seeking to detect the causes of the stagnation of expenditure in the nineteenth century, Malthus notes that '. . . . wants and tastes, and [a] desire to consume . . . are absolutely necessary to keep up the market prices of commodities, and to occasion an increasing demand for them, and for the capital which is to produce them.'[2] And he says elsewhere that it is the lack of variety in domestic commodities which leads to the stagnation of needs: '. . . if goods could be produced at home, which would . . . communicate the same enjoyments, and create a consumption of the same *value*, foreign markets would be useless.'[3] He includes weak incentives among the factors of stagnation. The situation is very different nowadays.

We know that the technical revolution produces goods which in the European countries, and particularly in France, stimulate demand to an extent that outstrips productive capacity. It is no longer necessary to travel abroad in order to find new things; appetites are whetted at home by the attractions of housing, tourism, hygiene, sport, motor-cars and so forth; greater transport facilities and glimpses of how rich people live reveal new things to covet; and needs are also stimulated by the prospects of economic growth revealed in the Plans. The more optimistic the forecasts of progress, the more rapidly they bring about changes in the demand for goods. It is safe to say that in France at present there is no prospect that demand will stagnate; the danger lies, on the contrary, in its fundamental tendency to increase faster than productive capacity.

If demand is to increase, the need felt must be able to find expression through a monetary purchase, the expenditure of income received. Nowadays, group pressure is enabling the individual to demand the income necessary for this. Even the wage-earners are not obliged, as they were in the nineteenth century, to keep their expenditure within the limits of whatever income the community is prepared to grant them. The worst-off sections of the population have united to defend their rights, thus setting an example which has not been wasted.

The formation of groups to present demands is becoming widespread, in different forms.

The *entrepreneurs*, regarded as consumers, have always occupied a privileged position. Their power to make investments puts them in control of what is really a public service, and brings in an income from which – especially in large companies – they can deduct a

[2] T. R. Malthus, *Principles of Political Economy*, p. 448. [3] ibid., p. 412.

proportion for themselves and their closest collaborators. They thus add to their private consumption in a way that is not open to criticism. This applies even in nationalized firms and in the Socialist countries; for though the entrepreneurs are then only salaried employees, they remain all-powerful. When they are owners, the mere increase in property which results from investment, whether in a big farm or in a factory, inevitably leads to an increase in their consumption. Whether or not the State is a Socialist one, their position is strengthened by the large measure of independence they have to be allowed if the very concept of business leadership is not to disappear; and the Eastern countries, which rejected that concept for a long time, learnt to their cost that it is indispensable. When business leaders unite to demand tax concessions or aid towards investment, they can use part of this assistance to add to their income or that of their creditors, and thus increase consumption. They disguise their demands by talking about the national interest and the development of their firms. Even without making demands they can unobtrusively increase prices, where these are not controlled. The strength of their position has been shown by the experience of the past few years. If the State lays heavier burdens on them, or withholds its aid, investment will decline. Little can be done to control rising consumption.

The *farmers*, when they demand higher prices and incomes, or tax rebates on their investments, are profiting, though to a lesser extent, by a similar confusion between the need for investment and the desire for a higher standard of living.

The *wage-earners*' demands are presented more directly, and the increase in their consumer expenditure is easier to estimate. In the low-income groups, at any rate, increased income in the form of wages cannot be obtained without an open struggle, though high-grade staff have more discreet methods of bringing pressure to bear.

At present the tendency to 'ask for more' is spreading like an epidemic. Strangely enough, it is aggravated by the existence of statistics and predictions about the increase of incomes, which make everyone feel he is not getting as much as the other fellow. Particularly since (I shall return to this later) all newspapers, and the spokesmen for all branches and levels of activity, make it their daily purpose to persuade their readers, to whatever class they may belong, that they are being unfairly treated, and display a shocking dishonesty in manipulating the statistics to serve their own ends. This attitude of 'divide and rule' is reducing the entire population of France to a state of 'psychological frustration' in which they feel themselves under-privileged, though the purchasing power of the majority has risen by over 25 per cent in the last five years. Expansion may be dangerously slowed down by this state of things.

CONSUMPTION AND GROWTH

All these demands are a burden on the Budget. Housing subsidies, tax rebates on consumer goods and wage-increases in the public and semi-public sectors, obtained by direct demand, create deficits which are swelled by investment subsidies, decentralization loans and loans for different types of equipment.

To this cause of inflation must be added the price-increases due to the widening of trading and manufacturing margins and to higher wages. Excessive purchasing power is also liable to drive up the prices of consumer goods and reduce investment.

The State, its Budget already swollen by expenditure relating to consumption, cannot increase its investments to keep pace with rising prices. Indeed, it is reducing them. Twice in six months, in the spring and autumn of 1957, the Government had to cut public investment because they were swamped by demands from different quarters. Producers cannot always increase their capital equipment – indeed, as Adam Smith pointed out long ago, they frequently sacrifice it in the interests of their consumption, especially in branches where prices are frozen. The manufacturers of capital goods are therefore likely to pass over this sector and concentrate on the consumer industries, with their rapid expansion.

In one way or another, consumption encroaches on investment. The latter is increasing, but not as fast as future security requires. The most serious aspect of this situation is that because some types of onerous investment need from ten to twenty years to produce results, governments jettison these first of all – though they are the most important – in order to escape the consequences of their policy. For example, with our present large fuel imports and our housing shortage we are paying the penalty of neglect of basic investment in the pre-war years.

If consumption increases beyond what was predicted, there is little the French Government can do about it. The Government cannot control those – so many in this country – who make capital gains or increase their margins of profit; any peremptory reduction of profit-margins by price-control, or of self-financing by taxation, leads to a decline in investment, not in consumption. Wages are easier to supervise, since they are the only form of income that cannot escape detection.

But the attempt to control them, even if it goes by the name of 'national wage-policy', will always be opposed by the wage-earners' organizations, who consider, quite rightly, that their members should not be the only people to have their consumption cut down.

There are several dead-ends a government may explore before it adjusts its plans to the reduced volume of capital goods available. It may allow the foreign trade balance to deteriorate by buying abroad, on credit, what cannot be manufactured at home. But in the autumn of 1957 the French Government discovered that such a policy and such a deficit have their limits. Another expedient is to allow prices to rise and thus reduce the consumers' purchasing power, in the hope that the incomes of at least some of them – the less well-organized and the less astute – will lag behind prices. But this policy of tolerated inflation not only victimizes the weakest section of the community, it may also disorganize the whole system of production.[4]

In point of fact it is virtually impossible to resist the pressure exerted by different groups to secure a rise in consumption so rapid as to outstrip the necessary investment. Such pressure does not cause a crisis, but it periodically slows down expansion. The only possible remedy is for the different groups to agree on a plan.

THE PLAN AS A MEANS OF AGREEMENT AMONG THE SOCIAL GROUPS

The role of planning is not to put an end to the class struggle, but to guide it in the direction of collective progress.

It has become obvious that the State can do little to control the increase in consumption. The average standard of living has improved, but the Government still has to grapple with all the different groups at once – with the farmers, who want higher prices; the manufacturers, who complain of rising costs; the workers and employees, who clamour for more pay. If all these demands receive

[4] That is why a Socialist government refused to accept a sliding scale of prices and wages, which they had formerly advocated but which might have led to rapid inflation, always a disaster for the small wage-earner.

satisfaction, as they probably will, investment is likely to be reduced and the national expansion considerably slowed down.

Whereas if private consumers would only adjust their consumption to current possibilities, their future standard of living could be all the higher.

The only form of constraint available to the executive is an inadequate means of limiting group demands. Even in the People's Democracies, increasing consumption has burst its bounds and compelled the Government to make changes in the rates of expansion originally planned.

One step towards a solution might be to focus the group struggle, in a small way, upon the Plan, so that behaviour could be adapted to the requirements of expansion.

This would call, at the outset, for an appreciation of the very close connection between the present situation and the future, and of the value of reaching agreement. The Plan encourages this by indicating the conditions on which development must depend.

There are unmistakable signs that matters are already taking this turn.

Though the short-term struggle between workers and employers still goes on, a number of longer-term agreements have recently been signed, in which both parties set aside their means of coercion and adopt measures to protect their respective incomes and the prosperity of the firm. The 'Renault' agreements, which are typical of these, provide for a limitation of the right to strike, for wage increases and practical advantages, and give evidence of an awareness that growth requires united effort.

The groups concerned are more prepared than formerly to allow for the long-term necessities of national equilibrium. A section of the public, having followed the discussions that take place in the Modernization Commissions and the Economic Council with regard to the preparation of the Plan and to compliance with its forecasts, has become keenly aware of the desirability of harmonious development. People have not forgotten the years between 1945 and 1951, when the pressure groups drove incomes up in a chaotic manner and everyone suffered from the ensuing inflation.

This sense of union in development explains why the workers' and employees' organizations kept their demands within comparatively modest limits at a time (1954–1958) when the price-index was being almost officially 'cooked'. They know that part of what is not paid out in wages goes to build up reserves for investment on which their own future prosperity depends. Public investment, such as that in the nationalized firms, which accounts for nearly half of French equipment expenditure, has helped to win acceptance for this idea, which had been obscured by the private ownership of the means of production. With or without inflation, any ill-regulated rise in wages represents a danger to the future. But would the unions agree to rates of remuneration laid down in a 'social plan', even if the other groups in the community were ready to do so?

By taking part in the work of the Commissions, the manufacturers' and farmers' organizations showed their interest in these long-term forecasts and it affected their attitude. They should go further and allow the public authorities to control their incomes.

That is the crux of the problem. The Plan has brought all the groups a step forward, and now, while not renouncing their means of defence, they realize the usefulness of a proper co-ordination of economic policy and of organization at a level above the struggle in which they are engaged. But they will not agree to control of remuneration unless it applies to everybody.

The present means of enforcement of the Plan do not, for instance, allow self-financing to be controlled to an extent that would convince the workers that all parties were pulling their weight. To strengthen those means is the first requisite if planning is to cover remuneration and lead to more harmonious expansion.

But even if the Plan were made appreciably more effective, would the trade unions and the large firms be willing to depart from their traditional policies? A long experience of frustration in the past makes the former cling to their aggressive attitude, while the latter cherish their freedom of action. Yet there can be no advance beyond the present Plan without some such undertaking, even if it covered only part of the field.

The class struggle has not so far destroyed capitalism. As a result of technical changes it has led to institutions such as the Plan, which have profoundly modified the system and increased its stability.

But the advance to a new stage of economic development is conditional upon a reinforcement and extension of the present Plans, and the question is, whether French opinion is in favour of achieving this by bringing remuneration under control.

General Conclusion

THE PLAN reflects a far-reaching transformation of the economic machinery, if not of the economic structure.

Liberated from certain inconsistencies, expansion seems to be speeding up. Until quite recently, it was disturbed by periodical depressions, with their train of unemployment and poverty, and that state of things was universally taken for granted. Now the different groups base their conduct on long-term forecasts and are trying to stabilize economic life. Their structure has changed considerably and – partly under the influence of technical progress – they have altered their behaviour.

They used to take a short-sighted, egotistical attitude towards such matters as production and investment; now they tend to fit in with the long-term forecasts of a national and international system in which the State asks them to observe at least some small degree of collective discipline. Their action used to be static, confined to the regular exchange of goods; it has now become dynamic, inasmuch as it is directed towards achieving maximum expansion by the projection of activities into the future.

The entrepreneur's attitude to fluctuations is typical. Formerly – and even today in some countries – an employer reacted to a decline in trade by dismissing redundant workers. The increasingly strict regulation of the conditions of employment now compels the entrepreneur to transfer his risks to his machinery. Chronic over-investment makes it possible to deal with peak demand. Many examples of this are to be seen in the United States. To avoid having to dismiss workers, managements prefer not to take them on; instead, they maintain a reserve of productive capacity. In France the Plan offers a general frame of reference, plots a line of development that everyone is supposed to follow, and thus narrows the margin of uncertainty regarding future expansion. So far, of course, the information provided is only quantitative. Studies of price-trends are much to be desired. But it must be acknowledged that an acquaintance with the Plans is already enabling managements and the nation to avoid under-employment of men and investments.

We may go further and suggest that the Plans, which express this tendency of the different groups to strive for future prosperity through united action in the present, may be a sign that capitalism is changing. The greater powers conferred upon the State are not, as Stalin asserted, merely the result of the leaders' determination to thrust the workers into the background and fight first against Germany and then against the Soviet Union.[1] If the employers' and workers' associations are beginning to allow the State to intervene by establishing development forecasts and working them into a Plan, it is because they are confusedly aware that collective long-term action will be to their advantage. Experience seems to bear them out, for a journalist behind the iron curtain declares: 'The role of distributor of the national revenue has devolved in France upon the State administration (though this is still the instrument of the power of a particular class) through planning, an appropriate policy of taxation, etc. The French State plays this part none too well, but efficiently enough to contribute to the development of prosperity, however slowly and inconsistently, and thus to *tone down one of the fundamental contradictions in the capitalist system*.'[2]

In spite of the class struggle, organization is playing an ever greater part in the capitalist world.

It must be remembered, however, that the Plan is not a panacea; its fulfilment will not create perfection; other institutions are necessary and the Plan is no substitute for these. Moreover, it has defects which cannot be remedied without institutional, political and ideological changes at national and international level.

Among the *institutional changes* we will mention only those affecting the ownership of property. Experience in the iron curtain countries has shown the dangers accompanying general collectivization, such as loss of the incentive to work. But the private ownership of certain means of production leads to self-financing, which is not always compatible with the general interest and sometimes hampers the public authorities in their decisions. It also raises the problem of distribution, for any increase in investment puts more capital into the hands of one section of the population.

[1] Stalin, quoted by H. Chambre in *Le Marxisme en Union soviétique*, Editions du Seuil, Paris 1956, pp. 412–416.

[2] See M. Swymansky, 'Comment les Français établissent-ils leur plan?' in *Zyxie Warszawy*, 22 November 1956.

It remains difficult to ask the wage-earners to make sacrifices in order to add to other people's wealth. As a result of nationalization, the community now provides nearly 50 per cent of investment, and this has made the problem less acute, though it still exists.

The *political changes* are needed to intensify public participation, which is essential to the fulfilment of a flexible Plan, where decisions are to be accepted rather than enforced. The general public is not directly committed by its parliamentary representatives. The attitude of a trade union leader is more likely to win the support of a whole group.

In France, parliamentary representation has been paralleled by a kind of direct confrontation of interests in the Economic Council and the Modernization Commissions, but there are several flaws in this system. Being regarded as a method of group self-protection, and considered by some of the workers' representatives to have a bias towards reform, its effect is limited.

The different groups have not ceased, even temporarily, to demand increases in income which militate against the fulfilment of the Plan. This is because the Plan itself is still too alien to them. In Holland the trade unions took a more active share in things and, by accepting considerable sacrifices, made it possible for reconstruction to be achieved without inflation. Their example gives food for thought.

The French system not only fails to unite the different interests to full effect; it has the further drawback that the groups are not bound by decisions taken in the Commissions. While the Plan is in operation, the unions do not hesitate to bring pressure to bear, openly or furtively, on the administration or on Parliament, in order to secure concessions relating to credit, taxes or prices. To defeat this spontaneous tendency of the different interests to 'double-cross' one another, the Plan – or some other body with general powers – should be more closely linked to the executive and have real authority to co-ordinate economic policy.

If the *Commissariat du Plan* were given fuller powers, the Plan would be more effective. This would put an end to the dispersion of effort among the various Ministries – which is reduced but not prevented by the *Commissariat général* – and to a great deal of inconsistent and unhelpful administrative interference. It would relieve group pressure on the individual departments of the Civil Service. And it would facilitate supervision, without which the different interests cannot be expected to conform to the decisions that are reached. For how can manufacturers, farmers and wage-earners be asked to accept temporary financial restrictions when – as is the case today – some people are not subject to any form of supervision, even by the tax authorities?

There should also be more active participation in the political control of the Plan. The French parliamentary experience of the last few years has been disappointing. The two Chambers have shown little initiative in economic matters, and debates on the subject were attended only by a small minority of members – except on a few occasions, when the defence of local or professional interests received as much prominence as the concern for national prosperity. As a result, greater reliance is now placed on group representation and 'direct democracy'. But this invariably has a corporative aspect, which should not be forgotten. The present tendency is to advocate a skilful combination of both forms of representation – parliamentary and group. Is this a satisfactory compromise? Yes, if the democratic spirit is kept in evidence at the summit and in the firms. But no institutional structure, however ingenious, will get over the contradiction involved in calling for democracy at the national level and rejecting it at the level of the firms, as we in France are doing at present.

Lastly, the participation of the general public, or at least their awareness that the Plan exists and has its importance, is needed to offset the dangers with which the Plan inevitably threatens the political life of the country. One of these dangers is the emergence of a form of 'technocratic' power which, even if not exercised by technicians, would compel the individual citizens to comply with decisions taken without their consent, in obedience to alleged 'technical necessities'. The other is the danger that the individual may be crushed by a centralized system which would deny him the right to choose even in his own area of competence, where his liberty should be manifest.

The success of a plan also depends on *ideological changes*. The individualistic outlook is still dominant in politics, because economic theory is still based on eighteenth-century philosophy.

Despite what has already been said about changed behaviour, our political power is still cankered by a spirit which is individualistic and – in the widest sense of the term – radical. The general interest is still regarded as the sum of individual interests, however shabby they may be. Economic decisions are thus paralysed by a respect for individual liberties which are often outdated. The State needs the permission of the various groups if it is to act as arbiter, for it has to move among their different interests without trampling on any of them. The groups have an exaggerated idea of their rights and privileges, and their organizations pander to this. Listening to his leaders' speeches, reading his newspaper and observing the attitude of his party in Parliament, every Frenchman becomes convinced that he is getting a raw deal. The systematic distortion of statistics, and the skilful exploitation of marginal groups – certain firms, the unskilled workers, the small farmers – not only safeguard the jobs of certain leaders, who 'have the best interests of those groups at heart', but set up among our countrymen, most of whom live very comfortably, a serious psychological frustration which prompts them to push their claims at the expense of national development.

Economic theory too often paints a utopian picture of a world populated by individuals acting rationally in the sole light of their personal interests: individualism, rationalism and empiricism remain abstract ideals in a shadowy background, as they were with Jevons and Edgeworth in the nineteenth century. The theory fails to allow for new types of behaviour and technological advances. An illusory form of economic progress and its expression in drastically simplified equations will not make this image more realistic.

Economic thought is not only individualistic but anti-evolutionary. The physical and mathematical sciences have expressed the universe in the form of fixed equations in stable equilibrium, and this fully agrees with the picture of the world presented to us by this lingering philosophy. The idea of evolution and continuous progress, put forward by biology and history, encounters violent opposition, particularly as it has been associated from the first with materialistic concepts which denied the Creation. As a result, some of the thinkers who draw their inspiration from religion have allied themselves with the opponents of evolutionary theory. Despite present-day references to St Thomas,[3] who maintained that the creation was subsequent to the world, that it is

[3] The present tendency is to differentiate clearly between evolution, which is a matter of before and after, and creation, which is a problem of above, beyond, of meta-history – evolution being to creation what the secondary causes are to the primary causes. See Moretti, 'Le virus et la synthèse de la vie', in *Etudes*, April 1956.

merely an attribute of the world and of God who existed in the beyond, the anti-evolutionary attitude still finds wide acceptance, nourished by a certain indifference to worldly progress and by the fear of authoritarian determinism and collectivism.

This mental block is strengthened by the existence of Marxism, with its praise of collectivism and of a materialistic concept of evolution. The clash of ideas in France stiffens the class hostility which makes a rational reorganization of society so difficult. The wage-earners' struggles have undoubtedly been useful – as we have seen, they had a share in creating new institutions, such as the Plan – but they are now in danger of paralysing development.

It is less important to put an end to an inauspicious form of philosophy than to provide ideological support for the Plan, which has no meaning in itself alone.

Planning is successful in 1962 because it seems to be filling an ideological vacuum. But the Plan cannot exist without a certain political and philosophical content, consisting of decisions as to how the economy is to be guided, how incomes are to be distributed, what attitude is to be adopted towards the neutrals, etc. Unless these decisions are made, there is reason to fear that certain plans, grafted onto traditional economic and sociological concepts, will be no more than myths, discrediting the very idea of planning. A sociological study of decision, penetrating behind the façade of 'new policy', would discover conservative attitudes which alone are really decisive.

If we are to maintain a planned economy in France changes will have to take place not only in that country itself, but at the European level. As the economic frontiers are thrown open, entire sectors – energy, transport, motor vehicles, iron and steel, shortly to be joined by the chemical industry – are being swept into an international strategy aimed at the conquest of markets.[4] Unless

[4] 'European forecasting is becoming all the more necessary because national plans and programmes are growing more and more difficult to prepare and there is a danger that once the Common Market is set up, they may lose much of their significance. For a plan, or programme, assumes the existence of an economy whose relations with foreign countries are limited, or can be restricted in case of need. But the six economic systems of the Common Market are destined to become, to an increasing extent – and within a few years, completely – economies thrown open to Europe.' M. R. Marjolin, speaking at Arcachon, 25 May 1962.

international competition is regulated by European institutions, these sectors will be torn away from the French Plan and subjected to the alleged laws of international competition, or brought into the supranational plans devised by large private groups.

True, the French Plan cannot remain unchanged in a context of European unity. It will gradually become the programme of France, of one region in a greater area. But unless European planning takes over from it, French programming will fall back.[5] There can be no doubt that the spirit of the Treaty of Rome, and its actual application, are still somewhat unfavourable to planning, even after the distinct change evidenced during 1962. In order to bring about the ideological, institutional and political modifications which will be necessary at the European level, it is essential to preserve our economic system from contamination by other systems under cover of the Common Market. We must not, of course, go to the extreme of an autarchy which would reject Europe and justify the slogan 'Planning against Europe'. But an organized Europe will not be brought into existence simply by abolishing the French Plan.

[5] M. Lebrun, *Le Monde*, 17 August 1962 (*Tribune libre*).

Appendixes

APPENDIX I

LEGAL PROVISIONS RELATING TO THE ROLE AND OPERATION OF THE BODIES RESPONSIBLE FOR THE PLAN

I

Decree No. 46–2, of 3 January 1946, setting up a Council for the *Plan de modernisation et d'équipement*, to be responsible to the Head of the Government, and defining the attributions of the Commissioner-General for the Plan.

(*Journal Officiel*, 4 January 1946)

The President of the Provisional Government of the Republic,

Having regard to Act No. 45–1, of 24 November 1945, relating to the prerogatives of the Ministers of the Provisional Government of the Republic and the organization of the ministries;

Having regard to the Order of 23 November 1944, reorganizing the Economic Committee and determining the powers of the Minister of National Economy and the organization of his Ministry;

Having regard to the Decree of 7 July 1945, setting up the Interministerial Committee for German and Austrian Affairs;

Having regard to the Act of 13 August 1936, Article 5, paragraphs 2 and 3, determining the status of heads of mission attached to the Office of the Prime Minister;

The Council of State having been heard;

Gives Order:

ARTICLE 1. – Within six months of the date of publication of this Decree, there shall be drawn up a first general Plan for the modernization and economic equipment of metropolitan France and the overseas territories.

The particular purpose of this Plan shall be:

1. To increase output in metropolitan France and the overseas

territories and their trade with the rest of the world, more especially in those products in which their position is most favourable.

2. To raise the productivity of labour to the level of those countries where it is highest.

3. To ensure full employment of the labour force.

4. To raise the standard of living of the population and to improve housing conditions and the circumstances of community life.

The Plan shall cover the reconstitution of the public and private plant and equipment damaged or destroyed as a result of the war.

ARTICLE 2. – A Council for the Plan shall be set up, to be responsible to the Head of the Government, and shall make proposals to the Government concerning the Plan and the means of ensuring its fulfilment.

The said Council shall comprise:

The President of the Provisional Government of the Republic (Chairman)
The Minister of National Economy (Vice-Chairman)
The Minister for Foreign Affairs
The Minister of Armaments
The Minister of Finance
The Minister of Agriculture and Supplies
The Minister of Industrial Production
The Minister of Public Works and Transport
The Minister of Labour
The Minister for the Colonies
The Minister of Reconstruction and Town-Planning
The Commissioner-General for German and Austrian Affairs
The Commissioner-General for the Plan.

Not less than twelve and not more than fourteen persons selected in consideration of their special qualifications and appointed by Order of the Head of the Government after consultation with the Minister of National Economy.

The Rules of Procedure of the Council for the Plan shall be laid down in an Order to be promulgated by the Head of the Government.

ARTICLE 3. – The *Commissariat général* thus attached to the Office of the Head of the Government shall be directed by a Commissioner-General who shall be appointed by decree.

The Commissioner-General shall prepare the proposals to be submitted to the Council for the Plan for their consideration. He shall be the permanent delegate of the Head of the Government to the ministerial departments for all matters regarding the preparation of the Plan. The Commissioner-General for the Plan shall be an *ex officio* member of the Economic Committee, the Interministerial Committee for German and Austrian Affairs, the National Economic Council and the National Credit Council.

ARTICLE 4. – The Commissioner-General shall address any inquiries he may deem advisable to the public offices and, with their co-operation, to the workers' and employers' associations, to industrialists and farmers, and to such other bodies and individuals as he may think fit to consult.

The public offices and other bodies connected with the operation of public services shall furnish him with all the statistical and other information he may request.

The appropriate Ministers shall give him their support in the fulfilment of his task, particularly with a view to the preparation of a general account, and shall transmit to him the production programmes already drawn up for the various branches of the national economy.

As from the issue of this Decree, all programmes relating to the country's economic activity, and more especially those concerned with production, reconstruction, armaments, investment, foreign trade and the requisitioning of enemy property by way of reparations, which are prepared by the appropriate ministerial departments, shall be communicated to the Commissioner-General. The Commissioner-General shall be informed of all projects in course of preparation.

ARTICLE 5. – The Commissioner-General for the Plan shall submit to the Head of the Government Orders providing for the appointment of working committees and co-ordinating committees, to be composed of senior officials of the Ministries represented on the Council for the Plan, and of modernization commissions comprising representatives of the administration, experts, and representatives of the trade unions and employers' associations.

ARTICLE 6. – During the period of preparation of the Plan, the Ministry of National Economy shall put the services of the following bodies at the disposal of the Commissioner-General: the *Institut de Conjoncture* (Institute for the Study of the Economic Situation), the *Service de l'Equipement* (Investment Service), and the *Service des Monographies* (Monographs Service) attached to the National Centre of Economic Information. These bodies shall follow all instructions and undertake all work for which they are called upon by the Commissioner-General for the Plan. For purposes of management and finance, however, they shall continue to form part of the Ministry of National Economy.

ARTICLE 7. – The *Commissariat général* shall comprise, under the authority of the Commissioner-General, certain heads of mission whose status is defined by Article 5, paragraphs 2 and 3 of the Act of 13 August 1936.

ARTICLE 8. – All provisions conflicting with those of this Decree are hereby abrogated.

ARTICLE 9. – The Minister of National Economy, the Minister of Armaments, the Minister of Finance, the Minister for Foreign Affairs, the Minister of Agriculture and Supplies, the Minister of Industrial Production, the Minister of Public Works and Transport, the Minister of Labour, the Minister for the Colonies and the Minister of Reconstruction and Town-Planning shall be responsible, each in his own province, for the application of this Decree, which shall be published in the Official Gazette of the French Republic.

Given at Paris, this third day of January 1946.

By the President of the Provisional Government of the Republic:

C. DE GAULLE

The Minister of National Economy, FRANÇOIS BILLOUX.

The Minister of State, Acting Minister for Foreign Affairs, FRANCISQUE GAY.

The Minister of Armaments, CHARLES TILLON.

The Minister of Finance, R. PLEVEN.

The Minister of Agriculture and Supplies, TANGUY-PRIGENT.

The Minister of Industrial Production, MARCEL PAUL.

The Minister of Public Works and Transport, JULES MOCH.

The Minister for the Colonies, JACQUES SOUSTELLE.

The Minister of Labour, A. CROIZAT.

The Minister of Reconstruction and Town-Planning, RAOUL DAUTRY.

II

Decree No. 47–119, of 16 January 1947, on the methods of fulfilment of the *Plan de modernisation et d'équipement*, in which the functions of the Council for the Plan and the Commissioner-General for the Plan are defined.

The President of the Provisional Government of the Republic,

Acting on the report of the Minister of State entrusted, as the delegate of the President of the Government, with the functions of Chairman of the Council for the Plan;

Having regard to Act No. 45–1, of 24 November 1945, relating to the powers of the Ministers of the Provisional Government of the Republic and the organization of the Ministries;

Having regard to the amended Order of 23 November 1944, reorganizing the Economic Committee and defining the powers of the Minister of National Economy and the organization of his department;

Having regard to Decree No. 46–2, of 3 January 1946, setting up a

Council for the *Plan de modernisation et d'équipement* to be responsible to the Head of the Government, and defining the powers of the Commissioner-General for the Plan;

The Council of State having been heard;

Gives Order,

ARTICLE 1. – The provisions of the above-mentioned Decree of 3 January 1946, setting up a Council for the *Plan de modernisation et d'équipement*, to be responsible to the Head of the Government, and defining the powers of the Commissioner-General for the Plan, shall be supplemented, with a view to the fulfilment of the Plan, by the following provisions:

ARTICLE 2. – The Council for the Plan shall propose to the Government, for the whole territory of the French Union, annual programmes covering production, the distribution of essential raw materials, reconstruction, investment, imports and exports.

These programmes shall be submitted to the Council for the Plan by the Commissioner-General, who shall be responsible for co-ordinating their preparation and for adapting them to the framework laid down by the Plan and to the resources available.

ARTICLE 3. – The Commissioner-General shall be responsible for supervising the fulfilment of the Plan. Should he consider that its fulfilment may be jeopardized for whatsoever reason, he shall inform the competent Ministers and, if need be, shall carry the matter before the Prime Minister and the Interministerial Economic Committee.

Important decisions affecting the fulfilment of the Plan or its adjustment in the course of the year, such as those relating to the distribution of essential materials, shall be prepared by the appropriate public offices and other bodies, in agreement with the various sections of the *Commissariat général du Plan.*

ARTICLE 4. – Every six months, the Commissioner-General shall submit to the Council for the Plan a report on the progress achieved towards the fulfilment of the Plan; this report shall be made public. Any important amendments it may be advisable to make to the annual programmes shall be submitted to the Council on this occasion.

ARTICLE 5. – The Directorate of Economic Programmes at the Ministry of National Economy shall be at the disposal of the Commissioner-General for the Plan in all matters pertaining to his duties. The Directorate is hereby instructed to carry out such tasks as may be assigned to it by the Commissioner-General for the Plan, as delegate of the Prime Minister. From the standpoint of administration and finance, it shall continue to form part of the Ministry of National Economy.

ARTICLE 6. – In the exercise of his powers, the Commissioner-General acts as the permanent delegate of the Prime Minister to the ministerial departments and organs concerned. He shall be assisted by a Standing Committee of the Council for the Plan, the members of which shall be appointed by an Order of the Prime Minister. He shall have the further assistance of the working committees, the co-ordinating committees and the modernization commissions set up by the above-mentioned Decree of 3 January 1946.

ARTICLE 7. – All provisions conflicting with those of this Decree are hereby rescinded.

ARTICLE 8. – The Minister for Foreign Affairs, the Minister of the Interior, the Minister of National Defence, the Minister of National Economy and Finance, the Minister of Agriculture, the Minister of Industrial Production, the Minister of National Education, the Minister of Public Works, Transport and Reconstruction, the Minister of Postal, Telegraph and Telephone Services, the Minister for Overseas France, the Minister of Labour and Social Security and the Minister for Public Health and Population shall be responsible, each in his own province, for the application of this Decree, which shall be published in the Official Gazette of the French Republic.

Done at Paris, this sixteenth day of January 1947.

By the President of the Provisional Government of the Republic, Minister for Foreign Affairs: LÉON BLUM.

Decree No. 47–119, on the methods of fulfilment of the *Plan de modernisation et d'équipement*, in which the powers of the Council for the Plan and the Commissioner-General for the Plan are defined.

Correction to the *Journal officiel* of 17 January 1947, page 590, col. 3, among the signatures.

After:

The Minister of State, GUY MOLLET,

Insert:

The Minister of State, FÉLIX GOUIN.

III

Decree No. 51–1417, of 11 December 1951, prescribing the preparation of a second *Plan de modernisation et d'équipement* and defining the attributions of the Commissioner-General for the Plan.

(*Journal officiel*, 12 December 1951)

The Prime Minister,

Having regard to the Act No. 45–1, of 24 November 1945, on the prerogatives of Ministers and the organization of the ministries;

Having regard to Decrees No. 46–2, of 3 January 1946, and 47–11, of 16 January 1947, defining the powers of the Commissioner-General for the Plan,

The Council of State having been heard,

Gives Order:

ARTICLE 1. – Within six months of the date of publication of this Decree, there shall be prepared a Second General Plan for the modernization and the economic and social equipment of metropolitan France and the overseas territories. This Plan shall cover the period 1952–1956 and shall have as its particular purpose the increase of agricultural and industrial production and productivity considered in relation to a European Community.

The Commissioner-General for the Plan is hereby instructed to draft proposals to this end, in consultation with the Ministries and public and private bodies concerned in the matter, and to submit those proposals to the Government.

ARTICLE 2. – The Commissioner-General for the Plan shall have the further duty of providing for the study of questions which necessitate a general view of the long-term development of the French economy and the repercussions of its prospective integration in an economic system directed by supranational institutions. He may also arrange for the study of any question put before him by the Prime Minister.

ARTICLE 3. – The Minister of National Defence, the Minister of Finance and Economic Affairs, the Minister of State for Relations with the Associated States, the Minister for Foreign Affairs, the Minister of the Interior, the Minister for the Budget, the Minister of National Education, the Minister of Public Works, Transport and Tourism, the Minister for Industry and Power, the Minister for Trade and Foreign Economic Relations, the Minister of Agriculture, the Minister for Overseas France, the Minister of Labour and Social Security, the Minister of Reconstruction and Town-Planning, the Minister of Public Health and Population, the Minister of Postal, Telegraph and Telephone Services, the Minister of the Merchant Navy and the Deputy-Minister of National Defence shall be responsible, each in his own province, for the application of this Decree, which shall be published in the Official Gazette of the French Republic.

Done at Paris, this eleventh day of December 1951.

By the Prime Minister: R. PLEVEN.

The Deputy Prime Minister, Minister of Finance and Economic Affairs, R. MAYER.

IV

Decree No. 61–729, of 12 July 1961, setting up a Higher Council for the Economic and Social Development Plan.

The Prime Minister,

Acting on the report of the Minister of Finance and Economic Affairs,

Gives Order:

ARTICLE 1. – A Higher Council for the Plan shall be hereby established, with the Prime Minister as its Chairman.

ARTICLE 2. – The Higher Council for the Plan shall be kept informed of the different phases in the preparation of the Plan. It shall draw up a report on the draft Plan prepared by the Commissioner-General for the Plan, before it is referred to the Government and considered by the Economic and Social Council.

It shall annually consider the reports on the fulfilment of the Plan. It shall compare the results with the objectives selected for the principal activities and the different regions, and propose to the Government any measures calculated to ensure the fulfilment of the Plan, with especial regard to its social objectives.

The Government may further instruct the Higher Council for the Plan to undertake any study connected with the application of the Plan.

ARTICLE 3. – The Minister of Finance and Economic Affairs and the Chairman of the Economic and Social Council shall be *ex officio* Vice-Chairmen of the Higher Council for the Plan.

ARTICLE 4. – The composition of the Higher Council for the Plan shall be as follows:

1. The Governor of the *Banque de France*.
2. The Chairman and the two Vice-Chairmen of the Planning and Investment Section of the Economic and Social Council.
3. Eight members of the *Commission des Comptes de la Nation* (Commission for the National Accounts), to be appointed by the Economic and Social Council.
4. The Chairmen of seven of the recognized regional Economic Expansion Committees, appointed by rota for a twelve-month period, in the alphabetical order of the 'regional action' districts.

5. The Chairman of the Permanent Assembly of the Chambers of Commerce and Industry;

The Chairman of the Permanent Assembly of the Chambers of Agriculture;

The Chairman of the Permanent Assembly of Chambers of Trades.

6. Qualified representatives of the following organizations, to be appointed by the Government in consultation with the said organizations:

The *Conseil national du patronat français* (employers' association);

The *Confédération générale des petites et moyennes entreprises* (association of small firms);

The *Fédération nationale des syndicats d'exploitants agricoles* (National Federation of farmers' unions);

The *Confédération nationale de la mutualité, de la coopération et du crédit agricole* (farmers' mutual aid association);

The *Cercle national des jeunes agriculteurs* (Young Farmers' Club);

The *Confédération générale des cadres* (federation of associations of executive and supervisory personnel);

The *Confédération générale du travail – Force ouvrière;*

The *Confédération française des travailleurs chrétiens*;

The *Confédération générale du travail.*

7. Specially qualified persons, appointed by Order of the Prime Minister and the Minister of Finance and Economic Affairs, their number not to exceed one-third of the total membership of the Council. These shall include the Chairmen of four of the Modernization Commissions of the Plan.

ARTICLE 5. – *Ex-officio* members are appointed for the period during which they remain in office. Members appointed by the Government shall serve on the Council for four years.

ARTICLE 6. – Ministers shall attend meetings of the Higher Council for the Plan at which matters affecting the sectors for which they are responsible are discussed.

ARTICLE 7. – The Commissioner-General for the Plan shall act as Rapporteur to the Higher Council. Secretarial services for the Council shall be provided by his staff.

ARTICLE 8. – This Decree shall be published in the Official Gazette of the French Republic.

Done at Paris, this twelfth day of July 1961.

The Prime Minister: MICHEL DEBRÉ.

The Minister of Finance and Economic Affairs, WILFRID BAUMGARTNER.

V

Establishment of an Interministerial Committee for the Economic and Social Development Plan.

The Prime Minister and the Minister of Finance and Economic Affairs

Give Order:

SINGLE ARTICLE. – There shall be hereby established an interdepartmental committee, to be known as the Interministerial Committee for the Economic and Social Development Plan, which shall be responsible to the Prime Minister and instructed to follow the preparation and fulfilment of the Plan.

This Committee, of which the Prime Minister shall be Chairman, to comprise the following members: the Minister of Finance and Economic Affairs, and the Ministers responsible for the activities covered by the Economic and Social Development Plan. The Commissioner-General for the Plan and the Chief of Staff of National Defence shall participate in the work of the Interministerial Committee.

As and when the need arises, the Committee shall call upon the services of persons with an expert knowledge of the questions on the agenda.

Secretarial services for the Interministerial Committee shall be provided by the Secretariat-General of the Government.

Done at Paris, this eleventh day of July 1961.

The Prime Minister: MICHEL DEBRÉ.

The Minister of Finance and Economic Affairs, WILFRID BAUMGARTNER.

VI

Act No. 62–900, of 4 August 1962, approving the Economic and Social Development Plan.[1]

[1] Act No. 62–900.
National Assembly:
Bill No. 1573.
Letters correcting the Plan (Nos. 1728 and 1783);
Report by M. Marc Jacquet, on behalf of the Finance Commission (No. 1712);
Opinion of the Production Commission (No. 1707);
Opinion of the Cultural Commission (No. 1714);

The National Assembly and the Senate have adopted, and

The President of the Republic hereby promulgates the law set forth below:

ARTICLE 1. – The fourth Plan, known as the Economic and Social Development Plan, appended to this Act, is hereby approved as the framework of the investment programmes for the period 1962–1965 and as the instrument determining the direction to be followed by economic expansion and social progress.

In this latter respect, its aims shall be:

On the one hand, to improve the circumstances of the under-privileged categories of the population, such as old people, those with family responsibilities, repatriates, small farmers, self-employed craftsmen and low-wage groups;

On the other hand, to speed up economic and social progress in the under-developed regions.

ARTICLE 2. – Before issuing its instructions to the Commissioner-General for the Plan, the Government shall submit to Parliament a Bill approving a report on the principal options in the light of which the Plan must be drawn up from the standpoint of territorial development, particularly those relating to:

Economic expansion;

The division of gross domestic production between investment and consumption;

The most desirable pattern of final consumption;

The lines to be followed in social and in regional policy.

Debates of 22, 23, 24 and 29 May 1962 and 6, 7, 14, 19, 20 and 21 June 1962;
Adopted 21 June 1962.

Senate:

Bill adopted by the National Assembly, No. 237 (1961–1962);
Letters correcting the Plan, Nos. 274 and 275 (1961–1962);
Reports, submitted on behalf of the Commission for Economic Affairs and the Plan, No. 238 (1961–1962);
Opinion of the Cultural Commission, No. 239 (1961–1962);
Opinion of the Social Commission, No. 243 (1961–1962);
Opinion of the Finance Commission, No. 247 (1961–1962);
Debates of 3, 4, 5, 6, 9, 10, 11 and 12 July 1962;
Adopted 12 July 1962.

National Assembly:

Bill amended by the Senate (No. 1850);
Report by M. Marc Jacquet on behalf of the Finance Commission (No. 1857);
Debate and adoption, 23 July 1962.

ARTICLE 3. – In the Report accompanying the annual Finance Bill, which describes the economic and financial balance, the known results and the prospects for the future, the Government shall make known the stage reached in the fulfilment of the Economic and Social Development Plan, with the measures taken to apply it, the results obtained, the difficulties encountered and any amendments which may appear necessary.

The Finance Bill shall furthermore be accompanied by a General Appendix giving a general recapitulation of the financial effort for which the State Budget makes provision with a view to completing the successive operational stages into which it has been decided to divide the fulfilment of the Economic and Social Development Plan.

This document, to be tabled not later than 1 November, shall comprise:

A recapitulation of loans granted, programmes authorized and deferred payment terms arranged, for each economic and social sector;

A recapitulation of the same credit arrangements for each region of the programme.

This Law shall have the force of a State Law.

Given at Colombey-les-deux-Eglises, this fourth day of August 1962.

By the President of the Republic: CHARLES DE GAULLE.

The Prime Minister: GEORGES POMPIDOU.

The Minister of Finance and Economic Affiairs, V. GISCARD D'-ESTAING.

APPENDIX II

1

LEGAL PROVISIONS RELATING TO THE ESTABLISHMENT OF THE ECONOMIC AND SOCIAL DEVELOPMENT FUND (F.D.E.S.)

Decree No. 55–875, of 30 June 1955, establishing an Economic and Social Development Fund (*Journal Officiel* No. 156, 2 July 1955).

The Prime Minister,

Acting on the report of the Minister of Finance and Economic Affairs,

. . . .

Having regard to the Act of 2 April 1955, conferring special powers upon the Government in economic, social and fiscal matters,

The Council of State having been heard,

The Cabinet Ministers having been heard,

Gives Order:

ARTICLE 1. – A single Fund, entitled 'The Economic and Social Development Fund', shall be hereby established to finance the projects set forth in the Plan for Modernization and Equipment and in the regional action programmes, and in particular those relating to construction, rural equipment and economic expansion, to increase of productivity, to industrial or agricultural conversion, to the resettlement of workers and to the decentralization of industry.

This Fund shall replace the various Funds by which these functions have so far been carried out and, subject to the conditions set forth in the following articles, shall have the same resources at its disposal.

ARTICLE 2. – The Economic and Social Development Fund shall be under the management of the Minister of Finance, assisted by a Governing Body whose composition shall be fixed by decree.

The Governing Body shall be entitled to delegate part of its functions to specialized committees.

The powers hitherto vested in the Committee described in Article II of the Decree of 14 September 1945 shall be transferred to one of these specialized committees, having the same composition.

ARTICLE 3. – The Economic and Social Development Fund, which is a special-purpose Fund opened in the books of the Treasury, shall comprise four sections:

1. Section for the equipment of industry, agriculture, trade and tourism.

This section shall be responsible for loans to firms, bodies or local authorities which carry out the investment programmes advocated in the Plan for Modernization and Equipment and in the regional action programmes.

2. Section for industrial and agricultural adaptation and industrial decentralization.

This section shall be responsible for:

– loans granted to firms to enable them to convert their activity, to achieve greater concentration, or to specialize;

– loans granted to industrial firms to facilitate construction, extension or transfer programmes contributing to the decentralization of industry.

3. Productivity section.

This section shall be responsible for loans to help in financing schemes calculated to increase the productivity of the firms concerned.

4. Construction section.

The construction section shall be responsible for State loans for the construction of dwellings, meeting specifications determined in Orders to be issued by the Finance Minister for Reconstruction and Housing, and in particular for the enforcement of the legislation governing the *H.L.M.* (*habitations à loyer modéré* – low-rent housing).

Such loans shall continue to be granted to the H.L.M. societies, subject to the conditions stipulated by Article 196 of the Town-Planning and Housing Code.

The construction section shall receive:

(1) Sums paid into the Fund under Article 2 of Decree No. 53–701, of 9 August 1953, on the participation of employers in the building campaign, together with the amount of the subscriptions mentioned in Article 3 of the said Decree.

(2) Payments made by the Treasury as a counterpart to the annually authorized borrowing by the Finance Ministry to finance the loans it makes to the Building Societies for the construction of low-rent dwellings.

ARTICLE 4. – The Finance Minister is hereby authorized to issue, during the year 1955, loans to finance housing construction, industrial, agricultural and tourist equipment and, in general, the investment programmes advocated in the Plan for Modernization and Equipment; such loans to be charged against sections 1 and 4 of the 'Economic and Social Development Fund' and not to exceed the total of expenditure authorized for the Construction, Rural Investment and Economic

Expansion Fund by Law No. 55–359 (3 April 1955) on Special Treasury Accounts for the year 1955.

ARTICLE 5. – The Economic and Social Development Fund shall be operated in accordance with the rules laid down in Articles 42, 44, 45 and 46 of Law No. 53–1336 (31 December 1953) on Special Treasury Accounts for the year 1954.

The provisions of Article 12 of Law No. 48–406 (21 March 1948) amended by Article 14 of Law No. 55–359 (3 April 1955) shall likewise be applicable to the operation of the Fund.

ARTICLE 6. – The rules laid down in Decree No. 53–656, of 30 July 1953, setting up the National Productivity Fund, shall apply to section 3 of the Economic and Social Development Fund.

However, the opinion of the Investment Commission, required by Article 2 of the Decree of 30 July 1953, shall be replaced by the opinion of the Governing Body of the Economic and Social Development Fund.

ARTICLE 7. – The Governing Body of the Economic and Social Development Fund shall give the opinion called for by Article 35 of Law No. 53–79 (7 February 1953).

ARTICLE 8. – As from 1 January 1955, the special investment account opened by Article 40 of Law No. 53–1436 (31 December 1953) shall be known as 'Treasury Payments to the Economic and Social Development Fund'.

It shall be divided into three parts: the first for payments intended to finance loans for the construction of H.L.M., the second for payments intended to finance loans for the equipment of industry, agriculture and tourism, and the third for payments intended to finance loans to firms under the programme of decentralization of industry.

ARTICLE 9. – As from 1 January 1955, the special purpose account opened by Article 41 of Law No. 53–1336 (31 December 1953) shall be known as 'Resources allocated to the Economic and Social Development Fund'. In addition to the sums specified by the above-mentioned Article 41, this account shall receive the sums appropriated in the Budget to finance loans for industrial and agricultural conversion.

ARTICLE 10. – The Cabinet, acting on reports from the Finance Minister or other Ministers concerned, shall be entitled to issue Decrees making available to the Development Fund the resources of various existing special Treasury accounts of a similar character, the Fund to assume responsibility for the corresponding charges.

ARTICLE 11. – The conditions of application of this Decree shall be established as need arises by a Decree adopted by the Council of State and countersigned by the Minister of Finance and Economic Affairs, the Minister of Public Works, Transport and Tourism, the Minister of Industry and Trade, the Minister of Labour and Social Security, the Minister of Reconstruction and Housing, the Minister of Agriculture and the Secretary of State for Finance and Economic Affairs.

ARTICLE 12. – This Decree shall come into application on 1 September 1955.

ARTICLE 13. – Subject to their remaining in force for the implementation of decisions adopted prior to 1 September 1955, the following are hereby rescinded:

– Decrees No. 48–964, of 10 June 1948 and No. 48–1762, of 19 November 1948;

– Article 8 C and Article 9 of Law No. 53–611 (11 July 1953);

– Article 43 of Law No. 53–1336 (31 December 1953) on the Treasury accounts for the year 1954;

– Decree No. 54–951, of 14 September 1954, the purpose of which was to facilitate the adaptation of industry, the retraining of manpower and the decentralization of industry, in so far as it conflicts with the provisions of the present Decree, and, in general, all provisions which conflict with this Decree.

ARTICLE 14. – All agreements concluded by the Minister of Finance and Economic Affairs, the Minister of Industry and Trade, the Minister of Labour and Social Security, the Minister of Public Works, Transport and Tourism and the Minister of Reconstruction and Housing with a view to carrying out the transactions of the Fund for Construction, Rural Equipment and Economic Expansion, the Fund for the Conversion of Industry, the Fund for the resettlement of Manpower and Section B of the Territorial Development Fund, shall be applicable in all respects to the transactions of the Economic and Social Development Fund.

ARTICLE 15. – The Minister of Finance and Economic Affairs . . . shall be responsible, each in his own province. . . .

EDGAR FAURE

2

LEGAL PROVISIONS RELATING TO THE OPENING AND OPERATION OF THE ACCOUNT ENTITLED 'LOANS BY THE ECONOMIC AND SOCIAL DEVELOPMENT FUND'

I

Finance Act for 1960, No. 59–1454, of 26 December 1959. (*Journal Officiel*, 26 and 27 December, page 12,363).

ARTICLE 87. – There shall hereby be opened on the books of the Treasury a special loan account entitled 'Loans of the Economic and Social Development Fund', which shall be administered by the Minister of Finance and Economic Affairs.

The debit side of this account shall show disbursements in respect of the loans granted for the fulfilment of the Plan for modernization and equipment and for the productivity, conversion and decentralization programmes; the credit side shall show the capital sums repaid by the borrowers.

Within the limits of the receipts from the repayment of loans granted for the development of productivity, further credits may be opened in the course of the year, under the account mentioned in paragraph 1 of this Article, by order of the Minister of Finance and Economic Affairs.

The balance outstanding at 31 December 1959 in the special-purpose account known as the 'Economic and Social Development Fund', established by Articles 1 and 3 of Decree No. 55–875 of 30 June 1955 and closed by Article 88 of the present Law, may be used in full to finance the opening in 1960, by order of the Minister of Finance and Economic Affairs, of supplementary credits under the account entitled 'Loans of the Economic and Social Development Fund' opened by the present Article.

ARTICLE 88. – 1. The special accounts or subdivisions of special accounts listed below shall be permanently closed on 31 December 1959:
Treasury Payments to the Economic and Social Development Fund;
Resources allocated to the Economic and Social Development Fund;
Economic and Social Development Fund

II

Decree No. 60–703, of 15 July 1960, organizing the special account entitled 'Loans from the Economic and Social Development Fund' (*Journal Officiel*, 21 July 1960).

The Prime Minister,

Acting on the report of the Minister of Finance and Economic Affairs:

Having regard to Order No. 59–2, of 2 January 1959, formulating an organic law relating to the Finance Acts, and in particular to Articles 23 and 29 of that Order;

Having regard to Article 87 of the Finance Act for 1960 (No. 59–1454, of 26 December 1959),

Gives Order:

ARTICLE 1. – The special loan account entitled 'Loans from the Economic and Social Development Fund', opened by Article 87 of the Finance Act for 1960, shall record all disbursements in respect of loans granted to businesses, industrial firms or collectivities which are pursuing investment schemes intended either to promote the objectives laid down in the Plans for modernization and equipment, or to carry out specific projects in such matters as productivity, regional action, conversion and decentralization.

On the credit side, it shall record capital repayments on the said loans and capital repayments on loans granted by the Fund for Modernization and Equipment, the Fund for Construction, Rural Equipment and Economic Expansion, and the Economic and Social Development Fund.

ARTICLE 2. – Decisions for the allocation of funds shall be announced by an Order of the Minister of Finance and Economic Affairs, who shall take into consideration the proposals made by the Governing Body of the Economic and Social Development Fund regarding the distribution of funds available for loan. The sums lent shall be transferred to the beneficiaries either direct, by the Treasury, or through the specialized establishments.

The terms of these loans shall be specified in agreements to be concluded between the Minister of Finance and Economic Affairs, of the one part, and the establishment or the direct borrower, of the other part.

ARTICLE 3. – Within the framework of the above-mentioned agreements, the establishments authorized to act as intermediaries shall be permitted to carry out transactions of two types:

1. They may use the funds lent to them from the special account to make loans at their own risk, the rates of interest and conditions of

redemption being governed by the legislation or regulations in force and by the statutes of the establishment concerned;

2. They may use the sums put at their disposal to grant loans on behalf and at the risk of the Treasury, the rates of interest and duration of such loans being determined by the Minister of Finance and Economic Affairs, acting on the opinion of the Governing Body of the Economic and Social Development Fund.

ARTICLE 4. – The loan credits to be available in the special account entitled 'F.D.E.S. Loans' shall be announced annually in the Finance Act. They may be augmented:

a. By the addition of all or part of any loan appropriations not yet allocated at 31 December of the preceding year, within the limits established by orders for the carrying forward of such sums, signed by the Minister for Finance and Economic Affairs;

b. by the appropriations for 'miscellaneous State loans', transferred by Orders signed by the Minister of Finance and Economic Affairs;

c. By the amount of the credits opened during the year by an Order of the Minister of Finance and Economic Affairs, up to the total of receipts paid into special-purpose accounts, either as repayments of loans granted by earlier funds, or in the form of resources allocated to those accounts and intended as security for loans. These augmentations shall be conditional upon the exhaustion of the corresponding appropriations made to the special-purpose accounts.

ARTICLE 5. – Within the special account, the loans shall be classified as follows:

0. Agriculture;
1. Energy;
2. Transport;
3. Private industries;
4. Outside metropolitan France;
5. Special loans;
6. Conversion, decentralization;
7. Productivity.

In each sector, the loans shall be divided into different lines.

The full nomenclature of the special account shall comprise the list of sectors and lines, the name of the borrower and the category of the loan.

These data shall be given decimal numbers for the purpose of mechanical classification.

ARTICLE 6. – The methods of application of this Decree shall be announced as need arises, by instructions issued jointly by the Directorate of the Treasury and the Directorate of Public Accounts.

ARTICLE 7. – Decree No. 55–1367, of 18 October 1955, organizing the Economic and Social Development Fund, is hereby rescinded.

ARTICLE 8. – The Minister of Finance and Economic Affairs shall be responsible for the enforcement of this Decree, which shall be published in the Official Gazette of the French Republic.

Done at Paris, this fifteenth day of July 1960.

By the Prime Minister: MICHEL DEBRÉ.

The Minister for Finance and Economic Affairs, WILFRID BAUMGARTNER.

APPENDIX III

STRUCTURE AND ORGANIZATION OF THE GOVERNING BODY OF THE ECONOMIC AND SOCIAL DEVELOPMENT FUND

The Investment Commission, established by Decree No. 48–964, of 10 June 1948, amended by Decree No. 48–1762, of 19 September 1948, was replaced, as from 1 September 1955, by the Governing Body of the Economic and Social Development Fund, established by Article 2 of Decree No. 55–875, of 30 June 1955.

I. COMPETENCE

(*a*) The Governing Body exercises the general functions formerly entrusted to the Investment Commission in regard to public investments or investments financed from public funds.

Decree No. 55–1368, of 18 October 1955, states among other things that the Governing Body shall consider the investment programmes of the public offices and public corporations, and any investment programmes financed with the direct or indirect assistance of the State. The Governing Body is to give its opinion regarding the order of priority and speed of execution of the work to be undertaken, and the most appropriate method of financing it.

Before 30 September of each year, the programmes to be carried out during the following year are submitted to it.

In the course of the year, it considers any proposals for the revision of these programmes. It is periodically informed of the stage reached in their fulfilment.

(*b*) The Governing Body assists the Finance Minister in the administration of the Economic and Social Development Fund established by Article 1 of Decree No. 55–875 (30 June 1955).

The Council is called upon for its opinion regarding the amount and distribution of the Fund's authorized annual expenditure.

It gives its opinion on the allocation of loans by the Fund and on the terms of such loans.

The agreements concluded with the establishments which act as agents for these loans are submitted to the Governing Body.

(*c*) Certain special functions have been conferred upon the Governing Body of the Fund in connection with the policy of conversion and the policy of regional action:

– by virtue of Article 2 of Decree No. 55–875 (30 June 1955), the Governing Body exercises the functions formerly devolving upon the Committee appointed by Article II of the Decree of 14 September 1954, in matters concerning conversion, the decentralization of industry and the retraining of manpower;

– by virtue of Article 3 of Decree No. 55–874 (30 June 1955), the Governing Body gives its opinion regarding the allocation of the sums appropriated in the budget of the Ministry of Labour for vocational retraining and for the payment of indemnities to workers moving to another area;

– by virtue of Article 4 of Decree No. 55–876 (30 June 1955), the Governing Body gives its opinion regarding the minimum-dividend guarantee which may be given to the regional development companies; the Order of 7 October 1955 states that agreements concluded between the Finance Ministry and the regional development companies shall be drawn up after consultation with the Governing Body of the Fund.

The Governing Body is asked to consider the work programme of companies wishing to obtain a guarantee of dividend, and the different opinions which are to be expressed on this programme by the terms of Article 3 of the Order of 7 October 1955.

The public administration regulations set forth in Decree No. 55–877, of 30 June 1955, provide that official recognition of associations of industrial managers shall be contingent upon their approval by the Governing Body of the Economic and Social Development Fund.

The Governing Body is called upon for its opinion as to the award of the special investment bonus provided by Decree No. 55–878, of 30 June 1955, for firms which set up or enlarge their business in critical areas suffering from serious and permanent under-employment or from insufficient economic development.

Lastly, Article 1 of Decree No. 55–874, of 30 June 1955, requires the Governing Body to give its opinion on the guarantees and interest remittals granted by the State to loans raised to finance measures of conversion, concentration, specialization or decentralization, or any other operation conducive to regional development.

(*d*) Various other functions have since been entrusted to the Governing Body.

By virtue of Article 1 of Decree No. 57–967 (29 August 1957), the Governing Body is consulted on the question of whether companies may deduct from their taxable profits any dividends paid on the occasion of issues of new capital made before 31 December 1961.

By virtue of Article 6 of the Act of 29 March 1958, the approval of the

Governing Body must be obtained by firms applying for a reduction of their licensing fees.

The Governing Body gives its opinion, or approval, concerning the granting of various tax exemptions for which provision is made in Articles 3, 4 and 5 of Order No. 38–382 (25 September 1958) on taxation in connection with scientific and technological research.

Article 44–1 of Order No. 58–1372 (29 December 1958) stipulates that the Governing Body shall give its views as to which of the 'mixed economy' companies concerned with investment or territorial development shall be dispensed from registration fees and turnover tax on sales of real estate following the conclusion of development and investment schemes.

By virtue of Article 4 of Decree No. 59–733 (16 June 1959), the Governing Body grants the loans for which provision is made in Article 2 of that Decree, to assist in financing French films and contributing to improvements in cinemas operated by small proprietors.

Article 2 of Decree No. 60–560 (14 June 1960), on the granting of the State guarantee for which provision is made in Article 90 of the Finance Act for 1960, states that the Governing Body shall give its opinion on the award of that guarantee to loans contracted by private firms with a view to facilitating the economic and social development of the Member States of the French Community.

II. MEMBERSHIP

The membership of the Governing Body of the Fund, laid down by Decree No. 55–886, of 30 June 1956, amended by Decree No. 57–52, of 17 January 1957, Decree 58–575, of 5 July 1958, and Decree No. 59–826, of 4 July 1959, is as follows:

The Minister of Finance and Economic Affairs or his representative (Chairman);

The Secretary of State for Economic Affairs or his representative (Vice-Chairman);

The Secretary of State for Finance or his representative;

The Minister for Industry and Trade or his representative;

The Minister of Agriculture or his representative;

The Minister of Public Works, Transport and Tourism, or his representative;

The Minister of Labour and Social Security or his representative;

The Minister of Construction or his representative;

The Governor of the *Banque de France*;

The Chairman-Director-General of the *Crédit National*;

The Governor of the *Crédit Foncier*;

The Commissioner-General of the *Plan d'Equipement et de la Productivité*;

The Director-General of the *Caisse des Dépôts et Consignations*;

The Director-General of the *Caisse Nationale de Crédit Agricole*;

The Director-General of Prices and Economic Surveys;

The Director of the Treasury;

The Director of the Budget.

Ministers who are not members of the Governing Body take part in its discussions of matters within their province.

The Commissioner for Construction and Town-Planning also takes part in the discussion of all matters concerning the Paris area.

The Directorate of the Treasury provides the Secretariat of the Governing Body.

Applications are investigated by the appropriate technical Ministry.

The work of the Governing Body is prepared by twelve specialized committees. At a meeting held on 21 October 1955, the Governing Body decided that any unanimous expression of opinion by one of these specialized committees on a specific matter should have the force of an opinion from the Governing Body, which need only be informed thereof.

The following list gives an up-to-date version of the structure, membership and functions of the specialized committees set up by the Governing Body of the F.D.E.S., taking into account the reorganization of the committees responsible for State aid to private firms, and measures adopted in other respects.

Specialized Committee No. 1

Subject: State intervention on behalf of investment by industrial and commercial firms in the private sector.

Chairman: The Commissioner-General for the Plan for Investment and Productivity.

Membership: A representative of the Secretary of State for domestic trading;

The Director of Industrial Expansion at the Ministry of Industry;

The Director of Territorial Development at the Ministry of Construction;

The Director-General of Labour and Manpower;

A representative of the Governor of the *Banque de France*;

The Chairman-Director-General of the *Crédit National*;

The Director-General of the *Caisse des Dépôts et Consignations*;

The Director of the Treasury.

Representatives of the Minister of the Interior, the Minister of Public

Works and Transport, the Minister of Agriculture and the Minister responsible for Scientific Research take part in the work of the Committee during the discussion of subjects within their respective provinces. The Prime Minister may also be represented when he deems it advisable.

The Budget Directorate attends meetings of Committee No. 1 when the latter is allocating subsidies to facilitate investment for purposes of technological research. Similarly, the Director-General of Taxes attends any meetings at which the agenda includes questions involving tax concessions.

Secretariat: The Secretary of the Governing Body of the F.D.E.S.

Committee No. 1 *bis* (acting on the authority of Committee No. 1).

Subject: Allocation of any financial advantages granted by the State to promote investment in certain branches of activity.

Applications for loans, guarantees or bonuses submitted by firms or groups in certain branches of industry;

Loans for the investment in hotels, from the *Caisse centrale de crédit hôtelier, industriel et commercial* (Central fund for loans to hotels, industrial and commercial establishments);

Applications for loans, tax concessions or subsidies to promote scientific or technological research;

Applications from individual firms or from professional organizations in a particular branch to be admitted to the system of quasi-contracts introduced in the interim Plan.

Chairman: The Chairman and Director-General of the *Crédit National.*
Membership:

The Directorate of Industrial Expansion at the Ministry of Industry;

The Directorate of Territorial Development at the Ministry of Construction;

The Directorate-General of Labour and Manpower;

The Secretariat of State for domestic trade;

The Commissariat-General of the Plan for Investment and Productivity;

The *Banque de France*;

The *Crédit National*;

The *Caisse des Dépôts et Consignations*;

The Directorate of the Treasury.

Secretariat of the Governing Body of the F.D.E.S.

Representatives of other Government Departments attend meetings of the Committee for the discussion of matters within their respective provinces.

Secretariat: *Crédit National.*

Committee No. 1 *ter* (acting on the authority of Committee No. 1).

Subject: Allocation of any financial advantages granted by the State to promote regional development, productivity, and collective investment for the tourist industry.

Applications for special investment bonuses, loans, interest rebates and guarantees to facilitate conversion, specialization or industrial decentralization;

Applications for change-of-residence grants and subsidies for vocational retraining;

Applications for productivity loans;

Operations to promote collective investment in the tourist industry.

Chairman:

The Director-General of the *Caisse des Dépôts et Consignations.*

Membership:

Directorate of Industrial Expansion at the Ministry of Industry;
Directorate of Territorial Development at the Ministry of Construction;
Directorate-General of Labour and Manpower;
Secretary of State for domestic trade;
Directorate-General of local authorities at the Ministry of the Interior;
Commissariat-General of the Plan for Investment and Productivity;
Banque de France;
Crédit National;
Caisse des Dépôts et Consignations;
Directorate of the Treasury;
Secretariat of the Governing Body of the F.D.E.S.

A representative of the Prime Minister also takes part in the work of this Committee.

Secretariat: Caisse des Dépôts et Consignations.

Representatives of other Government Departments attend meetings of the Committee for the discussion of matters within their respective provinces.

Sub-committee acting on the authority of Specialized Committees 1 *bis and* 1 *ter.*

Subject: Tax exemption for capital increases and tax concessions for subsidiaries.

Chairman:

The representative of the Commissioner-General of the Plan for Investment and Productivity.

Membership:

The representative of the Commissioner-General for the Plan for Investment and Productivity;

The representative of the Director-General of Taxes;
The representative of the Director of the Treasury;
The representative of the Director of Economic Relations with Foreign Countries;
The representative of the Minister of Industry and Commerce;
The representative of the Minister of Construction (Directorate of Territorial Development);
The representative of the *Crédit National*;
The Secretariat of the Governing Body of the F.D.E.S.

Secretariat:
Commissariat-General of the Plan for Investment and Productivity.

Specialized Committee No. 2
Subject: Ways and means of financing investment by local authorities.

Chairman:
A member of the Council of State (M. VOIZARD).

Membership:
Ministry of the Interior;
Ministry of Agriculture;
Ministry of National Education;
Ministry of Construction;
Ministry of Public Health;
Ministry of Public Works and Transport;
Directorate of the Budget;
Directorate of the Treasury;
Commissariat-General of the Plan for Investment and Productivity;
Crédit Foncier de France;
Directorate-General of Prices and Economic Surveys;
Caisse des Dépôts et Consignations;
Secretariat of the Governing Body of the F.D.E.S.

Meets at the offices of the Commissariat-General of the Plan for Equipment and Productivity.

Secretariat:
Direction de l'Administration départmentale et communale (Directorate of Departmental and Municipal Administration), at the Ministry of the Interior.

Committee No. 2 *bis.*
Subject: Preparation of multi-annual programmes for collective investment in urban areas; preparation of annual lists of priority operations and statement of an opinion on the financing of those operations; consideration of plans for financing large housing projects.

Chairman:
The representative of the Commissioner-General for the Plan for

Equipment and Productivity (M. GOETZE, Deputy-Governor of the *Crédit Foncier*).

Membership:

Ministry of the Interior;
Ministry of Agriculture;
Ministry of National Education;
Ministry of Construction;
Ministry of Public Health;
Ministry of Public Works and Transport;
Directorate of the Budget;
Directorate of the Treasury;
Commissariat-General of the Plan for Equipment and Productivity;
Directorate-General of Prices and Economic Surveys;
The Commissioner for Construction and Urban Development of the Paris area;
Crédit Foncier de France;
Caisse des Dépôts et Consignations;
Secretariat of the Governing Body of the F.D.E.S.

Secretariat:

Commissariat-General of the Plan for Investment and Productivity.

Committee No. 2 *ter.*

Subject: Co-ordination of urban investment in the provinces and programmes for large housing estates.

Chairman:

The representative of the Commissioner-General for the Plan for Investment and Productivity (M. BLOT, Deputy-Governor of the *Crédit Foncier*).

Membership:

Ministry of the Interior;
Ministry of Agriculture;
Ministry of Industry;
Ministry of National Education;
Ministry of Construction;
Ministry of Public Health and Population;
Ministry of Public Works and Transport;
Directorate of the Budget;
Directorate of the Treasury;
Crédit Foncier de France;
Caisse des Dépôts et Consignations;
Commissariat général of the Plan for Equipment and Productivity;
Directorate-General of Prices and Economic Surveys;
Secretariat of the Governing Body of the F.D.E.S.

Secretariat:
Commissariat général of the Plan for Equipment and Productivity.

Specialized Committee No. 3.
Subject: Reconstruction and construction.
Chairman:
The Governor of the *Crédit Foncier*.
Membership:
Ministry of Construction;
Directorate of the Treasury;
Directorate of the Budget;
Commissariat général of the Plan for Investment and Productivity;
Directorate-General of Prices and Economic Surveys;
Banque de France;
Caisse des Dépôts et Consignations;
Sous-comptoir des Entrepreneurs;
Secretariat of the Governing Body of the F.D.E.S.
Secretariat:
Crédit Foncier de France.

Specialized Committee No. 4.
Subject: Fuel and power, with particular reference to the investment programmes of the nationalized companies (*Charbonnages de France*, *Electricité de France*, *Gaz de France*), the municipal gas and electricity systems and the *Compagnie nationale du Rhône*.
Chairman:
The representative of the Commissioner-General for the Plan for Investment and Productivity.
Permanent members of the Committee:
Ministry of Industry;
Directorate of the Treasury;
Directorate of the Budget;
Commissioner-General for the Plan for Investment and Productivity;
Directorate-General of Prices and Economic Surveys;
Representatives of each of the nationalized firms whose programmes are subject to the approval of this Committee (*Charbonnages de France*, *Electricité de France*, *Compagnie nationale du Rhône*, *Gaz de France*, *Gaz du Sud-Ouest*, *Société nationale des Pétroles d'Aquitaine*, *Commissariat a l'Energie atomique*).
Secretariat of the Governing Body of the F.D.E.S.

Specialized Committee No. 5.
Subject: Award of the State guarantee to loans floated to promote

the development of the overseas departments and territories, the States of the Community and the States linked to France by an association agreement.

Membership:

Ministry responsible for relations with the State or territory concerned;

Department of Overseas Economic Affairs at the Secretariat of State for domestic trade;

Caisse centrale de Coopération économique (Central Fund for Economic Co-operation);

Crédit National;

Commissariat général of the Plan for Investment and Productivity;

Directorate of the Budget;

Directorate of the Treasury;

Secretariat of the Governing Body of the F.D.E.S.

A representative of the Secretariat-General for Aid and Co-operation attends meetings of the Committee when the agenda includes the consideration of an application for the guarantee of a loan contributing to the financing of investment in States within the competence of that body.

The Directorate of foreign Finance attends meetings of the Committee when the agenda includes the consideration of applications for the guarantee of loans raised abroad or from international organizations.

Secretariat:

Caisse centrale de Coopération économique.

Specialized Committee No. 6.

Subject: Agriculture.

Chairman:

The representative of the Commissioner-General of the Plan for Investment and Productivity.

Membership:

Ministry of Agriculture;

Directorate of the Budget;

Directorate of the Treasury;

Directorate-General of Prices and Economic Surveys;

Caisse nationale de Crédit Agricole;

Crédit National;

Secretariat of the Governing Body of the F.D.E.S.

Secretariat:

Commissioner-General of the Plan for Investment and Productivity.

Specialized Committee No. 8.

Subject: Transport questions, with special reference to the S.N.C.F. (French National Railways), civil aviation (Air France, purchases of aeronautical equipment in foreign countries, Paris airport); the merchant navy, trading ports, sea-routes, local railways and public transport in towns, including the R.A.T.P. (Paris transport system).

Chairman:

The representative of the Commissioner-General for the Plan for Equipment and Productivity.

Membership:

Ministry of Public Works and Transport;
Secretariat-General for Civil Aviation;
Secretariat of State for domestic trade;
Commissariat général of the Plan for Investment and Productivity;
Directorate of the Budget;
Directorate of the Treasury;
Representatives of each of the nationalized firms (S.N.C.F., Air-France, Aéroport de Paris, R.A.T.P.) and other bodies whose programmes are subject to the approval of this Committee;
Secretariat of the Governing Body of the F.D.E.S.

Secretariat:

Commissariat général of the Plan for Investment and Productivity.

Specialized Committee No. 12.

Subject: Allocation of loans to the film industry.

Chairman:

The Chairman and Director-General of the *Crédit National.*

Membership:

The Governor of the *Banque de France*;
The Director of the Treasury;
The Director-General of the National Film Centre;
The Deputy Director in charge of production at the National Film Centre;
A representative of the *Crédit National.*

Secretariat:

Crédit National.

Decree No. 55–886, of 30 June 1955, on the composition and functioning of the Governing Body of the Economic and Social Development Fund.

The Prime Minister,

Acting on the report of the Minister of Finance and Economic Affairs, the Minister of Public Works, Transport and Tourism, the Minister of Industry and Trade, the Minister of Labour and Social Security, the Minister of Reconstruction and Housing, the Minister of Agriculture and the Secretary of State for Finance and Economic Affairs.

Having regard to Decree No. 55–875, of 30 June 1955, establishing an Economic and Social Development Fund,

Gives Order:

ARTICLE 1. – The Governing Body referred to in Article 2 of Decree No. 55–875, of 30 June 1955, establishing an Economic and Social Development Fund, shall be composed as follows:

– the Minister of Finance or his representative (Chairman);

– the Secretary of State for Economic Affairs or his representative (Vice-Chairman);

– the Secretary of State for Finance and Economic Affairs or his representative;

– the Minister of Industry and Trade or his representative;

– the Minister of Agriculture or his representative;

– the Minister of Public Works, Transport and Tourism or his representative;

– the Minister of Reconstruction and Housing or his representative;

– the Minister of Labour and Social Security or his representative;

– the Governor of the *Banque de France*;

– the Chairman-Director-General of the *Crédit National*;

– the Governor of the *Crédit Foncier*;

– the Commissioner-General for the Plan;

– the Commissioner-General for Productivity;

– the Director-General of the *Caisse des Dépôts et Consignations*;

– the Director of the Treasury;

– the Director of the Budget.

ARTICLE 2. – Ministers who are not members of the Governing Body shall take part in its discussion of matters within their respective provinces.

ARTICLE 3. – Secretarial services for the Governing Body of the Economic and Social Development Fund shall be provided by the Directorate of the Treasury at the Ministry of Finance.

ARTICLE 4. – An information Office shall be attached to the Governing Body of the Economic and Social Development Fund.

Applications shall be investigated by the appropriate technical Ministry, which shall transmit them to the Governing Body of the Fund or to the specialized committees for which provision is made in Article 2 (2) of Decree No. 55–875 (30 June 1955), establishing the Economic and Social Development Fund.

ARTICLE 5. – The Minister of Finance and Economic Affairs,

EDGAR FAURE.

FINANCING OF INVESTMENT UNDERTAK

Public Funds

Sectors	*Budget appropriations*		*War Reparations*		*Loans from the F.D.E.S. and H.L.M.*		*Loans through agents, from the F.D.E.S.*		*Miscel- laneou*	
Agriculture	140		205		18		176		279	
Farmers		43		205		—		167		2
Regional development		77		—		18		—		
Agricultural industries		10		—				9		
Energy	1,019		—		2,226		—	—	45	
Charbonnages de France		—		—		150		—		
Electricité de France		—		—		1,620		—		
Compagnie nationale du Rhône		—		—		130		—		
Gaz de France		—		—		156		—		
Gaz de Lacq		—		—		—		—		
Atomic energy		940		—		170		—		
Fuels		—		—		—		—		
B.R.G.G.M.		79		—		—		—		
Transport	245		70		417		—		693	
S.N.C.F.		—		66		200		—		
R.A.T.P.		—		—		—		—		
Local railways		—		—		—		—		
Road transport		—		—		—		—		
Sea transport		226		4		—		—		
Air transport		—		—		150		—		
Independent ports		—		—		8		—		
Paris Airport		—		—		50		—		
Inland waterways and canals		19		—		9		—		
Postal and Telecommunication services		—		—		—		—		6
Industries, Trade and Services	18		247		—		299		—	
Ores and non-ferrous metals		—		—		—		—		
Iron mines, iron and steel		—		—		—		16		
Engineering and heavy electrical goods		—		—		—		—		
Building and building materials		—		—		—		—		
Chemicals		—		—		—		45		
Textile industries		—		—		—		—		
Miscellaneous industries		—		—		—		—		
Trade		—		—		—		—		
Tourism		—		—		—		47		
Services, unclassified		18		247		—		191		
Social and Cultural Investment	78		—		—		—		—	
Hospitals		78		—		—		—		
Broadcasting, Television		—		—		—		—		
TOTAL, FIRMS		1,500		522		2,661		475		1,0
Households (including rented housing)		14		776		2,026		—		
State		1,374		—		—		—		2
Local authorities		1,142		175		60		40		5
TOTAL		4,030		1,473		4,747		515		1,7
Funding of special loans		—		—		—		—		
Financial firms		—		—		515		—		
Companies for financing the oil industry		—		—		—		—		
Overseas territories and foreign countries		2,111		13		390		—		3
C.A.R.E.C. Stock		—		—		—		—		
Miscellaneous		78		—		—		—		
GRAND TOTAL		6,219		1,486		5,652		515		2,1

[1] See Report for 1961–1962 of the *Conseil de Direction du Fonds de Développement économiq*

IN METROPOLITAN FRANCE IN 1960 (*in millions of NF.*)

Total		Loans from specialized bodies (Other Resources)		Medium-term bank advances (Other Resources)		Shares (Other Resources)		Bonds (Other Resources)		Balance of of other resources and uses		Gross investment	
818		1,370		−173		77		44		1,935		4,417	
	672		1,250		120		—		—		1,088		3,230
	127		—		—		—		—		10		137
	19		20		53		77		44		837		1,050
3,290		222		−25		100		1,232		2,074		6,893	
	150		—		—		—		384		606		1,140
	1,620		—		−99		—		798		1,049		3,368
	130				—		—		—		33		163
	156		134		−39		—		209		—		510
	—		3		110		—		—		74		187
	1,110		—		—		—		—		−343		767
	45		35		3		100		50		446		679
	79		—		—		—		—		—		79
1,425		139		207		3	—	544		3,322		5,640	
	266		—		—		—		444		1,820		2,530
	—		46		—		—		—		54		100
	—		5		—		—		—		23		30
	—		—		—		—		—		700		700
	230		25		112		3		100		262		732
	150		—		95		—		—		377		622
	8		—		—		—		—		92		100
	50		50		—		—		—		38		108
	28		13		—		—		—		47		88
	693		(150)		—		—		—		−63		630
564		609		185		1,532		1,103		10,327		14,320	
	—		—		—		99		15		86		200
	16		68		−12		61		384		1,283		1,800
	—		194		139		397		351		2,625		3,706
	—		91		−101		79		48		1,550		1,667
	45		234		112		338		302		542		1,573
	—		1		10		30		15		914		970
	—				5		17		7		686		715
	—		—		32		60		—		1,892		1,984
	47		20		—		—		—		133		200
	456		1		—		451		−19		616		1,505
78		178		—		—		—		414		670	
	78		178		—		—		—		324		580
	—		—		—		—		—		90		90
	6,175		2,518		540		1,712		2,923		18,072		31,940
	2,816		1,138		400		222		3		6,951		11,530
	1,624		—		—		—		—		−44		1,580
	1,940		2,152		—		—		25		503		4,620
	12,555		5,808		940		1,934		2,951		25,482		49,670
	—		—		—		—		—		—		—
	—		—		—		402		1,227		—		—
	—		—		—		25		250		—		—
	2,833		—		380		14		123		—		—
	—		—		—		—		—		—		—
	—		—		—		—		—		—		—
	15,388		5,808		1,320		2,735		4,551		—		—

social, p. 38–39.

APPENDIX V

TABLES ACCOMPANYING THE QUESTIONNAIRE SENT TO THE COMMISSIONS FOR THE FOURTH PLAN

PRODUCTION AND CONSUMPTION

Commission:

Branch:	*Index of volume (base* 1959)							1965 *(provisional)*		1965	
	1956	57	58	59	60	61	*Value* 1959	*Index base* 1959	*Value*	*Index base* 1959	*Value*
1. Branch output at real prices*											
2. Adjustment of export prices*											
3. Branch output at domestic prices* ..											
4. Imports (value C.I.F.)											
5. Import dues and taxes											
6. Trade margins											
TOTAL......											
Use of resources											
7. Intermediate consumption											
8. Household consumption											
9. Consumption by public offices											
10. Fixed asset formation by firms, households and public offices											
11. Exports (value F.O.B.)* .... public offices											
12. Adjustment of export prices											
13. Variations of stocks											
TOTAL....											

* It was found advisable to include two estimates of production in this table. The first, taking into account what was said above about the shrinkage of transactions within each branch, comes close to the concept of the turnover figure; this is the estimate 'at real prices', in which exported products are entered at the F.O.B. prices at which they were actually sold by the firms concerned. The second, the aim of which is to establish a more accurate basis for projections of intermediate consumption, investment and manpower, comes closer to the concept of volume, for it makes a homogeneous valuation of all products sold; this is the estimate 'at domestic prices', in which exported products are valued on the basis of the price ex works. In both instances, valuation includes all taxes.

MANPOWER

Commission:

Branch:

	1956	1959	1965 *provisional*	1965
1. Active population employed in the branch (in thousands)				
2. Index of production of the branch (at domestic prices)				
3. Index of annual *per capita* production				
4. Actual hours worked per week......				

	1959	1965 *provisional*	1965
Breakdown of active population employed in the branch (in percentages):			
1. Engineers and staff of similar grade			
2. Other high-grade staff			
3. Technicians			
4. Other middle-grade staff			
5. Foremen			
6. Skilled workers			
7. Specialized workers			
8. Unskilled workers.........................			
9. Other manual workers			

Regional distribution of active population employed in the branch, for each of the 21 regions included in the Plan......

INVESTMENT IN THE BRANCH

Commission:

Branch:

	1965 *Provisional*			1965	
	Value 1959	*Index base* 1959	*Value*	*Index base* 1959	*Value*
1. Gross fixed asset formation by the branch					
Breakdown (in percentages)					
1. According to type of investment.					
2. (*a*) Replacement or extension					
3. (*b*) Maintenance					
2. According to nature of investment					
4. (*a*) Building and civil engineering					
5. (*b*) Plant and equipment					
6. (*c*) Motor vehicles..........					
Methods of financing (in percentages)					
7. (*a*) Firms' own resources					
8. (*b*) External resources					

	1956	1957	1958	1959
Gross fixed asset formation by the branch (estimated in current francs)....................				